# ADVERTISING:
Concept
and
Copy

GEORGE FELTON
The Columbus College of Art & Design

Prentice Hall, Englewood Cliffs, New Jersey 07632

**Library of Congress Cataloging-in-Publication Data**

Felton, George
    Advertising : concept and copy / George Felton.
       p.   cm.
    Includes index.
    ISBN 0-13-189655-5
    1.  Advertising.    I.  Title.
HF5823.F43    1994
659.1--dc20                      93-31862
                                  CIP

Acquisitions editor: Sandra Steiner
Editorial assistant: Wendy Goldner
Production supervision: Elaine Lynch
Copy editor: Donna Mulder
Cover design: Violet Lake Studio
Manufacturing buyer: Patrice Fraccio

 ©1994 by Prentice-Hall, Inc.
A Paramount Communications Company
Englewood Cliffs, New Jersey 07632

Printed in the United States of America

10 9 8 7 6 5 4 3 2 1

ISBN 0-13-189655-5

Prentice-Hall International (UK) Limited, London
Prentice-Hall of Australia Pty. Limited, Sydney
Prentice-Hall Canada Inc., Toronto
Prentice-Hall Hispanoamericana, S.A., Mexico
Prentice-Hall of India Private Limited, New Delhi
Prentice-Hall of Japan, Inc., Tokyo
Simon & Schuster Asia Pte. Ltd., Singapore
Editora Prentice-Hall do Brasil, Ltda.,Rio de Janeiro

## DEDICATION

This book is for Debbie Warrenfeltz,
who taught me what love is.

# CONTENTS

# PREFACE

## *ORIGIN AND OVERVIEW*

*Advertising: Concept and Copy* has arisen from my teaching at the Columbus College of Art & Design. Our students—many of them training to become graphic designers, art directors, and creative directors—are visually oriented, design oriented. My copywriting courses work to invest their visual skills with language. We meet on the dividing line between image and word. And we spend a lot of time on strategic thinking—the concepts that underlie those images and words and are their driving wheels.

Like many textbooks, this one began innocently enough, with classroom handouts. I'd been teaching copywriting for 16 years and practicing the craft as a freelance writer, and somewhere in there I began to think I knew what I was doing. I found my handouts growing larger and more numerous, eventually straining the limits of both copying machines and in-class attention spans. So I've done with them what they seemed to be asking me to do: treat them right, turn them into a book.

The result you hold in your hands. Just what sort of book is it? What were my guiding principles?

Fundamentally, I've tried to give practical advice. Whenever I attempt something new or work to get better at anything, I want someone to show me how. I want hands-on, usable, specific advice: Do this, then this, try it that way, and so on. Thus the point of view from which I wrote the book: What do you want to know, need to know, to make good ads? And in what order?

I also wanted to strike a balance between market-oriented issues of creative strategy and ad-oriented issues of headline, visual, and copy. Many copywriting books lean one way or the other—much on copywriting techniques but little on strategy; long on strategy but short on ad-making. I tried to give adequate space to both issues, since each is essential to memorable, effective advertising.

Third, I feel that any copywriting text that isn't also a book about how to write well is missing its own point. You are first and finally copy*writers,* so I tell you everything I know about how to write, from creating a powerful, appropriate, persuasive voice, through fusing that voice with imagery, to getting, or trying to get, all the right words in all the right places.

Another obligation of a copywriting text, I think, is some advice on how to be creative. As a copywriter, you're going to be expected not only to write well but to think well—generating unusual, provocative ideas, visual as well as verbal ones. How this is done is a great mystery, of course, and no book can tell you enough. But I've often felt that we teachers of advertising have told you too little. We've accompanied assignments with pep talks no better than: "Go forth and be creative. Use that brain of yours. Find your originality. I'm sure you'll come up with something." Somehow many of you do. But a greater number don't, so throughout the text, and especially in Part 3, The Toolbox, I've tried to give you the best advice I can find on developing your creativity. If you become a copywriter, you'll be selling that creativity, so learn as much about it as you can.

In this light, I wanted the book to be inspirational and exciting. So I've filled it with ads, great ones, to show you what's possible, to challenge you to be as good. Reading about an advertising idea only goes so far; seeing it stunningly embodied does what explanations often can't. I've also blended in classic ads from previous decades—seminal work with which you should be familiar, work essential to your education.

Finally, I've tried to make this as readable, as conversational, as possible. Too many books, however well-intentioned, never transcend the dry, voiceless tone of text talk. Their ideas aren't heard because no one is listening. I hope that whatever ideas are here you'll find because you like reading the book and feel that it's talking to you.

## ORGANIZATION

As you see, I've divided the book into 3 large parts. The first two sections correspond to a natural sequence in the solving of an advertising problem: First you create a strategy, then you execute it.

Part 1, Strategies, operates on the premise that the selling idea beneath an ad's surface ultimately determines its success. You get that good idea by researching your product, understanding who buys it and why, and studying the marketplace in which it competes. In doing those things you'll discover the problem that your advertising must solve, you'll find the strategic approach that best solves it, and you'll be able to write the creative platform that focuses this strategic thinking into specific advertising objectives.

Now how will you put that strong selling idea into action? How will you express it? In Part 2, Executions, we examine all the tools at your command, from the elements of print advertising—headlines, visuals, body copy, graphic design—to the wide variety of media and advertising genres available to you. These are the means by which you turn strategic thinking into real-world effectiveness. Thus the movement of the first two sections: What are you going to say? How are you going to say it?

Part 3, The Toolbox, is what it sounds like: a place you can go to find problem-solving tools. Here I discuss some basic principles of creativity and follow that with an array of techniques that advertising professionals have used, over and over, to produce funny, attention-getting, and persuasive work. As I mentioned earlier, the idea of putting many of these techniques together in one place arose from my asking students to be creative without ever quite telling them how. Study these techniques. Try them out whenever you wish or as I suggest them to you in the text. I hope they will prove much more helpful than the earnestly offered but almost useless advice to "THINK."

So, will this book tell you everything you need to know to be a good copywriter? Hardly. Advertising is such a crossroads, such a jumble of influences: sociology and psychology, marketing and consumer behavior, graphic design and visual thinking, rhetoric and literature, filmmaking and photography, creativity and cold-eyed analysis, commerce and aesthetics, the fleeting and the eternal. No one book can do much more than take a pass through part of that.

To really be a good copywriter, you must soak up influences from everywhere. Develop your curiosity. Use your energy. Learn at least a little bit about lots of things. Sample a wide variety of undergraduate courses, keep your eyes on the culture as it flows by, and write and read as much as possible. Use this book, get from it what you need, then keep going. I hope that one day you'll create advertising that invigorates us all, in the process raising the level of the genre itself.

## *ACKNOWLEDGMENTS*

Writing a book may seem the most solitary of tasks, and in some ways it is, but it is also the labor of many hands and minds. Foremost among those in whose debt I stand are my reviewers, those critics whose insight and expectation pushed me to make a book better than I thought was in me. I thank them all:

J. Thomas Russell, the University of Georgia; William D. Ryan, Syracuse University; Gary Soldow, Baruch College; Lee Barlett, Brigham Young University; Lee Wenthe, The University of Georgia; Stan Harrison, University of Miami; Peggy Kreshell, University of Georgia; and Tommy Smith, University of Mississippi.

I am also indebted to Sharon Brock at Ohio State for her time and help in conversation and to Tom Jordan of San Jose State for his valuable points of view about advertising education. To the young women at the Packard Library and the Grandview Heights Public Library, who knew where things were when I so frequently didn't, I extend my thanks.

# CHAPTER 1

# CREATING AN ADVERTISING STRATEGY

*To do well what should not be done
is to do badly.*
—Theodore Levitt[1]

## FIRST THINGS FIRST

Probably the greatest danger you'll face as a copywriter is trying to get to the ad too fast. You'll rush for a headline or selling idea before making sure it works. And since most great ads do employ some kind of a twist (you can't just put clichéd ideas in clichéd places), it's tempting to start playing with language and image right away, trying to create some "pop," usually with puns, double-entendres, and other jokes. But cleverness is useless if you're saying something beside the point. Until you discover the real reasons—whatever they may be—that people buy this or that good or service, you create ads for no one.

So great ads really begin with the grunt work, the legwork, digging around in the issues, getting up to speed on the selling situation, working to know enough even to begin playing with the language.

If, for example, you're creating advertising against teen-age drinking and driving, writing headlines like "don't drive yourself to drink" or "don't take the car for a spin if your head's spinning" or "how can you stay in a single lane if you're seeing double?" is a waste of time. The real problems of drinking and driving are elsewhere, and you need to understand them. Why, in the face of repeated warnings and omnipresent advertising against it, do many young people still drink and drive? The answer isn't something you can come up with sitting around in

[1]Theodore Levitt, *The Marketing Imagination*, new, expanded ed. (New York: Free Press, 1986), p. 135.

1

search of a line. You can only begin to discover it by researching the problem, its social and psychological dimensions. You've got to get out there and talk to some people and do some thinking.

Most don't-drink-and-drive advertising stresses the risk of death on the highway. It's a reasonable argument. (See Figure 1.1.) But suppose, in your research, you discover that it's far more likely people will lose their licenses than their lives by drinking and driving. Suppose you also discover that many teens, young and strong, consider themselves almost immortal and are largely unable to imagine their own deaths. They can, however, understand the value of driving—seeing it as an essential initiation into adulthood—and they can feel the weight of peer pressure. Knowing all this, you may want to make a different argument. (See Figure 1.2.)

**Figure 1.1**  A reasonable advertising strategy for the teen-age drinking and driving problem. Courtesy of Reader's Digest Foundation and Ruhr/Paragon.

**Figure 1.2**   Perhaps strategically even stronger, this ad directly understands its audience. Courtesy of Reader's Digest Foundation and The Martin Agency.

## *STRATEGY VERSUS EXECUTION*

An ad really has two parts: WHAT you're saying and HOW you're saying it. The **what** is your strategy—the plan of attack, the ad's big idea, its selling argument; the **how** is the execution of that strategy—the particular form it takes: the images, language, layouts, and media that you use. (Employing the battlefield distinction, some advertisers split these two into *strategy* and *tactics*.)

Looking at the preceding ads, we might say that the strategy of the first is: Don't drink and drive because you may die. The strategy of the second is: Don't drink and drive because you may live. Obviously these are fundamentally different propositions, different **what**s, and each proposition could have been differently expressed, given a different **how**, as well. We consumers respond to both the underlying selling idea and its particular expression. (See Figure 1.3.)

When creating ads, you want to be smart at both strategy and execution. Often it's easy to admire the clever "creative" on an ad's surface, for example, the well-crafted, parallel headline on the kids-in-the-backseat ad, their wonderfully worried looks,

**Figure 1.3**   Here the same two underlying strategies each receive a different execution. As an advertiser you will frequently be asked not only to develop a strategy but then to express it in different ways. Courtesy of Bozell, Inc. and Reader's Digest Foundation and Chiat/Day/Mojo.

Mom's irritation, the point of view of the camera—all of it—and think that those make the ad great. But what also makes that ad great is the idea behind it: What if you live?

> We place a lot of importance on strategy. It's not worth anything to be creative if you're not going to make that turnstile turn. Creative and strategy are so integral, one depends upon the other.
> —Jean Robaire, art director, Stein Robaire Helm[2]

> Advertising based on a sound strategy but executed poorly is as dull as another snowy day in January. Advertising executed brilliantly but based on a weak strategy may be entertaining—but it won't work. So you have to do the whole job, not just half. Strong strategy. And strong execution.
> —Ron Anderson, executive vice president, Bozell & Jacobs[3]

## HOW TO CREATE STRATEGY

To develop a strong strategy, you need to understand three things: the product, the consumer, and the marketplace.

1. **The product.** What are you selling, really? This can be something more and different than it might at first appear. It's certainly something about which you need to know more than you do right now.

2. **The consumer.** Who are you selling to, exactly? Have you located those people who are your best market? How well do you know them? The key to selling products is understanding people's relationships with them, what they want from them. What needs and motives does your product address? What problems does it solve?

3. **The marketplace.** How does your product (and its advertising) fit into the array around it? No sale occurs in a vacuum; there are probably other products like yours, and your category has been advertised to consumers before. In short, they've seen it all and used it all, twice. How will your product stand out in the marketplace? Why choose it instead of a competing brand?

[2]Jean Robaire, quoted in Julie Prendiville, "Stein Robaire Helm," *Communication Arts* (May/June 1992), p. 66.

[3]"Right On, Ron," interview with Ron Anderson, *Creative Leaders Advertising Program*, collected reprints of its advertising series, published by *The Wall Street Journal*, 1991, p. 4.

All interesting questions—and all related: You can't locate your target market until you know what you're selling exactly, but you can't know what exactly you ought to promise until you locate a target market and decipher its needs. Nor can you create an effective strategy until you analyze the marketplace positions your competitors occupy and successfully differentiate your product from theirs.

Sorting your way through all this isn't easy, and each advertising situation will prove different from the one before it, too, so your job never reduces to a formula. Your goal is to understand the parts of the advertising scenario so well that you see how they all fit together—to know enough to write an ad that works, that talks to real people about real needs. You'd like to convince a teen-ager, perhaps for the first time, that "don't drink and drive" isn't simply someone else's argument. It's something he or she truly believes—because of the advertising you created.

Let's begin.

CHAPTER 2

# RESEARCH YOUR PRODUCT

*Do your homework.*
—David Ogilvy[1]

In truth, advertising starts with consumers and what they want, but you will never be given the assignment simply to make some market segment happy. Instead, you will usually begin with a product and the assignment to help sell it. Thus, in practice, advertising problems start with your clients, who have a product—a good or service—with which they'd like help. You are called in initially to do something for a client's product.

So steep yourself in information. Become an expert in that product and its category. Get overinformed. I once knew a student who wanted to sell Aloe & Lanolin soap to her classmates as a course project, but it never occurred to her to find out what aloe and lanolin were, exactly, and what they were doing together in a bar of soap. Needless to say, her success was limited. Strive not to be that student.

Let this be your model instead: Before creating their legendary ad campaign for the Volkswagen Beetle, the creative team at Doyle Dane Bernbach first headed for the manufacturing plant in Wolfsburg, West Germany, to do their homework. Says William Bernbach: "We spent days talking to engineers, production men, executives, workers on the assembly line. We marched side by side with the molten metal that hardened into the engine, and kept going until every part was finally in place...."[2] And only

[1]David Ogilvy, *Ogilvy on Advertising* (New York: Random House, 1985), p. 11.

[2]William Bernbach, quoted in *Is the Bug Dead? The Great Beetle Ad Campaign* (New York: Stewart, Tabori & Chang, 1983), pp. 8–9.

through this effort did they find their selling proposition, the VW as an "honest" car—simple, functional, and incredibly well made. Whenever you see reprints of these classic VW ads, study them, not only because the ads are great, but because each ad shows so clearly the homework required to think it up. Read enough VW ads and two things will happen: (1) you'll learn a lot about the cars, and (2) you'll want one. Sufficient testimony to the power of that campaign. (See Figure 2.1.)

**Volkswagen's unique construction keeps dampness out.**

**Figure 2.1** Too many ads fail to find the drama in the product, "borrowing" interest from elsewhere instead. The VW ads, however, made the car itself *consistently* interesting, a remarkable feat in a campaign that ran from 1959 to 1977. Courtesy of Volkswagen United States, Inc.

## HOW TO LEARN ABOUT YOUR PRODUCT

1. Learn what's in it and how it works, read the label, study the packaging. If possible, use it: wear it, eat it, drive it, bathe with it. Become its student. Also try to know as much about the product *category* as you can.

2. Ask people why they do or don't use the product. Word of mouth, actual information from real people, is essential. If you can be organized enough to use **focus groups** (collections of consumers brought together to talk about products and their own buying habits), great. If not, cultivate sources who understand their own consumer behavior fairly well, who can talk about shampoos for a while, or tennis rackets. You need to study the marketplace.

3. Call or write the company for information. If they have an 800 number, call it. Get whatever you can from them about their product. Brochures abound, from both your brand and the competition. Study ads by everybody in the field. Accumulate a file.

4. Go to local dealers and ask them about your product and its competition. Ten minutes with a retailer can give you a lot of information about the types of buyers, the heavy users, the competitive advantages and disadvantages of the major brands, the whole playing field.

5. Do library research. Tap the computerized information bases: ProQuest, InfoTrac, and the like. Sometimes, if you can't get enough information on your brand, you'll feel stymied, but try to bypass dead ends. For example, if you're selling vitamins, you can drop into a local bookstore and survey the health books. It's likely that quite a few authors will use interesting facts as chapter headings, on their covers, and so on, some of which might work for your vitamins. We often see sentences like, "Did you know that your body misses eight essential vitamins every day?" That fact can fit Centrum vitamins, or any other brand, right? Remember: The *product category* can often serve as a source of information for your particular brand. (See Figure 2.2.)

## STUDY THE COMPETITION: TWO KEY ISSUES

1. Who is your competition, exactly? Usually we simply assume it's a competing brand. But if your product owns dominant market share, its true competition isn't other brands so much as

**Figure 2.2** You can't use facts like these until you find them. The moral? Do your homework. Courtesy of the California Prune Board and World Wildlife Fund.

other ways we spend our money to satisfy the same need—its indirect competitors, if you will. For example, Hallmark and American Greetings are direct competitors of each other, but they also face the telephone as an indirect competitor. Each is a delivery system for feelings; they're all after the consumer's "sentiment message." "When an advertiser dominates its category, as Hallmark does, an indirect competitor can be more formidable than a direct competitor."[3]

So ask yourself who are the major players, both direct and indirect, with which you compete. Assess their strengths and weaknesses. Where do you fit in the array? And what competitive benefit do you offer that they don't? (See Figure 2.3.)

---

[3]William Wells, John Burnett, and Sandra Moriarty, *Advertising: Principles and Practice* (Englewood Cliffs, NJ: Prentice Hall, 1989), p. 174.

THE HUMBOLDT PENGUIN

IN THE AGE BEFORE MAN,

THE EARTH LOST ONE SPECIES EVERY THOUSAND YEARS. TODAY, WE LOSE ONE EVERY TWENTY MINUTES.

THE WORLD WILDLIFE FUND VANISHING SPECIES CAMPAIGN NEEDS YOUR HELP.   1-800-CALL-WWF.

**Figure 2.2** (continued)

2. What product category(ies) should you compete in? This corollary of the first question can also be answered too quickly. If you're selling Wheaties, you may assume you're just competing with other cereals. But there are other categories you might want to compete in as well: Wheaties is a kind of vitamin; it's a snack food for the healthy-minded; it's a breakfast, not just a

**Figure 2.3**  Although there are two newspapers in San Francisco, the *Examiner* recognizes that its competition also includes TV. (Developed by Goodby, Berlin & Silverstein, advertising agency for the *San Francisco Examiner*.) *The Oregonian* realizes that it competes with TV as a medium for retail advertising. Courtesy of *The Oregonian*.

cereal. So remember to ask what product categories you can compete in and which ones are best. (For more on turning competitive position into the entire advertising strategy, see "Positioning" in Chapter 6.)

## *WHAT ARE YOU LOOKING FOR IN YOUR RESEARCH?*

1. Don't get hung up in corporate this and earnings that. You're looking for information about this product that makes it worth buying. It's not a lump of wet clay, so look for features, particularities, whatever makes it more than a commodity, and whatever distinguishes it from its competition. What's in it? (For example, when oat bran became a national obsession for its supposed cholesterol-reducing capability, foods containing it quickly said so in their packaging and advertising.) How is it made? Real slow? Real fast? At high temperatures? In the old Dutch tradition? By whom? European craftsmen? The latest robotic wonders? Where is it made? Use the reporter's questions to help you generate material: who, what, where, when, how, why.

2. What, if anything, do people have against your product? What's its greatest liability? Is that something you should address, either as the main strategy or as a subordinate copy point? What's its greatest strength?

> All products and all ideas are salable only as they flow with the tides of thought and feeling which are surging through a given society. Because the forces which create these tides are more powerful than advertising, it is futile for us to run counter to them. —James Webb Young[4]

3. What cultural tides flow around your product that affect our desire to buy it? Is it associated with any rites of passage, life transitions—like birth, graduation, marriage, retirement, and so on? (For example, coffee used to be and shaving products still are associated with entry into adulthood, and advertising campaigns, sensibly, have used the connection.) Is it tied—or could it be—to any major cultural issues (self-improvement, health, environmental concerns, recommitment to education, emphasis on the family, and so on)? (See Figure 2.4.)

Much of this information is divined, systematically analyzed, and then sold to advertisers by market research firms, but much is also available by simply paying attention to trends as they manifest themselves around you. Read newspapers and magazines, watch TV and movies, listen to what's said by radio talk show callers. We all have pop culture antennae; the good ad writers keep theirs up.

[4]James Webb Young, *The Diary of an Ad Man* (Chicago: Advertising Publications, Inc., 1944), p. 252.

**Figure 2.4** Intelligent advertising monitors socio-cultural trends (here, lower hard-liquor consumption) and tries to make the most of them. Notice how simply and effectively this headline gets drinkers' attention. Courtesy of The House of Seagram.

NOTE: Obviously I'm suggesting a lot of research here. You'll know by the nature of each assignment and its timeline how much you can realistically expect of yourself. Sometimes you'll have to do a quick study of your product and its competitors. Other times you'll be able to analyze more of the field. You can't be expected to do all this research all the time, but the more you do the better. It will pay you back.

## TRANSLATE FEATURES INTO BENEFITS

Let's say you've done your homework. You now know all sorts of things about the product—its manufacture, ingredients, moving parts, founding father and mother, everything. But it's all inert data until you make it matter to consumers, and you do that by promising benefits, not just enunciating features.

Here's the distinction: Unless it's a commodity, like salt or sugar, whatever product you're selling undoubtedly has aspects that we might call features: a key ingredient, a selector switch that scans for songs, a self-cleaning button for the oven, a column by George Will on the last page, three speeds to its motor, a lubricated strip above the blade, 1/3 the calories of the regular brand, no caffeine, extra caffeine, timed-release deodorant capsules, biodegradability, freeze-dried crystals, a hatchback, an angled brushing head, and on and on. In other words, every product has certain parts, ingredients, things it can do that make it what it is. Facts you discover when you do your homework.

Too often, however, we assume that features alone sell a product. But they're just things hanging off a product. The real question is, what do we get out of them? Learn to ask, of any product fact or feature, "Who cares? Can or does this matter to the consumer? What's the payoff for the user?" Link benefits to features. Complete the argument.

Using previous examples, we see that a self-cleaning oven button means no more smelly scrubbing, stinging hands, backaches, and all-day labor; 1/3 the calories means we can have our cake and eat it, too—indulge ourselves but still be attractively slim; a hatchback lets us load up our gear quickly and easily; George Will every week means we'll smarten up fast and have clever things to say to our friends; freeze-dried crystals mean brewed-coffee taste without hassle; timed-release deodorant capsules mean we'll never be embarrassed by wetness and odor, appearing unflappable and cool to everyone; no caffeine means we're being good to ourselves and extending our lives, not to mention being "safe" by following a trend. Now all these neutral features have been expressed as benefits, too, so we can see what's in it for us.

Remember this marketing maxim, simple but profound: People don't buy 1/4-inch drill bits; they buy 1/4-inch holes. As Theodore Levitt points out, people don't really buy gasoline either: "They cannot see it, taste it, feel it, appreciate it, or really test it. What they buy is the right to continue driving their cars."[5] When ad great Claude Hopkins was advertising patent medicines in the early 1900s, he realized that "People were not buying medicine, they were buying results," so he pioneered the idea of the druggist's signed guarantee.[6] This habit of mind, seeing products from the benefits end, seems obvious, but it's amazing

[5]Theodore Levitt, *The Marketing Imagination*, new, expanded ed. (New York: Free Press, 1986), p. 159.

[6]Claude Hopkins, *My Life in Advertising & Scientific Advertising*, rpt. (Lincolnwood, IL: NTC Business Books, 1991), p. 79.

**Figure 2.5**   This ad invites its target audience (liquor retailers) to see the real benefit of carrying Wild Turkey. Courtesy of Austin Nichols Co., Inc.

how often we overlook it when planning strategies and writing ads. (See Figure 2.5.)

Look at Figure 2.6, a full-page print ad for Samsonite luggage. As you see, the copy is a series of call-outs surrounding the bag. Notice how each one talks about features *in terms of* benefits. The product specific is stated and then the "so" follows. This rhetorical approach—"it has this feature so you get this benefit"—is the essence of good copywriting:

Samsonite's Ultravalet Garment Bag is like a closet and chest of drawers in one. And you can carry it on a plane and live right out of it in a hotel room.

With 12 inside pockets, the Ultravalet has a place for everything and keeps everything in its place.

Another nice thing about the pockets is the mesh material that lets you see everything you've packed. You can also get into major pockets from the inside or outside.

**Figure 2.6** Here features become benefits: The fundamental selling idea is made visible by a smart comparison, and the copy call-outs translate specific features into benefits meaningful to travelers. Courtesy of Samsonite Corp.

There's even a special pocket for ties that helps keep them wrinkle-free.

Unlike most other bags, the Ultravalet opens like a book so you don't have to keep flipping the bag over to pack or unpack.

Thanks to a lot of organized thinking, the Ultravalet is the easiest bag to pack and unpack that we've ever made.

With its special hooks, you can hang the open bag in a closet or on a door and live right out of it.

You'll also appreciate our unique telescoping bar that pulls out to let you remove suits and dresses without disturbing the ones hanging in front.

Our large, reinforced shoe pockets hold a lot more than shoes.

The bag holds all kinds of hangers so you can pack anything right from the closet.

The Ultravalet folds over backwards, instead of forwards like other bags, to help keep lapels, sleeves, and pockets looking great.

There's also a removable wet pack that keeps wet or soiled items separate from dry ones.

Last but not least, our extended length panel helps keep longer garments from wrinkling at the bottom.

See the Ultravalet at a luggage store soon. And you'll see why it's an idea that's really taking off.

Samsonite. Our Strengths Are Legendary.


## Exercises:

1. Research your product and write down a list of ten true facts about it. What separates it from its competitors? What particularities, what features, does it have? Remember that these may concern packaging or distribution, too; they don't have to be part of the physical object. Then ask of each fact, "So what?" Make yourself express each one as a benefit to the consumer. For example, if you discover that Levi's are the oldest jean made in the United States, so what? Right now all we can say is that we're happy for Levi Strauss, but what's in it for us? Well, buying them gives us authenticity because we are getting the original. If Levi's are the oldest, they're doing something right, and by buying them, so are we. That's one possible "benefit" latent in this fact. Can you find others?

2. Here are more product features. Translate them into consumer benefits (of each, ask "so?"):

   Maxfli golf balls fly farther than other ones.

   Pinnacle golf balls have cut-proof covers.

Norelco shavers have a "lift and cut" blade system.

A bowl of Trix cereal has less sugar than a banana or an apple.

Acura cars have passenger-side air bags.

Doing this, you realize that translating features into benefits requires an understanding of consumer motives. What do people want from the material world? How many needs do they really have? Let's take a closer look at consumer psychology.

# CHAPTER 3

# UNDERSTAND CONSUMER BEHAVIOR

*It took millions of years for man's instincts to develop. It will take millions more for them to even vary. It is fashionable to talk about changing man. A communicator must be concerned with unchanging man, with his obsessive drive to survive, to be admired, to succeed, to love, to take care of his own.*
—William Bernbach[1]

Remember that marketing's central idea, as Theodore Levitt phrases it, is that "people buy products...in order to solve problems. Products are problem-solving tools."[2] Remember, too, that products may solve any problem from a physiological one all the way up to a psychological, social, or even spiritual one, and often several at once. So, for example, when we buy clothes at The Limited instead of at Wal-Mart, we are meeting the civilized need to cover ourselves, certainly, but we aren't stopping there. We're also choosing to buy *insurance*—fashion insurance. We will pay more for these clothes because we want to reduce the perceived social risk of wearing the wrong ones.

## OUR HIERARCHY OF NEEDS

This idea that a product can solve more than one problem at the same time owes much to the psychologist Abraham Maslow, who posited in human beings a "hierarchy of needs " ascending from physiological needs up to psychological ones. He argued

[1] William Bernbach, quoted in Bob Levenson, *Bill Bernbach's Book* (New York: Villard Books, 1987), p. 210.

[2] Theodore Levitt, *The Marketing Imagination*, new, expanded ed. (New York: Free Press, 1986), p. 76.

that we are driven to fulfill them all, although lower-level needs must be met before we will attempt to satisfy higher-level needs.[3] Here is his hierarchy:

1. **Physiological needs:** hunger, thirst, warmth, pain avoidance, sexual release, and others.

2. **Safety needs:** housing, clothing, financial and physical security.

3. **Love and belongingness:** social acceptance and personal intimacy. (Maslow argued that much of mankind's frustration stemmed from inadequacy here, since lower-level needs had been met. We can often say that we have eaten enough or have enough clothes, but who among us can say, "I am loved enough"? It isn't surprising, therefore, that the greatest number of consumer goods appeal to this level of need.)

4. **Esteem needs:** feelings of adequacy and achievement, approval, prestige, social status.

5. **Self-actualization:** the need to understand, cognitively and aesthetically; the ultimate integration of the self and realization of one's highest inner potential.

As we saw with Limited clothing and we see anytime we look at advertising, most products intersect Maslow's ladder at more than one point. Even as apparently simple an act as having friends over for pizza involves three levels of Maslow's hierarchy: physiological, love and belongingness, and esteem needs. We feed our bodies, bond with others emotionally, and perform some work on our social status; and we do it all by means of that innocent-seeming, double-cheese-and-pepperoni pizza.

## CLIMB MASLOW'S LADDER

Rarely do we buy products simply for their minimal satisfaction of the lowest-level need; therefore, as an advertiser you always want to think about climbing the ladder: In addition to a product's obvious solution to a need, what else is at stake?

[3]Data (for diagram) based on Hierarchy of Needs from "A Theory of Human Motivation" in MOTIVATION AND PERSONALITY, 3rd Edition, by Abraham H. Maslow, revised by Robert Frager, James Fadiman, Cynthia McReynolds, and Ruth Cox. Copyright, 1954, 1987, by Harper & Row, Publishers, Inc. Copyright © 1970 by Abraham H. Maslow. Reprinted by permission of HarperCollins, Publishers, Inc.

Always ask yourself, what is the **highest possible benefit** I can claim for this product? And realize that such ladder climbing is smart. In a culture as surfeited with competing material goods as America's, *many* products can satisfy lower-level needs, so we often differentiate among them on the basis of what else they can do for us. (See Figures 3.1 and 3.2.)

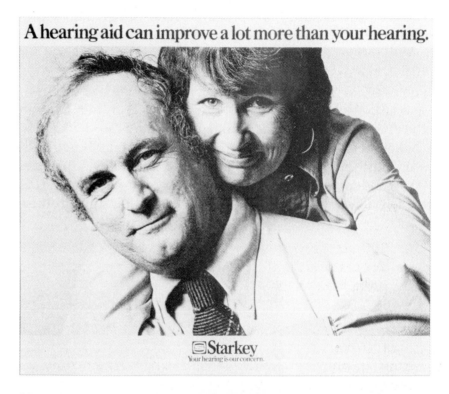

**Figure 3.1**    Smart advertising finds the strongest benefit, not simply the most obvious one. A hearing aid's highest possible benefit is more than just better audio, yes? Courtesy of Starkey Labs.

**Figure 3.2**    The highest possible benefit of changing your oil, or as this ad cleverly presents it, the highest possible penalty of not doing so. Courtesy of Jiffy Lube.

For example, the durable slogan for Jif peanut butter ("Choosy mothers choose Jif ") sails right past the promise of satisfying the physiological need of hunger (we understand that peanut butter fills stomach cavities) and promises to fill the higher-order needs of love, nurturance, and maternal competence. And those really are the psychological and emotional values at stake when a mother buys food for her children. Moreover, since peanut butter is a prepared food rather than something Mom made herself, since it's a convenience food, really, do you see that also embedded within that phrase is forgiveness for buying it, the assurance that such a food choice is more than convenience, or other than convenience: Buying Jif, far from being a labor-saving option, really reflects well on her. Do you see the promise there? Jif has climbed the ladder.

Nike doesn't just sell stylish, durable running shoes. With phrases like "Just do it " and "There is no finish line," they sell the transcendence of sweat, self-actualization through the testing of the self. (See Figure 3.3.) Rockport doesn't simply promise

**Figure 3.3** These multi-page Nike ads (first we see the type, then turn to the spread) understand the psychology of their audience, selling solutions to lifestyle problems, not simply sportswear. Courtesy of Nike, Inc.

well-made shoes; they write headlines like, "Shoes that help you live longer," and discuss in the copy the health-enhancing virtues of walking. (See Figure 3.4.) Margarine doesn't just promote its near-taste to butter or improved spreadability but often makes larger claims—like health through lower cholesterol, the implied promise of heart attack prevention.

**Figure 3.4**   Another highest possible benefit. Courtesy of Rockport/Reebok International Ltd.

Become sensitive to the problems being solved by a product; they are often more various and rise higher up the ladder than you suppose. Usually we are looking, not for a product that will do the least for us, but one that will do the most.

I note that all the really successful ad writers spend more time studying people's wants than anything else.
—James Webb Young[4]

---

[4]James Webb Young, *The Diary of an Ad Man* (Chicago: Advertising Publications, Inc., 1944), pp. 158–159.

## A SHOPPING LIST OF NEEDS

Maslow's hierarchy is so brief that a more specific catalog of our needs (and products associated with them) can be helpful. This list, not a hierarchy but a horizontal array, is from Robert Settle and Pamela Alreck's *Why They Buy: American Consumers Inside and Out.*[5]

1.  **Achievement:** the need to perform difficult tasks, exercise one's skills. [Professional tools, sports equipment, any skill-providing service: ballet, college courses, and so on. The Army's slogan: "Be all you can be."]

2.  **Independence:** the need to be autonomous, have options, be different. [Fashion makes this appeal; cars do, too. Hair care items "let you be you." Credit cards, alcohol, and cigarettes can be advertised this way; Virginia Slims has linked itself to women's rights: "You've come a long way, baby."]

3.  **Exhibition:** the need to gain public attention, show off, win notice. [Clothing and fashion accessories here, too. From big things like cars and homes to smaller items like hair styles, anything capable of asserting the self.]

4.  **Recognition:** the need for positive notice from others, to be held up as exemplary. [Many "badge" items symbolize this; so too do getting a college degree, joining social organizations.]

5.  **Dominance:** the need to exercise power over others, direct and supervise. [Any power item, from a big car or house to a pesticide or detergent that has punch.]

6.  **Affiliation:** the need for close association with others, for relationships. [Joining the Army, joining anything fills this need. Personal care items, breath mints, toothpaste, and so on facilitate closeness with others: "Aren't you glad you use Dial. Don't you wish everybody did?"]

7.  **Nurturance:** the need to provide care for others, to have and protect. [Child care and pet care products; gardening; cooking and housekeeping, laundry; volunteer or charity work.]

[5]Robert B. Settle and Pamela L. Alreck, *Why They Buy: American Consumers Inside and Out* (New York: John Wiley & Sons, 1986), pp. 24–27. Copyright © by John Wiley & Sons, Inc., used with permission.

8. **Succorance:** the need to receive help from others, be comforted. [Anything that functions as a care-giver: personal services, especially those that work on the body, limousines, salons, spas, counseling services; anything that "pampers" us.]

9. **Sexuality:** the need to establish and develop one's sexual identity, be sexually attractive. [All gendered products; colognes; fashion; dating accessories and entertainments.]

10. **Stimulation:** the need to stimulate the senses, pursue vigorous activity, engage the mind and body, sweat, stimulate the palate, be active. [Sporting goods, health clubs, restaurants, amusement parks, bubble baths, fabric softeners.]

11. **Diversion:** the need to relax, play, have fun, be entertained. [Vacations, amusement parks, sports, and so on.]

12. **Novelty:** the need to alter routine, experience change and diversity, learn new skills, have new experiences. [Travel, education, movies, books.]

13. **Understanding:** the need to learn and comprehend, make intellectual connections. [Self-improvement courses, education, movies, books.]

14. **Consistency:** the need for order and cleanliness, to control uncertainty and avoid ambiguity. [All cleaners, repair services, maintenance items; "matched" goods, organizers. The Holiday Inn's slogan "The best surprise is no surprise."]

15. **Security:** the need to be free from fear, acquire assets, avoid accidents. [Insurance, burglar alarms, investments, all safety equipment.]

Examining the list, we see, for example, that many need–product connections can easily be made: Why buy a smoke alarm? Security. Why go to college? Understanding. Why buy household cleaners? Consistency. And so forth.

But such easy connections can be too simplistic. The smoke alarm, for instance, may also signal independence, especially if you're living on your own for the first time. It may express affiliation if all your friends agree that no reasonable person should be without one. If you're a parent and put one in the baby's room, it becomes a form of nurturance. If you buy several and put them in many places, you could be expressing a need for consistency. If you're a landlord, you might buy them simply to

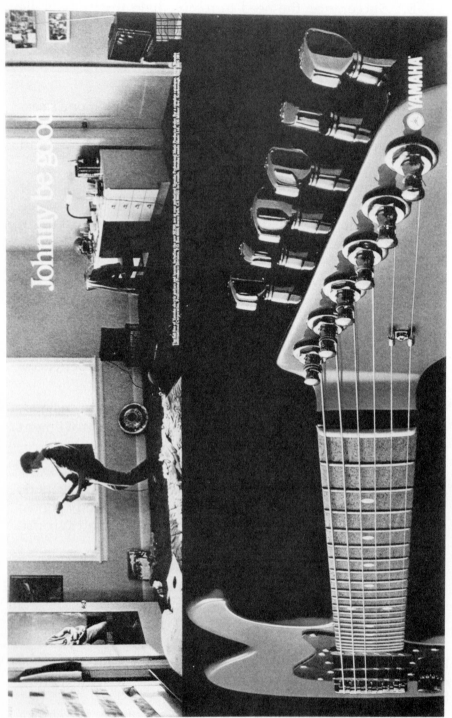

**Figure 3.5** This Yamaha ad understands the multiple needs of the adolescent American male—achievement, independence, exhibition, recognition, affiliation, and stimulation—and shows how a guitar can help. Courtesy of Yamaha International.

**Figure 3.6**  Appeals to health benefits aren't the only effective strategies for weight-loss programs. Courtesy of Pittsburgh Vista Hotel and Werner, Chepelsky & Partners, Inc.

comply with property statutes, for whom the alarms provide legal security. And all these people may be responding to more than one motive. (See Figures 3.5 and 3.6.)

## Exercises:

1.  Pick a product and set a quota, say five, from the preceding list of needs its use could satisfy. Learn to stretch yourself in these arguments; you are practicing associating products with motives, making little strategic arguments. Let's say you're advertising Wheaties. The obvious answer is that eating them satisfies the physiological drive for food. But keep going. What other needs might it be filling? Affiliation, if all the guys eat it. Since it has been considered a man's food, an "athlete's" breakfast, it's been a gendered product; eating it has expressed manhood. It's also an "adult" food and could signal independence, especially if younger friends are still eating Trix and Lucky Charms. Also since food always is a form of nurturance, Wheaties might, in some circumstances, become a surrogate parent.

2. Examine your list of benefits for a product. Try to rank them. What seems the highest possible benefit? What's next in importance, and so on?

If either of these exercises makes you think you should sell Wheaties one way to some of us, and another way to others, then you see the wisdom of **market segmentation**. Wheaties indeed means one thing to the health-conscious adult, another to the teen-age athlete, still something else to the senior citizen: The highest possible benefit varies with each segment. Let's examine market segmentation.

# CHAPTER 4

# ANALYZE THE MARKETPLACE

*There is no future for products everybody likes a little, only for products somebody likes a lot.*
—Laurel Cutler, VP-consumer affairs, Chrysler Corporation[1]

## THE PRINCIPLE OF MARKET SEGMENTATION

*If you're not thinking segments, you're not thinking.*
—Theodore Levitt[2]

Fewer and fewer products are sold today via a *total market approach*, that is, by creating one product and one argument for all humanity—One Size Fits All thinking, if you will. Sophisticated production techniques allow many product and packaging variations, so one size no longer need fit all. Plus mass media have so splintered and multiplied that broad-beaming an advertisement on major TV networks, for example, is often an inefficient and imprecise way to reach potential users. And given the heterogeneous lifestyles, media use, and consumption patterns in this country, a "mass audience" often rarely exists.

So we're usually selling via market segmentation strategies, that is, by creating separate selling arguments to separate segments or target markets of potential consumers, frequently with separate versions of the product.

Sometimes your advertising problem will present a fairly well-defined target market. For example, you'll be asked to write copy for your college to recruit students, so your audience is

---

[1]Laurel Cutler, quoted in "Is any niche too small for U.S. automakers," *Advertising Age*, April 9, 1990, p. 52.

[2]Theodore Levitt, *The Marketing Imagination*, new, expanded ed. (New York: Free Press, 1986), p. 128.

those people considering college, and you gain a good sense of who they are simply by looking around. Or you're asked to create a brochure for the local soccer club or Macintosh users club, and you know them, too. Other times you'll be asked to sell a product with a less firmly established target market; part of your creative task then will be to locate a likely segment. In all these cases you need to define your target audience well enough to tailor an argument just for them. How to do so?

## Demographics

Usually you begin by targeting product or category users. (For example, if you're selling running shoes, you target runners. If you're selling Wheaties, you target cereal eaters.) Then you further define your market through those physical attributes, including socioeconomic and cultural variables, commonly known as **demographics** and including such indexes as population size and shifts; sex and age; geographic location and mobility; income and expenditures; occupation and education; race, nationality, and religion; and marital status and family status.[3]

Every person is a sum of such parts, and not only can you be so defined but much of your buying behavior is a direct result of one or a combination of these characteristics. If, for example, you're a 20-year-old college student, think of the things you are interested in and buy as a consequence. If you go to college in San Diego instead of Minneapolis, consider how the geographical differences dictate everything from clothing to leisure activities to utilities use to food and so on. If you're a single, thirty-something, working woman, look at how many of your product needs spring directly from those facts. (See Figure 4.1.)

But demographics alone often prove insufficient as a way of defining your target market. One problem is that a demographic index may include various consumer patterns; various demographic indexes may contain the same pattern. Runners, for example, share certain product choices, yet they cut across many demographic segments. A 40-year-old single male with an income of $45,000 may be a plumber, a college professor, or an airline pilot, each with an obviously different lifestyle and consumption pattern. The "green revolution" of the 1990s, the environmental concern that has affected so many of our attitudes toward product use, can't be measured by demographic indexes at all. People haven't changed quantitatively; they have changed

---

[3]See Joel R. Evans and Barry Berman, *Principles of Marketing*, 2nd ed. (New York: Macmillan, 1988), pp. 72–79.

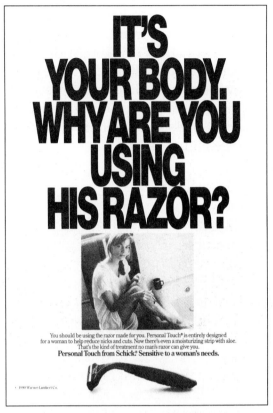

**Figure 4.1**   Two ads demonstrating the defining power of a demographic. Gender alone can be sufficient reason for picking one product and not another. Many products not intimately related to sexual differences have been successfully genderized, including cigarettes, diapers, magazines, beverages, and radio and cable channels. Courtesy of The Gillette Company and Schick®, Division of Warner-Lambert Co.

qualitatively, in their attitudes. Yet another problem with demographics is that they're too vague: If you're targeting "urban, college-educated women, 22–30, with incomes of $30–50,000," what pictures does this create in your head? Not many. Demographics become numbers and stats, not people, so you're writing ads to nobody.

## Psychographics

Thus, to demographics we add psychographics, people's activities, interests, consumer habits—their psychological and emotional traits. Think of psychographics as the opposite of demographics: not the outside of our lives, but the inside. And think just how much those insides have been changing over the years—the continual redefinition of women, men, and sex roles in this society; the rise of alternate lifestyles (and our changing attitudes toward them); the psychological effects of single parenting and latch-key childhoods; the "post-literate" but visually sophisticated mindset of today's adolescents; the rising health consciousness of the past decade; the demand for convenience across almost all product categories—the list is both endless and ever evolving. Since we express our values and lifestyles with the things we buy, psychographics help define markets, describe consumers, and determine advertising strategies themselves. (See Figure. 4.2.)

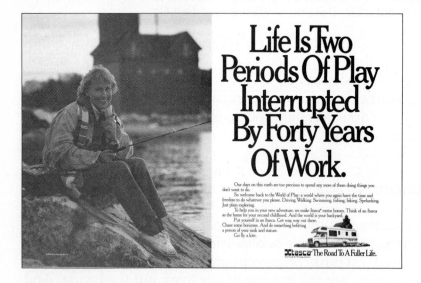

**Figure 4.2**    Demographics and psychographics combined: These ads target the upscale gray market (many of them "empty nesters"), understand what they're thinking, and tie recreation vehicles to the lifestyle change. Courtesy of Winnebago Industries, Inc.

## What can you do?

Short of taking a course in market research, subscribing to a market research firm's data, or becoming a market researcher yourself, you may assume that there's no realistic way to generate psychographic/demographic target information. And to some extent you're right. But no matter how sophisticated such research becomes, it still remains simply the *assertion* of buying categories by people thinking about consumers; it's not revealed, unalterable, inscrutable Truth. So you, too, can think about who's out there buying your product and how many kinds of whos there might be.

First let's look at a real-world example. Chiat/Day/Mojo, Nissan's ad agency, recently used psychographic segments of new-car buyers created by a market research firm to help them devise strategies.[4] The study postulated six consumer categories based on people's attitudes toward cars and the "driving experience." Here are brief summaries:

> *Gearheads*, the true car enthusiasts, actually work on cars and are mostly male, blue collar. They are the most likely to believe that the car you drive says a lot about you. They love sports cars, both domestic and Japanese.
>
> *Epicures*, the largest group, like fully equipped, comfortable cars; are looking for style and elegance; and have the second highest percentage of women, the highest household incomes, $100,00 or more. They especially like convertibles.
>
> *Purists*, the youngest group, are skeptical and not brand loyal but like driving and love sports cars. They have high concentrations of laborers and Asian Americans.
>
> *Functionalists* are conservative homeowners, often with children, who want sensible, fuel-efficient transportation. They buy small to mid-sized domestic cars.
>
> *Road-Haters*, tied with the Epicures as the largest group, are safety conscious, strongly prefer large domestic cars, don't enjoy driving, and have the highest share of women, the highest ages, and the lowest incomes.
>
> *Negatives* are uninterested in cars, regarding them as necessary evils, hassles. They're the most educated, with large incomes, and frequently buy small foreign cars.

You can see that these categories really are just assertions (who knows for certain how many kinds of new-car buyers there really are?). But they combine psychographics and demograph-

---

[4]"The Hearts of New-Car Buyers," reprinted with permission © *American Demographics* (August 1991), pp. 14–15.

ics in ways that seem to jibe with your intuitive sense of who
might be out there. You can also see that if you're Nissan this is
helpful material. You can target as many segments as you feel
you have cars for, and you can create advertising that talks about
those cars in ways that fit the needs of the targets. (You can also
use this material to change the kinds of cars you make, another
virtue of good research.) (See Figure 4.3.)

**Figure 4.3**   Porsche® targets Epicures; Volvo, Road-Haters. Copy of the
advertisement used by permission of Porsche Cars North America, Inc.
Porsche and the Porsche crest are registered trademarks of Dr. Ing. h.c. F
Porsche AG. Use of advertisement courtesy of Volvo.

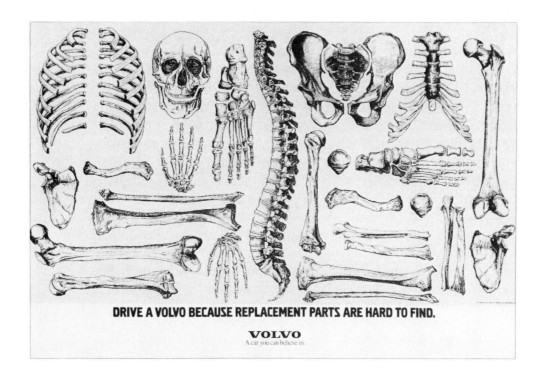

**Figure 4.3** (continued)

## Exercise:

Create your own psychographic/demographic segments in a product category you know well. Perhaps you play tennis or basketball, have a hobby like aerobics or know a lot about cosmetics. Create as many segments as you think there are of users in your category. For example, with basketball, you might divide the market into the Serious Street Player, The Aging Former College Athlete, the Young Wannabe, and the Weekend Hack. Briefly define each category. Who is this person demographically, psychographically? Now create a separate argument for each one: same product, athletic gear, but a different selling premise. For instance, you might argue that the gear will help the Young Wannabe rise to new heights; it will restore to the Aging Former College Athlete the edge he or she's lost. For the Hack, maybe your best argument says, "Hey, let's face it, looking good *is* most of it."

## Create a profile

Another way to combine demographics and psychographics and get a good sense of your market is to generate a brief character sketch of the typical target consumer. Based on your sense of who this person is, invent someone and write a few paragraphs about him or her. This is called a consumer **profile**, and it helps focus your thinking because now you're looking at someone. If, for example, you were creating ads for Limited Express, a clothing store for trendy women, you might be talking to this person:

> Today's fashion-forward woman, Debbie, is 27 and lives in her second apartment in an older suburb of Columbus, Ohio, while she saves money to buy a condominium in a newer suburb. She has a BFA degree in graphic design from Ohio State and uses her skills as a junior art director at a large design firm in the city, making $40,000 a year (a good amount in Midwestern dollars). She works hard and considers herself a woman with a career in progress; she is not just putting in time but is creating herself. Everyone dresses well at work, and clothes are part of the presentation she makes to others. Leading small groups is a common part of her job, so clothes become a professional asset and an expression of her own sense of design. Her dry-cleaning bills are large, as are her closets.

> She goes out on Fridays and Saturdays to the trendy nightspots with her friends. She has two cats, watches Lifetime cable and HBO, and is a big fan of *Seinfeld* and *Northern Exposure*. She watches TV while riding her StairMaster exercise machine. She subscribes to *Vanity Fair*, *Life*, and *Communication Arts* magazines and listens to the alternative rock station in her car to and from work. She does not get the daily newspaper, although reading the Sunday paper is a ritual. She travels overseas in her job and thinks of herself as cosmopolitan. Her immediate career goals are professional advancement to creative director within the design group. She'd like to be married and a mother some day, but right now her career is on the front burner. She thinks of herself as an experimenter and an edge person, willing to try new things and take chances.

If you were creating ads and brochures for Limited Express, don't you think that now you'd have a better sense of what to show and say? You'd write them to Debbie. That's the virtue of a profile.

## Exercises:

1. For whatever product you've been given, ask yourself, who is my most obvious target market? Try to define it demographically. What unifies it? Age? How big a spread? From what to what, can you say? Urban? Or suburban? City? Country? Men? Women? Regional? Religion? Is it ethnic in appeal? What income levels do you think are attracted? From what to what? Is marital status a factor? Occupation? Education level? How old are these people? Difficult and abstract, isn't it? Now add psychological data to it: Write a profile of the typical consumer. Invent a character and describe him or her.

2. A marketing rule of thumb is that 20 percent of a product's users consume 80 percent of that product. In other words, there is usually someone called the "heavy user." Many strategies target such heavy users for the obvious reason that they comprise the bulk of sales in a product category. Find the heavy user in your category. What is the person like who eats the most potato chips? Drinks the most pop? Buys the most stereo gear? Interview that person. What are his or her insides and outsides? What are his or her needs? Write a profile.

## *WHAT MARKET SEGMENTATION MEANS TO YOU*

[Aiming your advertising] is the same as hunting quail. You look up when a covey takes flight, and you think you'll hit something by just pulling the trigger. But you discover you have to choose a target—or you won't hit anything. Trying to sell anything to everyone isn't a strategy. It's wishful thinking.
—Hal Riney[5]

Segmenting the market clarifies your thinking. You understand what motivates each targeted segment of consumers, what they go to the product for, and what language they speak. If, however, you never decide on target markets and instead try to sell

---

[5]"How Now, Hal?," interview with Hal Riney, *Creative Leaders Advertising Program*, collected reprints of its advertising series, published by *The Wall Street Journal*, 1991, p. 42.

everybody in a language that offends no one—the "8 to 80" perplex—if you never place a particular person before your mind's eye when creating ads, then diffusion and blandness will undo you.

This holds true especially in the world of "let's pretend" advertising done for student portfolios. It can be hard to place a specific audience before your mind's eye—except perhaps the teacher—when doing assignments. Your ads become unrealistic because you forget, in the unrealistic setting of a college class-room, that you're really trying to reach actual, living people, not just hand in teacher-pleasing homework. So never content your-self with addressing fuzzy somebodies at best or demographic nobodies at worst, thinking, for example, that you are sufficiently precise if you say that your ad is "aimed at women 25–40." (Imagine for a moment the variety within those demographics. It varies all the way from the young woman sitting beside you in class to your mom.)

Instead always try to locate a particular person in your mind's eye: your roommate, your grandmother, the school's basketball players. Can you make him or her or them laugh? Can you get inside with the right talk and the right imagery? Try. (See Figures 4.4, 4.5, and 4.6.)

## Speak the audience's language

Look, for example, at these ads and note just how well they understand and locate, by their language and thought, highly specific market segments. This one, which appeared in London newspapers in 1900, was written by polar explorer Sir Ernest Shackleton:

> Men Wanted for Hazardous Journey. Small wages, bitter cold, long months of complete darkness, constant danger, safe return doubtful. Honor and recognition in case of success.

Response was overwhelming and immediate. The ad worked because it understood exactly what certain men wanted to hear, and said it to them, clearly, simply, and powerfully.[6]

Here's another ad, written 90 years later, and placed in men's magazines. It, too, understands what a certain market segment wants to hear and says it to them. Notice how precisely a particular type of person is evoked—the appeal combines demographics (thirty-something, urban) with psychographics (a

[6]Levitt, *The Marketing Imagination*, p. 129.

**Figure 4.4**   This campaign soliciting pizza delivery drivers knows what kind of language to use for its target market. The all-type format and wit also dignify the initial jokes, thus making clear the offer of professional opportunity. Courtesy of Godfather's Pizza, Inc.

particular lifestyle motive for running). The ad, a spread for Nike, shows a small figure running in what appears to be San Francisco, with these words as both headline and copy:

> He's fat and he's soft and he's wearing your clothes and he's getting too old and he was born on your birthday and you're afraid that if you stop running, he'll catch up with you.

Another ad from the same Nike campaign, this time showing an expanse of barren terrain with a road on which to run,

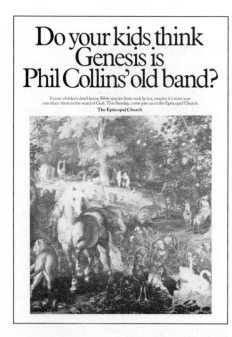

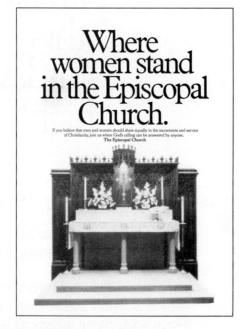

**Figure 4.5** This aggressive Fallon McElligott campaign for the Episcopal church realizes that more than one kind of person is missing from the pews, for more than one reason. Ads target specific segments of potential church-goers by addressing lifestyles and needs. Courtesy of Church Ad Project, 1021 Diffley Road, Eagan, MN 55123.

**Figure 4.6**   Here a product that might have been sold as a "home organizer" is wisely given a sharper focus. A specific audience is targeted, a specific benefit offered. A series of such ads, each singling out another potential user, would be stronger than any number of more generic ads. We look up when our names are called. Courtesy of California Closet Company.

evokes a different market segment, both an implied demographic (inner city, ethnic) and a psychographic (the motive for running this time: individuality and socioeconomic ascent):

> There are clubs you can't belong to, Neighborhoods you can't live in, Schools you can't get into, But the roads are always open. Just do it.

## Think like the market segment

It's easier to sell a product if you actually know someone who is part of its target audience. If, for example, you're selling golf equipment and you've played the game and know golfers, then you can become them in your mind while making ads.

One difficulty occurs when you must imagine an audience with which you have little experience: a different subculture or ethnic group, any audience a long way from you—maybe you're an undergraduate in New York City writing ads that sell farm equipment, or someone who's never taken more than a snapshot selling photography gear to pros. What to do? If possible, locate someone who is a part of the target and interview him or her. Find the magazines of that profession and read them. Study the ads to see what the issues are, what the selling arguments are, how the language works, what the slang is. You cannot write a good ad for a target audience until you become a surrogate member of it, and if you aren't born into it, then you must join it through empathy and effort. You must think and talk and want like your audience.

Another difficulty comes with business-to-business advertising: You must not only imagine two audiences, but neither one of them is a person. For example, you're asked to write an ad from a home construction firm to an architectural firm seeking to convince the latter that the former is the builder to choose. Even in this instance, however, the trick is to forget the corporations and become two people: a guy who builds houses talking to a guy who creates them. See it as a conversation between two people, one talking, the other listening. (We'll examine business-to-business advertising more completely in Chapter 13, "Other Media.")

## CONCLUSION

To create great advertising, you must examine, as we have, product, competition, consumer behavior, and target markets. But you can't simply weave your way through them impressionistically; rather, you combine them into a plan of action, a document in which you summarize the research and decide what your ads must accomplish. You write a creative strategy. Let's see what needs to be in it.

# CHAPTER 5

# WRITE THE STRATEGY STATEMENT

*Start with the right strategy. And follow that strategy relentlessly. We don't have a bunch of people just doing ads. We are structured and disciplined—and every job follows a step-by-step procedure.*
—Ralph Ammirati, founder, co-chairman, and creative director, Ammirati & Puris[1]

*Vague strategies inhibit. Precise strategies liberate.*
—Norman Berry, executive vice president, Ogilvy & Mather[2]

## *SET THE OBJECTIVE*

Even if you see the virtue of analyzing consumer behavior, creating target markets, and understanding your product in and out, you may not realize that a precise advertising objective is as important as anything else. Some of your assignments may sharply define your objective, others will be looser, and, if you're working on ads for your portfolio, you'll have no objective whatsoever until you give yourself one. Too often students think that an ad's purpose need be no more precise than, "This product is good, really, so buy it now." They regard a hearty, clever endorsement of the product a sufficiently precise task.

[1]"Ralph Revealed," interview with Ralph Ammirati 1989, *Creative Leaders Advertising Program*, collected reprints of its advertising series, published by *The Wall Street Journal*, 1990. Used by permission of Dow Jones & Company, Inc. publisher of *The Wall Street Journal*. *The Wall Street Journal* is a registered trademark of Dow Jones & Co., Inc.

[2]"Norman Conquest," interview with Norman Berry 1983, *Creative Leaders Advertising Program*, collected reprints of its advertising series, published by *The Wall Street Journal*, 1990. Used by permission of Dow Jones & Company, Inc. publisher of *The Wall Street Journal*. *The Wall Street Journal* is a registered trademark of Dow Jones & Co., Inc.

But unless you're creating "reminder" advertising, whose purpose may simply be to wave hello to the consumer, your advertising objective should be as specific as possible—utterance, not gesture. Otherwise you create ads whose effectiveness can't be determined partly because you've never asked what they ought to be doing. Advertising is too expensive for well-intentioned fuzziness.

So what's a good objective? That's obvious: one that solves your advertising problem. What's your advertising problem? That's often not so obvious, but it is something your research should suggest. Information about consumer behavior, target market, product, and position in the marketplace—all the issues we've been discussing—should be coming together to indicate what your advertising needs to do.

Maybe your product is new, so you need to announce, introduce, generate awareness. Maybe your product isn't new, but it's got new, more convenient packaging or better flavor, so here communicating that becomes your advertising objective. Perhaps your product is on the western slopes of its product life cycle, and you're injecting new life into it by proposing new uses, as Arm & Hammer did for its baking soda—encouraging us to put it in the refrigerator, sprinkle it on the carpet, in the cat litter, in our laundry tub, and so on. Maybe you're trying to expand product consumption among heavy users, as was the purpose of the long-running campaign, "Orange Juice. It's not just for breakfast anymore." Or you want to change attitudes about your brand or product category. Perhaps you face heavy competition, so you must communicate product superiority—by announcing a unique feature or creating a differential via a distinct brand image. Maybe you're targeting new markets, so you must create ads that speak their language and bind your product to their needs.

Who can say what your objective should be? That comes only from intelligent, creative analysis of all the forces in your product's force field. It's a complicated field, as we've seen, but now you must become simple and single-minded; now you must distill all that into one advertising objective. Just what—exactly—do you want to communicate? What one thing do you want the consumer to believe, or understand, or feel, or do about your product? Unless and until you focus on a specific objective, your ads will suffer from blurriness. Be an arrow, not an ink blot:

> Any premise that can't make up its mind or that is overburdened
> with more than one objective or idea is not a strategy.
> —John Lyons[3]

[3]John Lyons, *Guts* (New York: AMACOM, 1987), p. 124.

## *THE CREATIVE STRATEGY STATEMENT*

In its shortest form, all your creative strategy needs is three things:

> **What** benefit are you promising, what's your selling argument?
>
> **Who** are you making it to?
>
> **Why** should they believe you?

And you can put all that in a sentence or two:

> Ads will target current orange juice drinkers and convince them that orange juice is good any time of day or night; proof will be that it's nutritious, thirst quenching, and energy-giving, all benefits needed at various times in the day.

> Ads will target environmentally conscious users of household cleaners and convince them that Murphy's Oil Soap cleans thoroughly without damaging the environment. Support will be that it contains no harsh detergents or alkalis: it's 100 percent pure vegetable oil.

> Ads will target upscale women, 18–34, and convince them that Limited Express clothing will help make them successful, professionally and socially. Support will be the creation of a brand personality: fashion-forward, self-confident, hip.

Typically, however, ad agencies flesh this out into a couple of pages, and so can you. What an agency calls this planning document varies (sometimes *creative strategy*, *copy platform*, or *creative work plan*), and its length and information vary, too, but most advertising plans include the following:

| | |
|---|---|
| **Key Fact**<br>**Advertising Problem**<br>**Advertising Objective** | These three aspects combine to tell you what your ads need to do. |
| **Target Consumer**<br>**Competition**<br>**Key Consumer Benefit**<br>**Support** | These four aspects focus your approach. |

**1. Key Fact:** Bill Westbrook, corporate creative director at Earle Palmer Brown, begins his creative work plan with "a single-minded statement that sorts out from all the information about product, market, competition, etc., the element that is the *most* *relevant to advertising."*[4] Many advertising strategists concur: Begin your strategic thinking by looking for the *key fact* about your product. Why? Because it will cast the light by which to see the advertising problem you must solve.

**2. Advertising Problem:** What is that key fact telling you? What is your product's biggest consumer-related problem? For example, in researching Boku packaged juice drink, the key fact you discover may be that consumers have no firm sense of the brand: They don't know whether Boku is for kids or adults, for health or for fun. Your advertising problem is clear: You need to create a place for Boku in the consumer's mind; right now it's simply lost in the shuffle. If, as another example, the key fact is that the median age of Geritol users keeps rising, then your problem is also clear: You've got to expand the market for Geritol or vanish as a product with your current target market.

**3. Advertising Objective:** Once you find the key fact and understand the advertising problem, express this understanding as an advertising objective. What effect do you want to have on the consumer? An advertising objective is really a *communication* objective: what you want people to understand, believe, or feel about your product. (You can't set marketing tasks for yourself —like improving sales by 20 percent—since these can be realized only by the entire marketing effort operating in an economic climate, not by advertising alone.)

With Boku, your objective might be to create awareness of Boku as the *adult* juice drink. Or with Geritol, your objective might be to convince consumers that even though they're not yet old, they need Geritol's vitamins.

**4. Target Consumers:** To whom do you want to communicate this message? Which product users will you target? Define your target audience more specifically than simply demographically, just with numbers. What about psychographics—lifestyle and attitudes? Can you create a profile of the consumer you're addressing? Will Boku target pop drinkers, juice drinkers, health-conscious pop drinkers? Twenty-somethings or younger or older consumers? What specific attitudes should be addressed? Perhaps you'll target 18–25-year-old, health-conscious fruit juice drinkers, both men and women, concerned that they drink the right thing. Geritol might target health-conscious baby boomers —under 50, but aging and anxious.

[4]Bill Westbrook, quoted in Mill Roseman, "Bill Westbrook," *Communication Arts* (March/April 1991), p. 51.

**5. Competition:** Where does your product fit in the marketplace? How is your product perceived now and how do you want it to be perceived? What product category should it compete in? Who are its competitors, both direct and indirect? For example, is Boku competing primarily against soft drinks, Pepsi, Coke, and so on? Fruit drinks? Or since alcohol consumption is down and consumers are seeking alternatives, have beer, wine, and other alcoholic beverages become competitors? Is Boku really a packaging innovation and therefore should be sold as a new *way* to consume one of the preceding categories?

*What* something is (and therefore what products it should compete with) is obviously a key part of your strategy, one you should never consider pre-ordained. (Notice that you might make Boku fill a different need for each of several segments by creating more than one advertising campaign, each driven by a separate strategy.)

**6. Key Consumer Benefit:** If the *objective* is what *you* want to happen, the *benefit* is seen from the consumer's point of view: What benefit does your product deliver, what problem will it solve? This is the core of your strategy. Remember that our "problems" can be of all sorts, from product problems (we need a spaghetti sauce that isn't runny, a deodorant spray that doesn't punch holes in the ozone layer, bran that actually tastes good, and so on) to consumer problems (we want more spare time, we need more love and esteem, we'd like to succeed, and so forth). Should you emphasize product-related benefits or consumer-related benefits? Decide. With Boku you could either convince target consumers that Boku is the fruit juice made for adults or that they gain self-esteem by drinking it.

**7. Support:** Now, prove it. If you promise a benefit, what's your evidence? If your product will solve a problem, *how* will it do so? With its enhanced protein? Its button-fly? Its mentholated spray? Its sex appeal? Its German engineering? Its...what? You can't make people believe something without backing it up. This support is sometimes called the *reason why*. Boku needs to support the contention that it's an *adult* juice drink. This might be accomplished via brand image techniques, by appeals to its packaging or its fruit juice content, or by ads emphasizing who drinks it. Geritol must make the rational case for vitamins to a stressed-out, aging target market.

Say all this in one to two pages. Again, remember that the essence of your creative strategy is simply:

What benefit are you proposing?

To whom?

Why should they believe you?

The preceding seven sections are all that you need to put in your strategy statement, but often advertising plans contain other material helpful in focusing strategy. You may want to include it in yours:

**Tone Statement:** What *feel* do you envision for the campaign? Whimsical, no-nonsense, aggressively competitive, off the wall? An ad's tone is crucial, a large part of what that ad means. What tone do you want to communicate, what attitude is best for your product, target, and advertising problem?

**Mandatories and Limitations:** Westbrook includes in his creative strategy "any restrictions or client data which are necessary to a clear understanding of creative direction including legal cautions, carry-over of a successful slogan, items of line to feature, type of casting acceptable and corporate tags."[5] Usually you cannot simply start over with a clean slate but must deal with the advertising and brand image already in place. Taking the advertising in the direction you want it to go without rupturing current consumer perceptions in the process, making the transition toward your goals a seamless one, is often your real-world task.

## FINAL ADVICE

We spend more time finding out what the problem is than we spend solving it. Most designers skip the "identify-the-problem" step, they're so bristling with solutions, like puppies leaking everywhere.
—Stephen Doyle, Drenttel Doyle Partners[6]

The quality of the solution depends entirely on how well you state the problem.
—Craig Frazier, designer[7]

[5]Roseman, *Communication Arts*, p. 51.

[6]Stephen Doyle, quoted in "CSCA, Stephen Doyle, and a Punch," *3rd Thursday*, newsletter of The Columbus Society of Communicating Arts (July 1990), no pagination.

[7]Craig Frazier, quoted in *Communication Arts*, Design Annual, 1989, p. 143.

It sounds easy to find the key fact, but it often isn't. There are lots of facts about a product, and once you identify a major one, you're still not sure what to do about it. Sometimes, of course, the key fact is clear. For example, Citrus Hill marketed an orange juice with added calcium. Here the special ingredient was the key fact and dictated your advertising problem: You had to convince orange juice drinkers that calcium constituted an important differential, that orange juice without calcium was insufficient.

But often enough the key fact and hence the advertising problem you must solve are less obvious, so thinking the issues through becomes more difficult than our examples suggest. For instance, if you're advertising for AT&T, it's a fact that since AT&T's breakup in 1984 you've lost significant market share (down from 90 percent to 63 percent by 1991), especially to Sprint and MCI.[8] It's also a fact that you have some technological advances they don't. It's also a fact that people under 40, who didn't grow up with Ma Bell, have no special loyalty to AT&T (of course, another fact is that those over 40 do). It's yet another fact that many people age 18–34 regard AT&T as stodgy, not very youthful.

Which of these do you respond to? Do you target the young with a hip image campaign? Attack your competitors with ads emphasizing hardware differentials? Take the high road and reassure AT&T loyalists that Mr. Big is still big enough? (And we've grossly oversimplified the issues for brevity's sake. If we really opened them out, key facts and advertising problems would proliferate.)

Sometimes creative people mistakenly think that the strategy statement is at best a perfunctory outline, a simple condensation of the obvious, and at worst a straitjacket against good ideas. But neither is true. The genuine complexities of the marketplace are what make the strategic document so essential, and they're also why thinking one through requires intelligence and marketing savvy.

[8]Terry Lefton, "AT&T Spends $30M in Search of Youth," *Brandweek*, January 4, 1993, pp. 1, 6.

## CHAPTER 6

# KINDS OF STRATEGIES

Before making ads, let's survey the kinds of strategies advertisers use, not in order to pick one out like a shirt at a store, but to gain a sense of available ways to sell products.

If we were to say—in three words—what all good ads do, we'd say: "Dramatize the benefit." Advertisers differ, however, in what they consider the benefit in need of dramatizing—sometimes it's a product's feature or a marketplace position, other times a problem solved or a state of mind achieved.

Also, since ads sell a product to a consumer, advertisers can choose to emphasize one or the other. Thus, we can think of advertising approaches as residing on a continuum from product-oriented strategies, on the one hand, to consumer-oriented ones on the other, from hard product to soft lifestyle. We might also say that the approaches range from rational to emotional—product-oriented arguments frequently appealing to our sense of reason, the consumer-oriented approaches often stressing the emotional qualities of life with the product.

How many kinds of strategic approaches there are depends on who's counting and how. Here is our count; others, of course, may differ.

## *PRODUCT-ORIENTED VS. CONSUMER-ORIENTED STRATEGIES*

### PRODUCT-ORIENTED:

1. **Generic claim:** sell the product category, not the brand.
2. **Product feature:** sell a product feature; appeal to reason.
3. **Unique selling proposition:** sell a benefit unique to the brand.

4. **Positioning:** establish a distinct and desirable market niche.

## CONSUMER-ORIENTED:

5. **Brand image:** create and sell a personality for the brand.
6. **Lifestyle:** associate the product with a way of life.
7. **Attitude:** associate the product with a state of mind.

By artificially separating the flow of advertising, all categories—including these—are false, their distinctions neat on paper but messier in reality. Many ads borrow from several of these categories; other great ads can't be lodged in any of them. When you're making ads, use the idea of categories, but don't be bound by it. Don't worry over which one you're using so much as this: Is what you're doing working?

## Product-oriented strategies

### 1. Generic claim

Selling one of the principal benefits your product *category* delivers—fast headache relief for aspirin and other pain relievers; watery relaxation for cruise lines; clean clothes for laundry products, and so on—is probably the most widely used advertising strategy. Many ads simply make a generic claim, associate their brand with that claim, then count on the cumulative power of advertising and association, as well as the memorability of a strong execution, to link the principal benefit we seek with that brand. They do this even though competitors can (and do) make the same argument and deliver the same benefit. (See Figure 6.1.)

Selling the product category, not the brand, makes even better sense if you have dominant share in a market. Your main competitor is consumers themselves—their levels of usage—more than other brands. "When you own the pie, you should try to enlarge the pie rather than try to increase the size of your slice."[1] Arm & Hammer thus needs to sell the idea of baking soda, not its brand. Kodak's slogan "Because time goes by" invokes a fundamental motive for picture-taking. Likewise, Campbell's doesn't need to sell their brand but the generic product; their slogan "Soup is good food" encourages us simply to eat more soup. (See Figure 6.2.)

[1] Al Ries and Jack Trout, *Marketing Warfare* (New York: NAL, Plume, 1986), p. 66.

**Figure 6.1** All these ads' brands make generic claims—the optical retailer offers good-looking glasses, the bank promises to listen well, the YMCA promises to get us in shape—but they do so energetically. The strength of the execution (rather than the singularity of the strategy) is what makes these ads distinctive. Courtesy of Union Optical, YMCA of Metropolitan Minneapolis, and Bank One Corporation.

One of the best ways to insure good health, is to eat a well-balanced diet that includes nutritious foods like Campbell's Soup.

That's not just our opinion. The fact is university researchers found that soup plays a significant part in a nutritionally healthy diet.

That Campbell's Tomato Soup up there, for instance, is an important source of vitamin C. While Campbell's Vegetable Beef contains more than 1/3 of the day's allowance of vitamin A in just a single serving.

And not only are most Campbell's Soups a rich source of nutrition, they're also light on your stomach, and easy to digest.

So when you're picking out a good health insurance policy, remember to pick up a few cans of your favorite Campbell's Soups.

If you have any questions, talk to one of the best insurance agents around. Mom.

**CAMPBELL'S SOUP IS GOOD FOOD**

**Figure 6.2** The market-share leader makes a generic claim for soup. Courtesy of Campbell Soup Company.

New products (like fax machines and car phones) also need at first to sell the basic argument (why buy a fax? why install a car phone?) before worrying about brand differentiation. (See Figure 6.3.)

## 2. Product feature

Ask yourself why we buy your product. If our choice is largely rational, a sifting among product distinctions (most hardware, large and small; many household goods; packaged goods), and

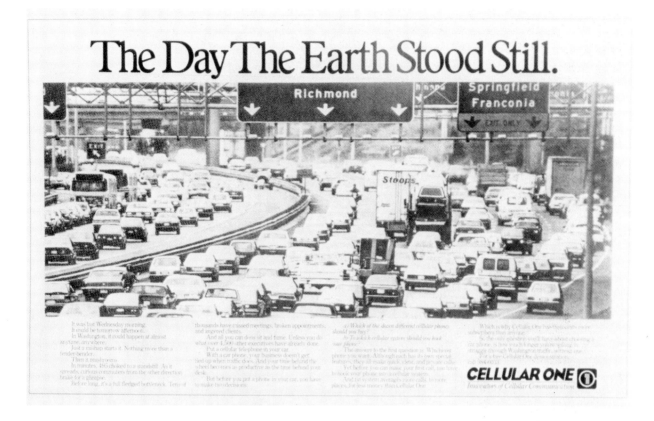

**Figure 6.3** Pioneering ads for cellular phones, like this one from 1985, made the generic claim. As the market grew and became competitive, ads focused on differentials, like better price or service. Courtesy of Cellular One®-Washington/Baltimore.

your product truly has distinctions that matter, then sell them. Focus, not on generic product benefits, but on competitive ones. Here you appeal to the logical choice based on sensible differences between brands. Ragu has real tomato chunks in its sauce. Volvo's passengers sit securely inside a steel frame. Keds tennis shoes are machine washable. (See Figure 6.4.)

This strategy can work in competitive markets, where you're fighting to distinguish yourself from others, and it can work whenever why we buy is a rational decision. You can emphasize either the product's virtue or our problem being solved—or both, as does this headline for an Acura coupe underneath a picture of the car in action, "Could your heart benefit from the use of another 24 valves?"

## 3. Unique selling proposition

The same idea as earlier but pushed further. Essentially your selling argument here is, "You should buy a _____ because it's the only one that _____."

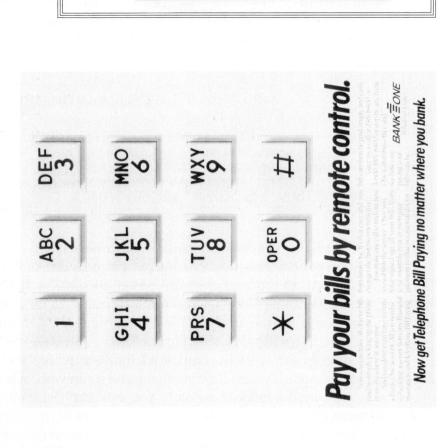

**Figure 6.4** Here both a bank and a newspaper offer distinct competitive benefits. Courtesy of Bank One Corporation and developed by Goodby, Berlin & Silverstein, advertising agency for the *San Francisco Examiner*.

Rosser Reeves, a famous American advertiser of the 1950s, built his career and legend on his idea that the best way to sell things was by making what he called a unique selling proposition (USP), a specific promise of benefit unique to the product, one that the competition either does not or cannot claim. So, for example, M&Ms "melt in your mouth, not in your hands," an argument implying that its competitors fail to do so. This singling out of some specific aspect of the product and then basing an ad campaign on it is predicated on our willingness to believe that products do differ from one another, that a given product can deliver something that others can't.

Although such product-oriented, hard-sell advertising has given way over the decades to softer, brand-image, style- and feelings-oriented advertising, the USP idea never really disappears. For example, what do we know about Folger's coffee? That it's "mountain grown." All coffee is mountain grown, but Folger's said it first, thus appearing to make an argument unique to itself, and now owns some territory in our brains as a consequence. (This first use of a generic feature by a brand is sometimes called a *preemptive claim* instead of a USP. You are preempting its use by competitors even though they too could have made the same claim, had they thought of it first.)

If you examine almost any array of advertising, you'll see such product-specific claims of uniqueness being made. VW's campaign theme, "Fahrvergnugen. It's what makes a car a Volkswagen," was based on convincing us that there was some design or engineering or ergonomic wisdom to VW's cars so unique that it deserved a name.

Do you see how this is a claim of a different order from Mazda's "It just feels right," Toyota's "I love what you do for me," or Chevrolet's "The Heartbeat of America" theme lines? All of them, whatever their merits, are generic claims, not claims that are product specific and unique. If you see the essential difference between the VW slogan and the other three, then you understand the idea of a unique selling proposition. (See Figure 6.5.)

## 4. Positioning

> The true nature of marketing today
> involves the conflict between corporations,
> not the satisfying of human needs and wants.
> —Al Ries and Jack Trout[2]

[2]Ries and Trout, *Marketing Warfare,* p. 7.

**Figure 6.5** USP advertising: Why drink Evian instead of another bottled water? Because it (alone?) comes from the French Alps. Courtesy of Evian/Great Brands of Europe.

We owe *positioning* to Trout and Ries, who developed the concept in a series of articles and later a book.[3] Simply stated, positioning is the perception consumers have of your product, not unto itself, but relative to its competition. Products are "positioned" in our minds, each being given an evaluation, a definition, a niche, in the product inventories we maintain. We condense our estimate of

[3]Jack Trout and Al Ries published a three-part series on positioning in *Advertising Age*, April 24, May 1, and May 8, 1972, and put it all in a book, *Positioning: The Battle for Your Mind* (New York: McGraw-Hill, 1981).

each product into one simple (and often permanent) perception and create hierarchies of similar products.

For example, among detergents, we consider Tide all-American, all-purpose; Cheer is all-temperature; Dreft is soft, for babies' things; Dash is the budget brand; Fab combines a softener with the cleaner; Bold is the enzymes cleaner; and so on. To be successful, a brand must carve out for itself an identity that's not only distinct—a handle by which we recognize it—but also viable—one for which we'll buy it.

### The power of positioning

> The starting point must be a distinct point of view. Bernbach taught us that if you stand for everything, you stand for nothing. That's why the essence of positioning is sacrifice—deciding what's unimportant, what can be cut away and left behind; reducing your perspective to a very sharp point of view.
> —Keith Reinhard, chairman, DDB Needham[4]

Positioning is a marketing idea so strong that whole campaigns can be based on it. We remember 7-Up as "the Uncola," a pure example of the power of positioning; we were asked to buy it for what it wasn't. Pepsi's slogan "The Choice of a New Generation" sought to reposition Coca-Cola as the drink of older people, while Coke's "The Real Thing" and "Coke Is It" campaigns tried to position it as the only authentic cola. (Many slogans and campaign theme lines are simply crystallized position statements. See the slogan discussion in Chapter 7.)

Positioning strategies are essential when products are new, since they occupy no place whatsoever in our minds. How you position them has much to do with their success. If yours is simply a "me-too" product, then your chances for survival may be poor. Discovering and then expressing a distinct, competitive position becomes a major goal of your advertising. Positioning can also determine advertising strategy when your product is not the category leader but an also-ran. After all, you have nowhere to go but up. If you're a strong # 2 or 3, say, you may want to go right after the leader. The key is finding a weakness inherent in the leader's strength. As Trout and Ries argue:

> What the leader owns is a position in the mind of the prospect. To win the battle of the mind, you must take away the leader's

[4]"Keith's Beliefs," interview with Keith Reinhard 1989, *Creative Leaders Advertising Program*, collected reprints of its advertising series, published by *The Wall Street Journal*, 1990. Used with permission of Dow Jones & Company, Inc., publisher of *The Wall Street Journal*. *The Wall Street Journal* is a registered trademark of Dow Jones & Co., Inc.

position before you can substitute your own. It's not enough for you to succeed; others must fail. Specifically, the leader.[5]

Avis's celebrated campaign in the 1960s against the market leader in rental cars, Hertz, is an example. Their "We try harder" campaign, based on Avis's second-place status, made us root for the underdog and doubt Mr. Big. Or you can "flank" the opponent, as did the VW Beetle, whose ad campaign established a unique niche for the Bug off to the side of the Detroit monster-wagons. (See Figure 6.6.)

# Avis is only No.2 in rent a cars. So why go with us?

We try harder.
(When you're not the biggest, you have to.)
We just can't afford dirty ash-trays. Or half-empty gas tanks. Or worn wipers. Or unwashed cars. Or low tires. Or anything less than seat-adjusters that adjust. Heaters that heat. Defrost-ers that defrost.
Obviously, the thing we try hardest for is just to be nice. To start you out right with a new car, like a lively, super-torque Ford, and a pleasant smile. To know, say, where you get a good pastrami sandwich in Duluth.
Why?
Because we can't afford to take you for granted.
Go with us next time.
The line at our counter is shorter.

**Figure 6.6** This classic Avis ad and recent discount broker ad both seek to reposition the competition. Another headline in the latter's assault on tra-ditional investment houses: "If you're still paying full commissions to your broker, you're not an investor. You're a philanthropist." Courtesy of Avis Rent A Car System, Inc. and Quick & Reilly.

[5]Ries and Trout, *Marketing Warfare*, pp. 68–69. I also draw my reference to VW's "flanking" maneuver from their discussion.

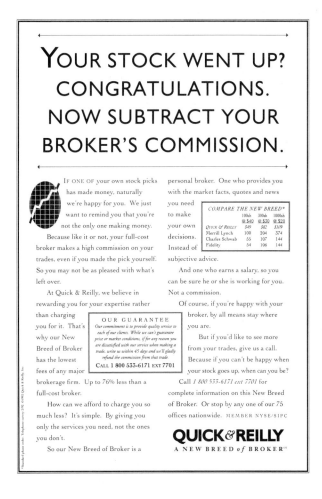

**Figure 6.6** (continued)

**Key positioning questions:**

What position do you now occupy?

What positions do your competitors occupy?

What new position do you want to occupy? Or how do you want to modify your current position?

What strategy should your advertising adopt as a consequence?

While many campaigns are based on positioning, its greatest value to you may be as an *idea*, an indispensable index by which to gauge your product and its relationship to the competition. You may never make positioning a dominant advertising strategy, but you should never be ignorant of your product's place in our minds. How we regard it, especially relative to other similar products, is essential information. No product is position-less.

# Consumer-oriented strategies

## 5. Brand image

> Image means *personality*. Products, like people, have personalities, and they can make or break them in the market place. The personality of a product is an amalgam of many things—its name, its packaging, its price, the style of its advertising, and above all, the nature of the product itself. Every advertisement should be thought of as a contribution to the brand image. It follows that your advertising should consistently project the *same* image, year after year.
> —David Ogilvy[6]

> When a customer identifies with the personality of a product, and finds its behavior attractive, he transfers that personality and behavior to himself by buying and using that product. It's like putting on a badge and wearing it proudly.
> —Keith Reinhard, chairman, DDB/Needham[7]

David Ogilvy is generally credited with developing the idea of brand-image advertising, and each of his great campaigns from the 1950s—Rolls-Royce, Schweppes, Hathaway shirts, and others—established a consistent style and sensibility that, once begun, were maintained. Brand-image advertising is the selling, not of specific product features, elements intrinsic to the object itself, but instead the selling of its aura, its personality, those aspects extrinsic to it that make up its (self-created) image.

All ads, regardless of strategy, contribute to a brand's image, so in this sense all advertising is brand-image advertising. If a brand has no image, then it's got a bad ad agency. Thus, discussing the *strategy* of brand-image advertising becomes tricky, since image is always at issue. But here let's use the term to mean a strategy *focused* on the personality of a brand. When you look at that product's advertising, you realize that you're being asked to buy into a personality, not an argument. That's the distinction.

What, for example, differentiates Reebok from Nike, Coca-Cola from Pepsi, BMW from Lexus? Primarily their advertising symbol systems. Each makes a good product; none is so advanced that its technical merit alone distances it from its competition. In our rational mind, we realize that, as an object, each is substantially equivalent to its major competitor(s). Since the product is intrinsically similar, the extrinsic brand image of the

[6]David Ogilvy, *Ogilvy on Advertising* (New York: Random House, 1985), p. 14.

[7]Keith Reinhard, quoted in David Martin, *Romancing the Brand* (New York: AMACOM, 1989), p. 92.

product, communicated through its advertising (often called advertising's "added value"), becomes the meaning we seek. The differentiated systems of language and design in which the products reside are what we buy. And we are happy to do so.

Here's Ogilvy:

> Take whiskey. Why do some people choose Jack Daniel's, while others choose Grand Dad or Taylor? Have they tried all three and compared the taste? Don't make me laugh. The reality is that these three brands have different images which appeal to different kinds of people. It isn't the whiskey they choose, it's the image. The brand image is 90 per cent of what the distiller has to sell.[8]

And so it is with many products: Most of what they have to sell is symbolic. You should consider this strategy when you're in a competitive, parity situation or when your product is almost a commodity: cigarettes, beer, liquor, cologne, soap, and so on (for which a unique feature or rational argument is often hard to find). Brand-image advertising is also a good idea for *badge* products, those items whose names are visible, whose identities are socially obvious (clothes, cars, and so on), unlike socially invisible products (canned goods in cupboards, detergents in the laundry room, and the like). Other products, invisible themselves, that contribute to our social esteem—personal care items, for instance—can also be sold via brand image.

If you think that's a long list, you're right. Brand-image advertising pervades so many product categories and has become so ubiquitous that some people argue that it's won the how-to-advertise war:

> Gone are the days of the left-brained "reason why" messages. Most of them are hokum...so insignificant and strained and boring and unbelievable they fall on deaf ears. It's a cliché to say the technologies of today can erase any product benefit overnight. Creating a brand image, giving the brand a personality, making it lifelike, building an aura around the brand so it seems like an old friend, is where the battles will be fought in the '90s.
> —Lou Centlivre, executive managing director, retired
> Foote, Cone & Belding/Chicago[9]

How to create brand-image advertising? For one thing, study the great campaigns: Marlboro, Nike, the image ads for

[8]Ogilvy, *Ogilvy on Advertising,* p. 14.

[9]Lou Centlivre, "The Joy of Discovery: Finding Dormant Talent," *Advertising Age,* January 29, 1990, p. 35.

various cars, and so on. Ask, what is a Volvo? (or Timex or whatever your brand) and see what answer you get. Either create ads that express that personality or reshape the personality to fit the answer you seek. Regard the product as a person; write up a profile of it as though it were a person, and study that. (See the voice discussion in Chapter 8, "Body Copy I.") Also, when you get to the design and typography chapter, realize that these two forces are powers behind brand images. Style *is* substance with brand-image advertising. (See Figures 6.7 and 6.8.)

## 6. Lifestyle

## 7. Attitude

> It is not sufficiently recognized—especially by the critics of advertising—that romance in its broad sense is the most wanted product in the world.
> —James Webb Young[10]

Closely related to brand-image advertising and each other are two more approaches that emphasize, not product hardware, but consumer states of mind—approaches we might call *lifestyle* advertising and *attitude* advertising. Rather than creating an image of the brand itself, they create an image of the consumer, making him or her, in effect, the product. The viewer is shown a desirable state of being, to which the product is appended.

**Lifestyle** advertising is what it sounds like: Ads show a desirable way of living and simply insert the product into it. Such advertising, by its nature, expresses the highest possible benefit because rather than arguing a narrow product advantage, it implies a large personal improvement: The lifestyle shown is one the viewers desire and can have, or begin to, if they buy the product that seems to be its indispensable accessory. (See Figure 6.9.)

Remember, the idea is that the target audience doesn't so much see the product (in fact, many such ads barely show it at all) as they see what it must be like to own it. When creating this kind of advertising, don't regard the product as some piece of hardware with features and USPs, some *thing* over there. Regard it as an indispensable accessory to a way of being; then use imagery that you think communicates this atmosphere—these psychological benefits, this alternate reality, if you will, that can be the audience's if it uses the product.

---

[10]James Webb Young, *Diary of an Ad Man* (Chicago: Advertising Publications, Inc., 1944), p. 24.

**Figure 6.7** Examples of brand-image advertising: What separates BMW motorcycles from Harley-Davidson motorcycles? Primarily the imagery that surrounds them. Courtesy of Carmichael Lynch Advertising and BMW of North America, Inc.

**Figure 6.8** In both these ads we learn not about products themselves but about their personalities: unconventional, assertive, on the edge. If we like these styles, then we can seek out specific items to which they are attached. Pure brand-image work. Courtesy of William Claxton, Photographer/Barneys New York and O'Brien International.

**Figure 6.9** Lifestyle advertising. Here the product accompanies a way of life that the target audience aspires to. By seeming indispensable to such a lifestyle, the brand becomes an incremental way of achieving it.Courtesy of Winchester/Olin Corporation, The Keds Corporation and The Lee Apparel Co.

$350 a month for rent.   $750 for the weekend.      Lee jeans.

**Figure 6.9** (continued)

With **attitude** advertising we are buying the expression of an inner feeling more than a particular lifestyle. We are presented a tone, a mood, an emotion, an *attitude*—the implication being either that this attitude is gained via the product or simply that the product is an accessory to it. Attitude ads are clearly a corollary of lifestyle advertising, perhaps its next development: the symbolic simplification of a complete narrative into its one purest emotion.

For example, the Budweiser beer campaign "Why Ask Why?" was less social scenarios than it was the hypothesized state of mind of the targeted beer drinker: a person interested in but confused by the opposite sex; hence, the shrug of the intellectual shoulders. This was the attitude of the Bud drinker. Buy the beer, get the attitude. Nike's great work often shows attitude more than lifestyle: Theme lines like "There is no finish line" and "Just do it," body copy heavy on inner psychological states, and TV ads wired to Beatles songs and John Lennon soundtracks—while sometimes situated in a slice of lifestyle—just as often seem almost purely mental states. (See Figure 6.10.)

## Corporate attitude

Some recent advertising has moved so far past both product and lifestyle as to present not a sought-after consumer attitude but the product as an expression of cultural force. For example, Benetton's controversial work has been an attempt, not so much to sell clothes as to present a provocative ethos and ask us to consider the clothes an objective correlative of it; that is, we're shown avant-garde social attitudes, aggressive social stances, and the clothes are meant to be fashion analogues. They become a parallel experience to the provocative imagery. (See Figure 6.11.)

Less controversial but still out there somewhere was 1989's prelaunch campaign for Infiniti cars that not only refused to show the cars themselves, but presented instead Zen-like nature

**Figure 6.10**  Attitude advertising. More than anything else, a state of mind is being sold. Courtesy of Nike, Inc. and The Donna Karan Company.

A WOMAN IS OFTEN MEA-
SURED BY THE THINGS SHE CANNOT
CONTROL. SHE IS MEASURED BY THE WAY
HER BODY CURVES OR DOESN'T CURVE, BY
WHERE SHE IS FLAT OR STRAIGHT OR ROUND.
SHE IS MEASURED BY 36-24-36 AND INCHES
AND AGES AND NUMBERS, BY ALL THE OUT-
SIDE THINGS THAT DON'T EVER ADD UP TO
WHO SHE IS ON THE INSIDE. AND SO IF A
WOMAN IS TO BE MEASURED, LET HER BE
MEASURED BY THE THINGS SHE CAN
CONTROL, BY WHO SHE IS AND WHO SHE IS
TRYING TO BECOME. BECAUSE AS EVERY
WOMAN KNOWS, MEASUREMENTS ARE ONLY
STATISTICS. AND STATISTICS LIE.

STATISTICS AND SIZES AND MEASURE-
MENTS DO NOT MAKE UP A WOMAN. THEY DO
NOT DESCRIBE HER FRUSTRATIONS OR HER VIC-
TORIES, HER EFFORTS OR HER INTENTS. BUT
THEY DO MAKE UP THE TOOLS SHE USES TO
COMPLETE HERSELF. WHICH IS WHY NIKE
DESIGNED THE AIR ELITE® ULTRA IN A SPECI-
FIC WAY, IN A WAY TO
CUSHION YOUR FOOT
AS IT LANDS, TO PRO-
TECT YOUR FOOT FROM IMPACT, AND TO SUP-
PORT YOUR FOOT WITH EACH AEROBIC MOVE
YOU MAKE. BECAUSE STATISTICS MAY LIE WHEN
IT COMES TO WOMEN, BUT THEY ARE
VERY IMPORTANT WHEN
IT COMES TO SHOES.

**Figure 6.10**   (continued)

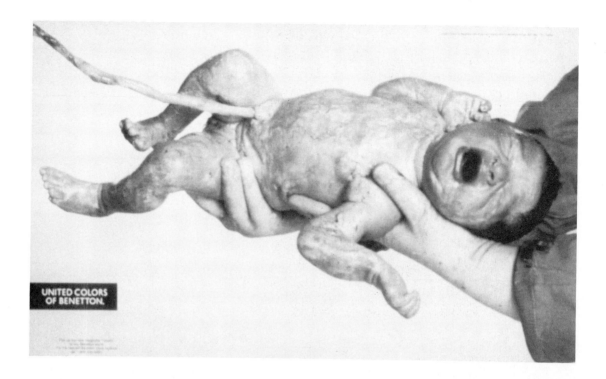

**Figure 6.11** These are, in their way, fashion clothing ads. (Benetton) Courtesy of Benetton Services.

images of sea, stones, haystacks, and the like, accompanied by elegant, abstract language. The idea was that the cars, wherever they were and whatever they looked like, were machine expressions of this state of mind. We were to admire the mind, and the cars would come tagging after. (See Figure 6.12.)

**Figure 6.12** This is a car ad. (Infiniti) Courtesy of Infiniti Division/Nissan Corporation.

## *STRATEGIES AS A CONTINUUM*

When you're making ads, it's not a case of either-or: Either you use this kind of strategy or you use that one; either you sell product features or you create a feelings-oriented brand-image campaign. These eight categories are really more a continuum than a rigid set of mutually exclusive approaches. In fact, given the unending discussion in the research journals about whether consumer behavior is cognitive or affective, whether we buy with our head or our heart and to what extent and when and how, it's best to neglect neither reason nor emotion in your ads. Focus on one but include the other:

> ...the best theoretical objective is to *surround the claim with the feeling.*
> —Rosser Reeves[11]

> Most often, a commercial is a blend of linear [rational] and non-linear [emotional] elements. The emotional setting helps make the rational message relevant and enjoyable. The copy message gives form and relevance to the imagery. Advertising, to be truly effective must appeal to both sides of the brain [the rational left brain, the emotional right brain], simultaneously and without conscious distinction.
> —Huntley Baldwin[12]

Look, for example, at Figure 6.13. At first glance it's a brand-image ad; we don't know what's for sale besides this girl's blissful communion with flowers. What product is responsible for her feeling? If we read the headline and copy, we discover that it's a herbicide; thus a product-specific argument—Accent is an environmentally safer agricultural chemical—is actually being made within this brand-image approach.

Also remember that although you're making only a few ads for your assignment or your portfolio (so you must choose just one approach), in the real world ads are parts of campaigns and work in concert to accomplish more than one aim. Some ads will establish the **umbrella** campaign theme so that other ads, operating underneath that umbrella imagery, can be product specific.

[11]Rosser Reeves, *Reality in Advertising* (New York: Knopf, 1961), pp. 82–83.

[12]Huntley Baldwin, *How to Create Effective TV Commercials,* 2nd ed. (Lincoln-wood, IL: NTC Business Books, 1989), p. 39.

**Figure 6.13** Here a product-feature ad is wrapped inside a brand-image approach. Courtesy of E.I. Dupont De Nemours & Co.

Look at the Timberland campaign (Figures 6.14 and 6.15). Brand-image ads establish the overriding feel of Timberland; they create the umbrella theme, setting the tone but selling no specific gear. Other ads can then pull in tighter on specific products within that brand image.

So realize that ads can, and usually do, blend strategies. And remember, too, that these categories are yours to use. They are suggestions for thinking—not binding, separate entities.

## Exercise:

Examine your product to see how many of the strategies you can use. Although your developing research should tell you what your ads have to do and thus what strategy or strategies might best do the job, you can experiment with these eight categories to see if you can create ads in each one, and then study them for their varying effects.

**Figure 6.14** A magazine spread that establishes the Timberland campaign's umbrella brand image. Courtesy of Timberland Corporation.

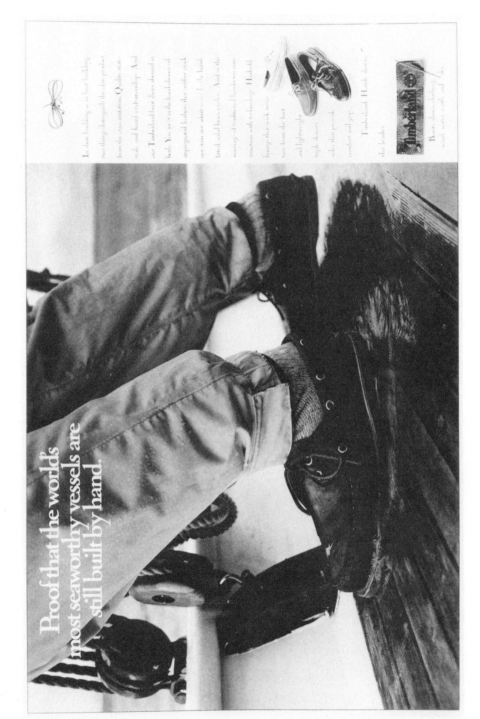

**Figure 6.15** A product-specific ad working within the overall brand image.

# CHAPTER 7

# HEADLINES AND VISUALS: Thinking in Words and Pictures

*The truth isn't the truth until people believe you; and they can't believe you if they don't know what you're saying; and they can't know what you're saying if they don't listen to you; and they won't listen to you if you're not interesting. And you won't be interesting unless you say things freshly, originally, imaginatively.*
—William Bernbach[1]

*Nobody reads advertising.*
*People read what interests them; and sometimes it's an ad.*
—Howard Gossage[2]

You've researched your product and your audience. You've decided upon your selling strategy and formulated your advertising objective: You know what argument you're making, to whom, and why. You've examined the kinds of strategies available to you. In short, you're as armed and loaded as you're ever going to get. Now it's time to execute your advertising plan, to create eye-popping, drop-dead ads. How to do so?

Remember that basically advertising is a relationship between language and imagery: Words are tied to pictures. There are complications and exceptions, of course. In television a soundtrack accompanies a series of images. In direct mail the words frequently dominate, even exclude, the visuals. And in radio there are no visuals at all (except in our heads, where there

[1]William Bernbach, quoted in Bob Levenson, *Bill Bernbach's Book* (New York: Villard Books, 1987), p. 116.

[2]Howard Gossage, *Is There Any Hope for Advertising?* (Urbana and Chicago: University of Illinois Press, 1986), p. xv.

can be plenty). But fundamentally the rhetoric of advertising involves some relationship between showing and saying: You show us a picture and then say something about it. Or you say something; then show us a picture about it.

## SYNERGY, NOT REDUNDANCY

Regardless of the sequence, you should create a relationship—tight, almost molecular—between words and pictures. The word *synergy* has been applied to the effect you seek between what you say and what you show.[3] (When two or more items combine to achieve a total effect greater than the sum of their individual effects, we say they are synergistic; so too are great headline/visual combinations.) The VW ad in Figure 7.1 is a classic example of two halves depending so utterly on each other that neither makes sense by itself, and their combined impact is stronger than a simple totaling of effects.

While not all great ads display so complete an interdependence between word and image, it's a good idea to seek a 1-2 complement, with no redundancy. Dumb ads show something and then say the same thing in words (1-1 instead of 1-2). They miss the higher energy of showing one thing while saying another, thus creating a third level of impact. So get in the habit of asking, If I say thus and such, what will I show? If I show thus and such, what will I say? And never content yourself with merely repeating in words what you show with visuals. Following this rule isn't easy, but you'll know it when you do. William Butler Yeats talked about the sound a poem makes when it finishes: like a lid clicking shut on a perfectly made box.[4] Your ad should make a similar sound when you get just the right fit between headline and visual. (See Figure 7.2.)

## ONE IDEA PER AD

Always pick one selling idea and let it dominate the ad. Even though you'll often be tempted, don't try to say several things at once. Your readers or viewers will simply get confused, and

[3]See A. Jerome Jewler, *Creative Strategy in Advertising,* 3rd ed. (Belmont, CA: Wadsworth, 1989), pp. 95–96; and Philip B. Meggs, *Type & Image* (New York: Van Nostrand Reinhold, 1989), pp. 64–65, 67.

[4]The poet Donald Hall, interviewed by George Myers, Jr., "For man of letters, contradiction is an eternal delight," *The Columbus Dispatch,* September 23, 1990, sec. G, p. 8.

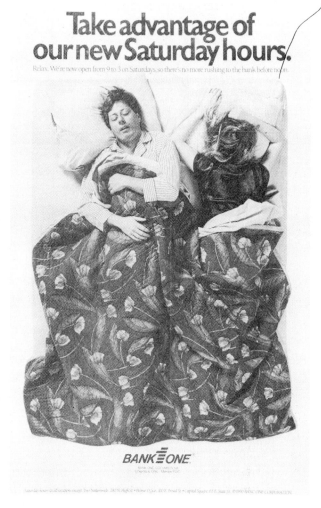

**Figure 7.1** Quintessential examples of synergy in a headline/visual. Neither half makes sense without the other. Courtesy of Bank One Corporation and Volkswagen United States, Inc.

you'll dissipate the power of one thought driven home. Force yourself to choose just one dominant idea, deliver it in headline and visual, and put subordinate ideas in the body copy:

> To break through, focus on one point and express it in words as strong, forceful, sharp, and penetrating as possible. The fakirs of India can fall asleep on a bed on nails with many points. Load up an ad with many points and none will penetrate. Make one point—and watch it penetrate.
> —Stavros Cosmopulos, founder Hill, Holiday, Connors, Cosmopulos[5]

[5]Stavros Cosmopulos, quoted in *The Wall Street Journal* advertising series, *Advertising Age*, April 22, 1991, pp. 6–7.

**WE DESIGN EVERY VOLVO TO LOOK LIKE THIS.**

**Figure 7.2** Not clever beyond compare, this ad shows how effective a good 1-2 working relationship between headline and visual can be. A strong, simple example of what synergy does for you. Courtesy of Volvo.

> It's natural...to want to boast about every last one of a product's benefits. *This impulse must be resisted.* Making an ad or commercial try to say more than one simple thing at a time is like inviting two people to give a lost driver directions at the same time.
> —Dick Wasserman[6]

## THINK VERBALLY AND VISUALLY

If you're more verbal than visual, you may want to start by writing down key words and phrases, by playing with lists of selling phrases, potential headlines, and campaign theme lines, slogans, and various ways of *saying* your strategy. Think also of what images might accompany any of these phrases.

If you're more visual, start making **thumbnail sketches**, little rectangles within which you place images and try to append headlines to them. Here you ought to sketch out the images that associate themselves with your product, with your strategy. When you look at your advertising problem, what do you see?

[6]Dick Wasserman, *That's Our New Ad Campaign...?* (Lexington, MA: D.C. Heath, Lexington Books, 1988), p. 28.

Let's assume, for example, that you're creating print ads for your portfolio and you've given yourself this problem: to expand usage of peanut butter by encouraging adults to consider it as a breakfast alternative. You're targeting health-conscious adults, aged 30–50, who have eaten peanut butter, but only as a lunch or snack food.

What do you see when you think of this problem? What images come to mind? Peanuts sprinkled on cereal as a surreal topping? One little peanut centered on a big white plate? The unopened jar on a plate or beside the morning paper? The morning sun shining through a window onto the jar? A half-shelled peanut sitting in an egg cup? (headline: "The breakfast egg, perfected," or "Funny. It doesn't look like an egg," or "Guess who's coming to breakfast?") Peanuts on toast? Or maybe crunchy peanut butter in the shape of a stick of butter in its tray? ("The better spread," or "Think of it as butter with muscles.") In short, when you visualize the argument *as* an ad, what do you see? And do any words seem to fit it?

## Start with the default ad

Another way to get started is to begin with the clichéd ad, the least wonderful ad you could make, ground zero. Ask yourself, what's my fundamental selling argument? What's the boring, clichéd, primal ad? Maybe beaming adults around the kitchen table spreading peanut butter onto their toast, under the headline, "I forgot how good peanut butter could be." Or "What a great way to start the day." Now do better. This is a bad ad right now; try to improve various parts of that. What can you change? Find a better headline? Close in visually on the product? Move your characters out of the kitchen? Show the *result* of a good breakfast instead (a smiling, productive moment in the day)?

In other words, start with the basic ad and then see if you can substitute for its parts, elevate it.

## How do you write a headline?

If I could answer this, I'd retire to Tahiti immediately with the money I'd make. Who knows how you write one besides just basically think it up? This book will give you techniques and advice, but finally you're alone inside your own head. As I mentioned earlier, once a visual does arrive, then you write the headline in response to or in consideration of that image, and you try to complement it, add to it. So what you show is always part of how you think one up.

One basic way to jump-start yourself is to write down in a plain and straightforward way your advertising strategy: the promise you plan to make to the consumer—the benefit(s) of the product, the problem(s) it solves. In other words, what's your appeal? What is your exact selling argument? Write as many of these as you can. They are your starting point, conceptually. They're *what* you want to say; they're just not *how* you want to say it yet.

You can be wrong at this level (that is, by choosing the wrong strategy), but if we assume you're making the right appeal, then the problem with most of your sentences is that they're not stoppers—they're too flat, too bald, too blah. No one is going to be compelled to consider them. So take each one and try to say it another way, spin it out sideways, heat it up. *Say the same thing another way.* Try to get that idea in our faces more, push it, be slangy, take some chances. Try to wrestle that reasonable idea out of its middle-of-the-roadness and into the ditch.

The benefit has to be on strategy, but its *expression* has to be a little twisted, lateralized, nonclichéd, or made more specific, more interesting. The dead clichés are usually right there in the middle, the first things you think up. You must go further. With this technique you must still supply the necessary wit and ingenuity, of course, but at least you have given yourself a method of operating and clarified your task.

## Create *walking strategy statements*

In a method similar to making a default ad, create default headlines. Write what Maxine Paetro calls *walking strategy statements.*[7] She uses this term negatively to criticize a finished ad that's not yet clever enough, one simply stating the selling idea in the barest, most painful way. While that's not where you want to end up, of course, it is where you want to start.

So here's a walking strategy statement for the peanut butter problem: "Try peanut butter for breakfast; it's a healthy alternative." Now just keep walking it. Keep trying to bounce the idea out another way:

> Peanut butter—the sticky stick-to-your ribs breakfast food.
> Start breakfast with lunch.
> Spread some energy on your toast.
> Peanut butter for breakfast—maybe your kids do know something.

[7]Maxine Paetro, *How to Put Your Book Together and Get a Job in Advertising* (Chicago: Copy Workshop, 1990).

There's not much so far, although the last item suggests tying the health argument to the product's kid appeal and therefore to the nostalgia of the target audience (for example, the headline "Ever wonder why you could run all day as a kid?" with a visual of the jar).

## Two examples

Here are two examples of headlines that are basically strategies, solid selling arguments, wrestled into the ditch. Watermark Water Centers, a California pure water bottler and seller, wanted to warn consumers that most of them were drinking water "contaminated" with one or another impurity. It was a "Hey, did you know your water's bad?" kind of argument. Research indicated that 90 percent of Californians could be said to have a water problem. Final headline over a glass of water: "9 out of 10 people in California have a drinking problem." That's the same idea as the original strategy, but now it's phrased hot enough to stop us. It's a solid idea made clever. (See Figure 7.3.)

Another example: Kaufman and Broad homebuilders advertised that their homes were very well made, so well made that customers were invited to walk through unfinished houses to see for themselves. The eventual headline, with a visual of an unwalled, half-finished house: "Walk through our homes naked." Again we see that the strategy's been played with until made clever enough, unusual enough, to stop the consumer. (See Figure 7.4.)

Remember, always try to express the selling promise as a consumer benefit; see it from the consumer's point of view. For example, in a contest for a membership to Scandinavian health spas, the big headline was, "Win Yourself a Brand New Body." The smaller subhead explained, "Enter For a Free 1-Year Membership." That's the way to say it. Why sell just a membership when you can express the benefit so much more powerfully? Here the big promise dominated, as it should, with the subhead simply clarifying the offer.

As you discover when you work on advertising problems, you often lose the selling idea in the act of trying to express it creatively. There is a continual push-pull between being on-strategy and being clever. Each wants to wrestle you away from the other. Your job as a thinker and problem solver is to keep both in mind, to spin the strategy without losing hold of it. As though to indicate this truth, the two most common rejections of your ideas will be "I don't get it" and "I've seen it before." In other words, either it's too weird or too obvious. That's why the great ones don't come easy.

**Figure 7.3** Keep rewriting your headline until it has stopping power: Here a solid selling idea that could have been boringly expressed ("Chances are your water is bad") is instead made memorable by the energy and specificity of its headline. Courtesy of Chiat/Day, Inc. Advertising.

## Visual advice

While you're free to show anything, of course, a good list never hurts. The most frequently used visual approaches are:

**1.** The product in use: Show it being spread on something, worn, getting things clean, and so on, or otherwise being demonstrated. If the product's got some motion or drama to it, show it.

**2.** The product itself, unwrapped or in its package. Great importance rests, then, on what you say about it. One technique is to be metaphorical, talk about the product *in terms of* something

**Figure 7.4** Another headline that invests its selling argument with enough wit to become arresting and memorable. Courtesy of Kaufman and Broad Home Corp.

else, express its benefit via language usually associated with something else. (See Figure 7.5.) For a longer discussion of this very common, very powerful headline approach, see "Verbal Metaphor" in The Toolbox.

**3.** A close-up of some critical part of the product: the hole-in-the-heel for Nike Air, the three stripes in the toothpaste for Aqua-Fresh, and so on. Very sensible for USP advertising, any feature-oriented approach.

**4.** A visually interesting aspect of the product story that you discover in your research: the unusual plant it's made in, the

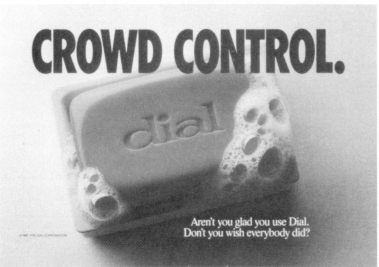

**Figure 7.5** Examples of verbal metaphor: These ads talk about their products in language we associate with other contexts. Courtesy of Volvo and The Dial Corp./DDB Needham Worldwide-Chicago.

founding city or founding father or mother, the valley where it's grown, a piece of historical data that captures the mind and eye.

**5.** Emphasize not the product but the "person" presenting it. This "person" may be a celebrity, an authority figure or expert, someone from history, a pop culture icon, even an invented character like Tony the Tiger or the Keebler elves. (See "Testimonials" in The Toolbox.)

**6.** The consumer benefit of using it: the people pleasures rather than the thing itself. In other words, show the payoff, the result, of using the product: the gleaming car, the well-cooked food, the white teeth.

**7.** Or go a step further and show the lifestyle the product helps create. Beyond the white teeth and smiles there is a desired lifestyle. Show this state of mind, this attitude or way of being that the product engenders. Good visual technique for brand-image/lifestyle/attitude advertising.

**8.** Use split-screen imagery; that is, before and after; a comparison with the competition or with some version of itself or with something unexpected. (See "Two-Fers" in The Toolbox.)

**9.** Show not the product but some modification of it, a transformation or metamorphosis that is visually arresting and communicates the selling idea. Or go further and show a metaphor for the product or service, something dissimilar that *stands for* its benefit. See Figure 7.6. (For further discussion of these techniques, see the metaphor chapters in The Toolbox.)

**10.** Show nothing. Use all type.

## Headline advice

You can't prescribe headline ideas so much as get them to come out of your approach, both strategic and visual. Nevertheless, these suggestions often apply:

**1.** Command headlines have power. You generate commands by using the imperative form of the verb, with "you" understood: "Join the Army." "Visit the zoo." "Just do it." Commands make us pay attention because someone is verbally pointing a finger, demanding a response. So, don't say, "people should discover the Bahamas." Say, "Discover the Bahamas." Similarly, avoid "-ing" verbs in your headlines: "Getting a life" is circular and headless; it makes us say, "so what?" By contrast, "Get a life" makes us say, "who, me?" It involves us.

**2.** Questions also make us pay attention, since they invite our participation. "Are your feet happy?" "Have you looked at your wife lately?"

Just this once, we'd like to give our vehicles the image they deserve.

**Figure 7.6** Metamorphosis of the UPS truck to express speed; metaphor of the sledge hammer to express golf clubs' power. Reprinted with permission of United Parcel Service of America, Inc. and The Richards Group-Ad Agency (Head ad): Grant Richards-Art Director, Stan Richards-Creative Director, and Rich Flora-Writer.

**3.** Adding "how" or "why" to a headline increases its pull and bonds it to its visual.

blah:
> We put a passenger-side airbag in our Acura.
> (visual of two open airbags.)

better:
> Why we put a passenger-side airbag in our Acura.
> (visual of a loving moment between husband and wife.)

"How" and "why" also gain reader interest by promising an immediate benefit: inside knowledge.

> How to cut your income tax in half.
> How to tell whether your house has termites.
> Why BMWs are worth $40,000.
> Why a college education is worth $80,000.

**4.** Ad legend David Ogilvy once wrote, in his elegance, that a print ad's "headline is 'the ticket on the meat.' Use it to flag down the readers who are prospects for the kind of product you are advertising. If you are selling a remedy for bladder weakness, display the words BLADDER WEAKNESS in your headline.... If you want mothers to read your advertisement, display MOTHERS in your headline. And so on."[8]

Writing that in 1963, Ogilvy now sounds dogmatic and dated, but he's still correct: You must flag down your consumer by communicating, one way or another, "This ad's for you." That message does not have to be in the headline, however, nor must it be as literal-minded and obvious as Ogilvy implies—in 30 years we've become very sophisticated consumers of public messages. Lots of elements besides the ad's language can be the ticket on the meat. In print it might be the images themselves, the typography, or the design of the page; on TV it might be the editing rhythms or the soundtrack; in radio the sense of humor or just the tone of voice. But it's got to be there. I only look up when someone flags me down, when someone calls my name, and so do you.

**5.** Other traditional advice has been to name the brand in the headline (or use great big product shots or large logotypes to identify the ad's commercial point). This is another "rule" that's not always wise, necessary, or graceful. How prominently, visually or verbally, you want your product's name in the ad should

---

[8]David Ogilvy, *Confessions of an Advertising Man*, 1963 (New York: Ballantine Books, 1971), p. 92.

be approached situation by situation. You want to sell the product, but shouting is not always the best way.

**6.** How long should a headline be? As long as it needs to be to say itself, not one word longer. The tendency is to keep them short, although we can always find a great, long one. The classic is, of course, Ogilvy's 17-worder for Rolls-Royce:

> At 60 miles an hour the loudest noise in this new Rolls-Royce comes from the electric clock.

Since it was written 34 years ago, you may argue that we won't read that much anymore. But here's one written in 1992 for PacTel Cellular phones:

> If there just don't seem to be enough hours in the day, maybe that's because you left two of them in your car.

Here's another, written in 1992 for Health-tex children's clothing:

> We've just made dressing your baby easier than ever. (Now it ranks right between juggling chain saws and catching a greased pig.)

The real trick is say what you want to, *then* tighten it. Don't limit your ideas by presupposing that you must have teensy ones or be terse.

For example, a tongue-in-cheek headline for a minor league hockey team, the Columbus Chill, could have been written this way:

> If you assault someone in America, you'll get five years in prison. But if you assault someone in hockey, you'll only get five minutes. So is this a great game or what?

Their actual headline, however, said the same thing without wasting a word. (See Figure 7.7.) Feel how much stronger it is:

> Assault someone, you get five years. In hockey, five minutes. Is this a great game or what?

**7.** Use both internal and end punctuation on headlines. Most ad writers use periods to close headlines (and often slogans), even when they aren't complete sentences. Periods add a sense of certainty and authority to the fragment or phrase.

**Assault someone, you get five years. In hockey, five minutes. Is this a great game or what?**

Deep down, they're really good kids. They're just dealing with a lot of stress right now. So why not bring $5 and a valid college I.D. to the Fairgrounds Coliseum this Friday or Saturday at 7:30 and watch some talented young men try to walk the straight and narrow. And, if they slip up and commit an act considered a felony in most states, well, a little time in the corner should straighten them out. You naughty boys.

*For more information, call 488-8000.*

CHILL
COLUMBUS

**Figure 7.7** An example of not only a tightly written headline but also an all-type ad. Courtesy of Concepts Marketing Group, Indianapolis, IN: Client-Columbus Hockey, Inc., Columbus, OH; Creative Director-Larry Aull; Copywriter-Mark LeClerc and Art Director-Tony Fannin.

**8.** Use subheads frequently. Learn to finish headlines, usually, with more straightforward subheads or underlines. Give yourself enough display type (the major language in the large point sizes) to communicate completely to readers. "Oh, they'll get it when they read the copy" is almost never a good excuse for an ambiguous, teaser headline or a headline/subhead combination that still doesn't make enough sense. An ad should work both fast and slowly; that is, a scanner should get something from it—at least the selling idea—and a true reader should get more—the complete story.

Here are two headline/visual techniques that may prove helpful:

## Combine understatement and overstatement

One kind of headline/visual synergy involves *tone*, combining understatement with overstatement. If your visual is wild and crazy or obviously excessive, then back off verbally. And vice versa. In other words, don't shout twice. This juxtaposition of loud and soft, big and little, really snaps that box lid shut. And it works as well in TV as it does in print—run one kind of soundtrack over another kind of imagery. If the car is undergoing a visual torture test, speak quietly about the "modest testing procedure" or play "Singin' in the Rain." (See Figure 7.8.)

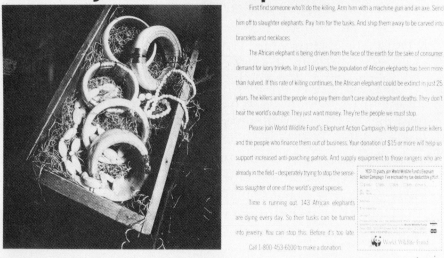

**Figure 7.8** Strong, ironic relationships between headline and visual, one funny, the other tragic. Courtesy of Copyright Bristol-Myers Squibb Company. Illustrations used with the permission of Bristol-Myers Squibb Company and World Wildlife Fund.

## Create alternative meanings

Another way to get synergy is to create alternative explanations for the visuals that come to mind. For example, if you're selling dental floss or toothpaste, you may come up with a visual of an old guy with no teeth. But then what to say? The obvious meanings would be things like, "Do you want to be this guy?" Or

"Don't let this happen to you." But they're too obvious; make yourself create alternative meanings for that image. What else could you say? "Relax. Baby food tastes better than it used to." "Hey, think of the time you'll save not chewing." Or "Smile. No more dental bills." And so forth. If, on the other hand, you use a visual of a smiling person with beautiful teeth (probably *the* visual cliché of the toothpaste genre), provide an alternate meaning: "Too bad he didn't use Crest." And explain in the copy that his teeth only *look* okay.

Some of these ideas need subheads to complete them, but do you see that finding alternate meanings creates an unexpected relationship and an arresting tone? You create nervy ads and avoid redundancy. Try it.

## PARALLELISM AS A HEADLINE TACTIC

Headlines (as well as slogans and body copy) often employ a rhetorical structure called parallelism. The best way to define it is to show it:[9]

Here are two sentences:

George liked Jean and often walked beside her on the way to school. Jean was also accompanied sometimes to school by Ronald, who also liked her, but who often could be seen walking behind her.

Made shorter:

George liked Jean and often walked beside her on the way to school. Jean was also accompanied by Ronald, who walked behind her.

Made *parallel:*

George liked Jean and walked beside her to school.
Ronald liked Jean and walked behind her to school.

Now you can actually *see* the meaning, can't you? Now you know who will win the girl, and who will worship from a distance. Parallelism is the notion that sentence elements identical in thought should be made identical in grammatical form, that form and function should coincide.

[9]Ken Macrorie, *Telling Writing*, 3rd ed. (Rochelle Park, NJ: Hayden, 1980), pp. 136–137.

**Parallelism** involves repetition, often of words, but more importantly, of structure; and, as you'll see, you can choose to repeat long structures or short ones. The point is to say similar things similarly. To do this, you'll need to realize which of your ideas are equivalent in meaning, and then express them in equivalent structures: a word for a word, a phrase for a phrase, a clause for a clause. Parallelism is to language what twins dressed alike are to childhood. Find your twins (or triplets or quads) and then put them in the same clothes.

As you see from the preceding example, parallelism throws a sharp light on your ideas, clarifying your distinctions. It also makes an otherwise ordinary idea *sound* better, if only because it now has new clothes. It looks dressed up, cleaned up, sharp:

> For the price of something small and ugly, you can drive something small and beautiful. (Fiat)

> If an air freight company can't fly on the ground, it doesn't matter how fast it flies in the air. (Emery Air Freight)

Notice that in addition to being parallel, these are balanced as well: The second parallel clause is about as long as the first one. It balances it. The virtue of this is that you raise an issue on the one hand and complete it nicely on the other. You appear both reasonable and complete—what more need be said? Balance parallel structures when you want to add resonance and authority to the expression.

A characteristic of parallelism is its completeness; it often makes a visual redundant. This isn't to say, however, that you can't complete parallelism with an image:

> *Headline:* You can tell from the outside which Scotch they serve on the inside.

> *Visual:* A mansion with its gates open (Johnnie Walker Black Label)

The double-headline for an American Tourister ad:

> We've made some hard decisions. (photo of hard-shell suitcase)
> We've made some soft decisions. (photo of soft suitcase)

A TV spot:

> *Voice-over:* The only time he removes his car from the road is when he removes the road from his car. (A dusty BMW is washed, then immediately driven back out onto the road.)

But with parallelism you often do lose the verbal-visual synergy discussed earlier, that tension between headline and visual so many good ads employ. Instead you place tension within the language itself, relying on a kind of verbal-verbal synergy embedded in the paired parallel phrases:

Life is too short to get there too fast. (Cunard Lines)

If it weren't so tough out there, we wouldn't make it so tough in here. (Pace University—A Real Education for the Real World)

Often you can establish a sequence, then surprise us with the last element, as do these two movie poster headlines:

Uncle Buck. He's crude. He's crass. He's family.

Black Rain. An American Cop in Japan. Their country. Their laws. Their game. His rules.

This cover headline, the most famous in *Rolling Stone* magazine's history, accompanied a photo of Jim Morrison:

He's hot. He's sexy. He's dead.

## How to think about parallelism

The key to any good parallel construction is having something to say in the first place. You cannot stick just any sort of mumbo-jumbo or throat-clearing into parallel structures and expect advertising miracles. As always, you need to create a real distinction, benefit, or promise.

How? Go to your list of benefits for your product and start looking for "two-fers," language that separates out into *this versus that*, or *this plus that*, or *this but not that, either this or that, not only this but also that*, and so on. You're trying to take your benefits and deliver them in a 1-2 punch. And you're usually looking for some kind of opposition, a contrast to throw into relief:

The best surprise is no surprise. (Holiday Inn)

Because she's old enough to have a baby, doesn't mean she's old enough to be a mother. (visual of 14-year-old pregnant girl) *Tag:* Planned Parenthood. Abortion is something personal. Not political.

We didn't forget the hard side of travel when we developed our soft luggage.
*Tag:* Beautiful on the outside. American Tourister on the inside.

Note that parallelism frequently relies on punning repetition, where the meaning of a repeated word or phrase changes:

Don't squander your disposable income on a disposable car. (BMW)

Stop handguns before they stop you.

Examining all the headlines I've given you here should show you the range of possibility. Parallelism is remarkably wide (and isn't even limited to two-ness, of course, though that's a good place to start). Yet it's not infinitely wide, as this disparity indicates:

Vermont. A lot goes on when the skis come off.

A world of wonder. A world of value. (Mexico)

The Vermont line is vivid and memorable, the Mexico line empty and absolutely forgettable. The moral? If you don't have much to say, parallelism won't say much for you. A cliché is still a cliché, however gracefully concealed.

## CREATING SLOGANS AND THEME LINES

Lots of products have slogans or tag lines. These usually run alongside the logotypes (as well as in voice-overs and supers in TV spots) and help state the purpose of the product, memorably, advertisers hope. Slogans, of course, are meant to stand by themselves as language, as a selling argument. They are purely verbal in this way, not requiring an accompanying visual. Certainly we remember the good ones, and they do help place the product in our minds, quickly identifying its value in our lives.

Some advertisers recommend distilling a product's selling idea into a slogan or theme line whenever you advertise anything to focus your own thinking, whether you end up using the line or not. Writing slogans also teaches you, in a compressed form, many of the lessons of good copywriting that longer exercises can obscure. Moreover, as a copywriter, you will often be asked to give short but interesting names to all sorts of things: speeches, exhibitions, events, and so on. Copywriters are in many ways phrasemakers. For all these reasons slogans are good practice.

If you examine slogans, you notice that they are often clever—rhyming, punning, or in some way using wit to create a rhetorical flair that makes them memorable. Slogans are indeed the art of the well-made phrase. But they had better do more than just be clever. Their real job is to be an ad in miniature: Make the case for the product, position it relative to its competition, justify it, make it a good thing we want. In short, more than being clever, they need to be smart.

## Make them smart, not just pretty

For example, one of the great slogans is Campbell's "Soup is good food." But at first it doesn't seem so great—it isn't witty, it's all monosyllables, and its promise seems banal. What it really is, however, is durable and right on a smart selling strategy. The monosyllables help emphasize soup's simplicity—its basic-ness—and the message positions soup (in case we might think otherwise) as real food itself, not just some accessory to a meal. Smart. But not glittery. The Campbell's slogan illustrates the difficulty in distinguishing a good line from a merely glittery one. So be thorough and thoughtful when creating and critiquing slogans.

The Campbell's line redefines soup for us in a positive way, and their strategy is fundamental. Often consumers need to be shown that products aren't just regular, boring, ordinary things, but are instead much more than that. Use slogans to elevate products in our minds, make us see them in the best possible terms. Bally's Scandinavian health spa slogan, "You don't just shape your body, you shape your life," is a classic example of this principle.

## Study slogans

The surest way to develop a feel for slogans as a genre is to look at a number of them. If you run enough of them through your mind, you'll see how similar their purpose often is and how variously it can be expressed. Here are several slogans for cars. Notice that we are never asked to buy just wheels and a chassis. Such high-ticket items must make us see the purchase in terms larger than that:

> "It's not a car. It's a Volkswagen." More recently VW has used, "German engineering the Volkswagen Way."

"BMW. The Ultimate Driving Machine." See how they make it seem like much more than merely a car?

"Acura—Precision Crafted Performance." Notice that this goes beyond BMW and sells pure design, not even naming the car.

"Lexus—The Relentless Pursuit of Perfection." Perhaps the purest expression of the tendency away from the car itself, this slogan ignores specific things altogether, selling instead obsession with an abstraction.

Other slogans:

"Timberland—More Quality Than You May Ever Need." Another instance of elevating the product; we're not buying a shoe here, either. This time it's the security of overequipping our feet.

"Speedo. Cut to cut through water." Effective use of a punning repetition.

"UPS. We run the tightest ship in the shipping business." Another example of punning repetition.

Various travel agents have nicely called themselves: "The Vacation Store." This makes the service more tangible, doesn't it?

The television game show *Jeopardy* has called itself "The most fun you can have with your brain."

"Beef—Real Food for Real People." An attempt to reduce the supposed health negatives of beef by insulting the bean-sprout eaters and flattering beef eaters.

Interestingly, the Pork Producers, realizing that lots of people just weren't eating pork, renamed themselves, too, and nicely allied themselves with ever-popular chicken: "Pork: the other white meat."

"The Armed Services—We're not a company, we're your country." This is meant to add significance while still selling the services as good career preparation.

"The Navy: It's Not Just a Job. It's an Adventure." Here the same strategy is differently expressed.

"Federal Express—It's Not Just a Package. It's Your Business." See how they raise the stakes? This slogan typifies the fundamental strategy, not only of slogans, but of advertising itself:

Claim the highest possible meaning for the product, assert its central importance to life well-lived.

"Saturn. A Different Kind of Company. A Different Kind of Car." This slogan, like the previous three, uses parallelism to make the case, here that an American automaker has restructured itself enough to make an internationally competitive car.

Maxwell House Instant Coffee has called itself, "Instant Sophistication," perhaps as overt a statement of selling strategy as we'll ever see.

"Amway. We're Your Neighbors." Slogans solve advertising problems. Since Amway isn't well understood, this slogan goes to work on that, reducing any stigma and making Amway seem as inevitable as the people next door. This slogan may do as much as any three words can.

Many people may have heard of this university but couldn't quite place it in their minds. They can now: "Seton Hall. The Catholic University in New Jersey."

"Apple—The power to be your best." You're not just buying expensive hardware; you're giving yourself the means to achieve.

"The Library. Know How. No Charge." Good pun, nice quick rhythm, and a true selling promise.

"A cookie is just a cookie, but Newtons are fruit and cake." A good slogan because it positions the product against its competition and upscales it in the process. More fundamental sales technique: inviting us to imagine the product at its highest possibility.

*Ameritech Yellow Pages* say of themselves: "Next to the phone, there's nothing better." (a great pun)

Federal Express: "When it absolutely, positively has to be there overnight."

"Overnight, not overpriced." (Purolator's response to Federal Express)

American Express Gold Card: "Worth Its Wait." Another high-quality pun that not only asserts the achievement of getting one, but also deftly invites us to complete its meaning: "(worth its weight)...in gold."

Mitsubishi: "Technically, Anything Is Possible." Adverb as pun, and a very good one, too, considering the wide range of Mitsubishi hi-tech products, from TVs to cars.

Nice N Easy hair color: "You. Only Better." Perhaps the quintessential ad claim. Many products base their strategy on the assumption that we are incomplete without them. So they'll help us win the war against our inherent insufficiency.

Here are the slogans for several magazines:

*TV Guide:* "The best thing on television" (a real sweet pun, yes?)

*Lear's* magazine, for older women, has used this as its subtitle, nicely identifying its target audience, "For the woman who wasn't born yesterday."

*Life* magazine: "The power of pictures" A very clear statement of *Life's* fundamental strategy as a magazine and its market niche.

*Sassy* magazine, targeted to teenage girls: "There are five years in a woman's life when she really needs a best friend."

Instead of renaming products or corporations, slogans often tell us either what they do or what we're doing when we buy them:

"G.E.—We bring good things to life." They're not just a TV and toaster outfit; they make our life better. (Nice quiet little pun about electricity animating things, too, don't you think?)

"Olympic House Stain—Protecting the American Dream for Over Half a Century" This one, like so many slogans, upgrades the product. We are not simply repainting that old house, we are preserving the national purpose itself. The Highest Possible Benefit.

"When you've got Epson, you've got a lot of company." A strong pun, inviting us to think of Epson as widely used and powerful—"a lot of company" in both senses of the term.

## How to think up slogans

When creating slogans, ask yourself, What is this product? What does it do for people? If you had to say what this company or product is, if you had to put its whole purpose in a phrase or a sentence, what would that be? Slogans are miniature sales arguments that make the best possible case for the product and its benefits to us.

One way to do this is to begin by simply listing what it is or does. Say what it most obviously is. Be dull and boring but get all the sayings of what something is or does down on the page.

Then try to heat them up, say them another way, be more clever, verbally winsome. For example, if you're selling potatoes for the Potato Council, write down what potatoes are:

big brown vegetables

one of the four food groups

healthy food that's a little boring

ugly looking food but good for you

vitamins and minerals in a skin

a food that goes great with toppings

a simple food

Then look at each one and ask yourself if you can say it another way, extend it, free-associate on the basis of that phrase. Create bunches of phrases in the hopes that one or more may work:

big brown vegetables...we make other vegetables green with envy, it's not easy being brown

one of the four food groups...a quarter of your life

healthy food that's a little boring ...hug a potato today, ugly but we do the job, don't let looks deceive you, the rest of your life is exciting enough, ugly food makes pretty people

ugly but good for you...it's what on the inside that counts, get under our skin, go skinny dipping today, shred us up, open up to us, the vegetable with the great personality, the world's largest vitamin pill, a vitamin you can butter, butter us up, top this, we can be topped, as real as you are, the underground favorite, from the good earth, and so on.

Another approach is to ask yourself what your product's position is in the market. Or what position you seek. As we've seen, many slogans are simply position statements. Budget Gourmet frozen food is, for example, what?, expensive meals that don't cost that much—"fast food with style" (a good slogan if Rax restaurants didn't already have it). Try to say what your product is and how it's different from others.

Or ask yourself, what's its biggest problem? The Amway line shows how slogans can solve problems, help reposition products in consumers' minds. Maybe yours needs that done.

Yet another approach is to ask, what's its highest possible benefit? What's the most you can reasonably claim for this product?

# CHAPTER 8

# BODY COPY I:
# Voice

*In your natural way of producing words there is a sound, a texture, a rhythm—a voice—which is the main source of power in your writing.*
—Peter Elbow[1]

## THE IMPORTANCE OF ETHOS, PERSONA, VOICE

Body copy is really part of something larger—the rhetoric of the entire ad or campaign—and we need to discuss that before we can talk very well about copy itself. The literary critic M. H. Abrams, discussing Aristotle's theories of rhetoric, said this: "An orator establishes in the course of his oration an *ethos*—a personal character which itself functions as a means of persuasion; for if the personal image he projects is that of a man of rectitude, intelligence, and goodwill, the audience is instinctively inclined to give credence to him and to his arguments."[2]

Advertising is a form of public speechmaking, and whenever we consume ads, we confront a speaker delivering a persuasive message. Even if the ad has no literal spokesperson, it always has a consciousness, and our response to this frequently invisible but everywhere apparent speaker becomes central to the ad's success: We are never just buying a product, we're buying an *ethos*, too. Do we like this person or don't we? Are we interested

[1]Peter Elbow, *Writing Without Teachers* (New York: Oxford University Press, 1973), p. 6.

[2]M. H. Abrams, *A Glossary of Literary Terms,* 3rd ed. (New York: Holt, Rinehart and Winston, 1971), p. 123.

in this sensibility or aren't we? Do we want to bring this person home with us or not?[3]

When we talk about this sensibility behind the product, we are, of course, talking about the product's brand image, the personality behind the brand. We've all noticed how an advertising agency creates a persona for a corporation and its products and then maintains it through the years. (*Persona*, Latin for the mask once worn by classical actors, is another good word to use for this sense of self created by the ads, the implied speaker or personality behind the language and imagery.)

For example, Volkswagen's classic ads from Doyle Dane Bernbach seemed to have a self-deprecating, funny, modest-but-self-assured person behind all of them—we almost felt as though we'd enjoy having lunch and some laughs with the VW person, whoever he or she was. We also felt that the mind behind the car was the car's argument for itself: rational, practical, intelligent, whimsical, but finally serious.

BMW advertising in the 1980s, by contrast, was almost intimidating, with its all-caps, boldface headline voice and its copy tone veering toward arrogance. We didn't want to invite the BMW persona over for dinner (or if we did, we'd be nervous), but we were convinced that he (or she?) knew how to build an expensive, artful-but-muscled performance car. The personality of the ads matched our sense of the personality required to make those cars. It was the right voice, given the upscale target market and product positioning, as well as the aggressive business ethos of the decade. (See Figure 8.1.)

But times change, and so did the voice of BMW advertising. In Figure 8.2 we see an ad from 1993. Notice that the brand's image has softened: the voice, while still long-winded, has become more helpful, less intimidating. The language and point of view still express authority but turn it into authoritative advice. With America demanding less corporate aggression, with the excesses of the 1980s business climate replaced by a 1990s concern for limits, self-restraint, and responsibility, BMW has modified its persona to keep the cars in tune with cultural trends. Gone is the arrogance of the 1980s advertising, its strength now transformed into sophisticated know-how. We don't feel that this

[3]In this light all the Leo Burnett "critters," the Jolly Green Giant, the Keebler elves, Tony the Tiger, and others, reveal their value. By taking these fellows home with us, we add to otherwise mundane products an imagined but nevertheless sustaining emotional and psychological content. When I buy Jolly Green Giant peas, I feel that I've put more in my cart than simply frozen peas; I've added the mythic presence of that character.

**Figure 8.1** The 1984 BMW voice. Courtesy of BMW of North America, Inc.

is a different person, just—given the times—a better one, someone we *could* have dinner with.

In short, the advertisers for both Volkswagen and BMW have created personalities by which we identify the brands and relate them to ourselves. All great advertising understands this need not only to create a strong image for the brand, but also to manage it, modifying its characteristics to match changing circumstance and purpose. Says David Martin, founder of The Martin Agency and a strong proponent of sustaining successful brand images: "Personality is a buoy, not a dead weight. Great brands are built over a long period of time with advertising that is faithful to product personality....Brand personality is permanent. Lose it and lose the franchise."[4]

[4]David Martin, *Romancing the Brand* (New York: AMACOM, 1989), pp. 89, 96.

# HOW TO READ THE ROAD WITH YOUR FINGERTIPS.

No, this isn't a page out of your old driver's education textbook.

There will be no list of "do's" and "don'ts." No tips or tricks.

What we have to say isn't about *how* to drive. But *what* to drive in order to drive better.

INTRODUCING THE BMW 525i.

Instead of merely driving along the road, the BMW 525i feels its way along it. Transmitting information about the road's surface up through the tires, to the suspension system, to the steering column, to the steering wheel and, finally, to the driver.

Or, more accurately said, to the driver's fingertips.

This is no small feat. But rather, the result of a painstakingly planned and meticulously executed mechanical circuit.

One that begins with an internationally renowned front and rear suspension system that's specifically designed to know which parts of the topography to insulate you from and which parts to inform you about.

So when you travel across broken pavement you don't even feel most of the bumps and yet when you bend into a hard corner, both ends of the car dig in

for all they're worth. Sending critical feedback up to the driver through an engine-speed-sensitive power-assist steering system that has no rubber bushings which might dilute any of that feedback.

Which, we hasten to add, arms you with enough information to respond instantly and intelligently to that ever-changing slice of land we call the road.

A CAR BUILT AROUND THE DRIVER'S EYES, ARMS, LEGS AND BACK.

At BMW, we've spent decades studying driver physiology – the

physical relationship between the driver and the cockpit.

Toward that end, the BMW 525i is equipped with greenhouse-size windows to maximize your visibility of the world around you.

A seat you can position almost any way except backward.

As well as a steering wheel and pedals that have been designed according to the range of human response and reaction times.

Suffice it to say, the BMW 525i wasn't only built around your fingertips. But around your entire body.

And, like all BMW's, it's protected

by a 4-year/50,000-mile bumper-to-bumper warranty along with an around-the-clock nationwide Roadside Assistance program.

No wonder one editor at Motor Trend was moved to say it was "one of the best-handling, most civilized 4-door sedans on the planet."

To see how the BMW 525i moves you, schedule a test drive by calling 800-334-4BMW for the BMW dealer nearest you.

**THE ULTIMATE DRIVING MACHINE.**

**Figure 8.2** The 1993 BMW voice. Courtesy of BMW of North America, Inc.

## HOW TO THINK ABOUT IMAGE AND VOICE

Since you inevitably create your product's "self" when you write copy, brand image is always at stake: You add to or subtract from it with every word. To make sure that this self you're creating works, think about these issues:

1.  What image of the brand already exists?

2.  Is it the right one for your product? Does it fit your target market? Your competitive position in the market? The times?

3.  What modifications, if any, do you want to make to it? Once you've settled on the appropriate brand image, then consider these:

4.  What voice is the best expression of this image?

5.  How will you use this voice to communicate the objectives of the ads you're making? In other words, how would your brand's "person" make this specific selling argument? How would he or she say it? If you pose the problem this way, as the mimicking of somebody's voice, then you can more easily solve it.

So before you ever write a word of body copy, you need to determine—or to understand, if someone else has determined—these larger concerns of product personality, the overall voice and stance of the advertising. Not until they are resolved can you write effective copy. Once you start to write body copy, however, you'll make a pleasant discovery: You already know how, for the simple reason that you've already done it.

## HOW BODY COPY IS LIKE FRESHMAN COMPOSITION

Most, if not all of you, have had a college composition course in which you wrote essays. Body copy is really nothing more than English Composition 1: nonfiction prose written to support an argument. The ad's headline and visual advance the argument, and the body copy justifies it. Although well-written body copy does differ from the prose of a well-written essay (and we'll discuss those differences), the similarities far outweigh the differences. Good writing is good writing. Period.

If you apply what you learned in freshman composition to your copywriting, you'll be fine. Let's recall those principles of good prose your English professor taught you:

1. Voice: The writing has a natural, authentic sound, free of clichés.

2. Details: The writing is full of specifics; it's particular, not vague.

3. Style: Form matches content: the prose is not overwritten. It's stylistically graceful, with strong, clear sentences, and well-chosen language.

4. Thesis: The writing has one central, unifying idea. It hangs together.

5. Organization and structure: It develops this idea in some order; has a beginning, middle, and end; and coheres throughout.

That's a familiar and fundamental list, isn't it? The first item on our list—voice—is so important that we'll spend this chapter analyzing it and save the others for the next one.

## Voice

As I suggested earlier, the voice in a product's advertising should flow from the overall strategy; voice is the brand's image as expressed in language. For the voice of a specific ad, look to your headline/visual concept. If your headline relies on wit, then the copy had better share the same clever person. If the headline is brash and assertive, then the voice in the copy ticking off the selling points should be just as aggressive.

Voice is a concept so crucial to writing that in a sense, it's everything. As you remember from freshman composition, all good writing has a sound—the human, expressive rhythm that animates it. Good writing sounds like somebody particular uttered or thought it. If your language has no sound or rhythm, it's dead, and so is your ad.

But voice is difficult to talk about for several reasons. For one thing, you can't point to it exactly. It's just there, *between* all the words. For another, it's made up of myriad things: the words you choose, the sentences you write, the amount and kind of detail you use, what you're talking about, what your point is, how you organize the writing. Almost every choice you make as a writer plays a part in creating the voice of the copy—the sense we get, when we read it, of its living current. Throughout our discussion of good writing, remember that we're always talking about voice, too.

### Analyzing the voices of ads

Let's analyze some copy to see if we can isolate the characteristics that make up a voice, the parts that combine to create our intuitive sense of the speaker. Here, for example, is the copy for the ad for Nike's water socks (Figure 8.3).

*Headline:*
Hawaiian shirts for your feet.

*Copy:*
So, you're hanging ten in Maui or you're just stepping into your hot tub. Fine. You'll need a few things. First, you'll need a solid rubber outsole for traction. Then you'll need a spandex upper for breathability. Like gills, sort of. And you'll definitely need some wacky colors to make the fish think you're one of them. In short, you'll need NIKE Aqua Socks. Remember: when the going gets wet, the wet go Hawaiian.

How do we characterize this voice? It's hip and flippant, but it's got some steel, too. The tone is authoritative, telling us what to do, what's cool, but doing so with jokes. It's clearly a variant of the Nike voice ("Just do it.") that we've been hearing for years.

How do we know all this? The authoritative tone comes from the repetition of the near command, "you'll need," which doesn't allow room for disagreement, but the voice lightens that tone by mixing in whimsical allusions ("to make the fish think

**Figure 8.3** Nike's distinctive voice—hip, flippant, but authoritative— perfectly matches product with target audience. Courtesy of Nike, Inc.

you're one of them," and so on). Also, the language contains slang ("hanging ten," "wacky," "sort of"), contractions ("you're," "you'll"), and sentence fragments ("Fine." "Like gills, sort of."), all of which produce a very informal, almost chummy tone. By beginning in the middle of a thought ("So..."), the copy implies an already formed relationship; it seems to know us. The closing, clever twist on the cliché adds to our sense of a witty hipster. Finally, the diction (word choice) is unpretentious, so the voice is that of a peer—a fun but knowledgeable older brother, perhaps. Altogether, a perfectly created voice, given our sense of this product, the Nike audience, and the Nike campaign theme. Here, as elsewhere, they're telling us *how* to just do it.

By contrast, look at the ad for the Royal Viking Line (Figure 8.4). Here is some of the copy:

*Headline:*
Civilization is advancing at a stately 18 knots.

*Copy:*
Long before reaching your destination, you will experience a sense of having arrived. Such is life aboard our newest ship, the intimate *Royal Viking Queen,* and her larger, more stately companion, the elegant *Royal Viking Sun.*

Here, all that has made sailing Royal Viking Line so wondrous over the years is heightened as never before. Consider mingling with learned experts in World Affairs. Or collecting secrets of aquatic life from the Cousteau Society. Elsewhere, guest chefs the likes of the renowned Paul Bocuse will provide exquisite nourishment for areas found somewhere south of the mind....

The copy here obviously implies an older, more genteel speaker and audience. The implied distance between the two is greater also. This is not chumminess. How do we know? The sentences are more sophisticated, and so are the words. There are almost no fragments and no slang, no contractions. With adjectives like "wondrous," "exquisite," and "renowned," the copy is more intent on evoking a mood, an upscale one at that. Each element, from the self-congratulatory paradox of the opening sentence to the unusual details (the Cousteau Society, the chef Paul Bocuse), helps accentuate the copy's we-are-the-best attitude. The tone is self-assured, precise, authoritative but at our service. It sounds like this cruise might cost us something, but we'd have a fabulous time. The voice perfectly embodies the kind of experience they're selling.

You can simply *hear* how each piece of copy creates its own unique persona, can't you? Explaining the differing effects re-

**Figure 8.4** In this ad we hear a more sophisticated voice, one that works well for a more expensive product and an older, more urbane target audience. Courtesy of Royal Viking Line.

quires analysis, but clearly the right speaker is presenting each product, and each voice rings true. That's the goal: to sound like a real person, not an edifice of polished prose. As Elmore Leonard says, "If it sounds like writing, I rewrite it."

Two points: You don't create copy by analyzing it. You create copy by throwing yourself into a voice. But you do improve copy by analyzing it, and that requires a sensitivity on your part to what aspects of the language are creating what effects. Become a good critic of voices. It will help you rewrite yours.

## Write in the first and second person

To write well, you must become the sound of someone talking—not literally your own specific self but the self of the seller, the corporation, or the person talking to us in the ad. If you just write logical, institutional prose that *assembles* the case for a product, prose without someone inside it, then you're missing the essence of good writing. It must project a personality, a living voice, and that's always an "I," whether your copy uses one or not. As Thoreau said, "We commonly do not remember that it is, after all, always the first person that is speaking." He wasn't talking about ad copy, but he could have been.

So prefer the first person ("I" and "we") and the second person ("you") to the third person ("it," "they"). Don't say what "they're" doing at Nike for people and "their" problems. Say what "we're" doing at Nike for "you" and "your" problems. How will "our" products serve "your" needs? Copy that pulls the reader close this way is much more intimate and effective than stiff, third-person prose. Try to sound like speech, or at the least very warm thought.

Both the preceding examples use "you" and imply "we." (The Royal Viking's "her" is, of course, the feminine pronoun preferred for ships. It not only tells us they know what they're doing, but it also adds a touch of formality—a good idea, given their upscale product.)

## The rhetorical triangle

Let's add a couple more terms to the conversation; they've been implied so far, and if you know them, you can better analyze your writing. First, here's what's called the rhetorical triangle (see Figure 8.5). It's a helpful way of visualizing the relationships that occur when you're speaking or writing.[5]

[5]See Walker Gibson, *Persona* (New York: Random House, 1969), p. 52.

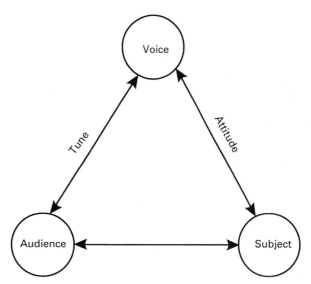

**Figure 8.5** The rhetorical triangle, based on figure in Walker Gibson, *Persona* (New York: McGraw-Hill, Inc., 1969), p. 52. Reproduced with permission of McGraw-Hill.

You're always dealing with speaker (voice), subject, and audience, and a change in one usually creates changes in the others.

## Tone

The implied distance between speaker and audience is called **tone:** In what tone of voice are you speaking to your audience? What's your relationship with them? Formal and reserved, intimate, amused, angry, what exactly? Your tone can vary from at-their-elbow, in-their-ear coziness all the way to the objectivity of a newspaper reporter or voice of the ages announcing product news. Usually, with copy, your tone is some version of *friendly*, sometimes almost best-friendly, other times more distantly pleased-to-be-having-a-conversation friendly. If you're trying to sell somebody something, being friendly is a reasonable idea.

But other tones are possible, too. Nike, as we've noticed, isn't exactly friendly toward us. They're often stern, telling us things we should do, acting as our self-improvement conscience, our "tough love" coach. Reebok's "Life is short. Play hard." voice is similarly aggressive. Many public service announcements (anti- and pro- various causes or issues) shame us with pointed, impatient tones, wagging their finger at our stupidity. You do not have to wear a big grin and say a big howdy to sell us something. (See Figure 8.6.)

## Attitude

The relationship of a speaker to his or her subject we call **attitude**. What is your attitude toward your product (or more precisely,

**Figure 8.6** Apparently less than friendly tones. *The Village Voice* coupon ad creates a humorously negative tone and attitude by using "our" voice, not theirs. Courtesy of *The Village Voice*, New York, NY and *The Des Moines Register*.

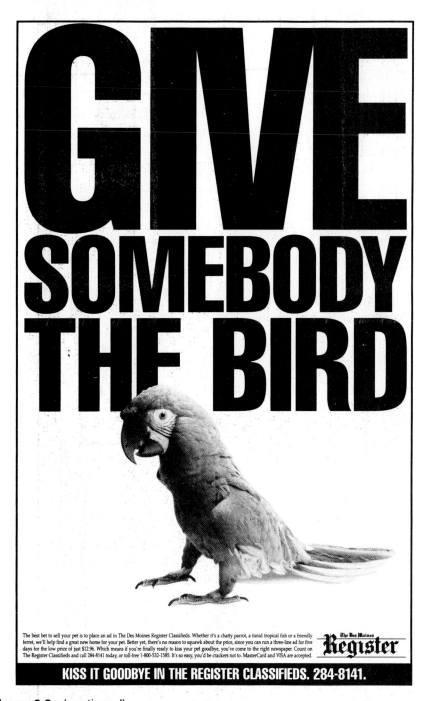

**Figure 8.6**   (continued)

toward your selling argument)? For example, Nike's attitude is that working out (in their gear) is a serious subject: They're really talking about our buried potential, what we should make of ourselves. So although they're often funny and hip, finally their attitude is serious: They're concerned, and so should we be. Usually in advertising the attitude toward the product is very positive, praising its virtues and its powers to improve living. In most ads most of the time the product is the hero—unambiguously so. But this can easily be overdone: The features are said to be great, the product is marvelous, the offer here nothing short of astounding. This tendency toward an overinflated attitude is a real danger. What we consider unpersuasive overselling is often a case of overinflated attitude. So watch the tendency toward hype. Experiment with various relationships toward your product: Be flippant, be apparently unconcerned, be surprisingly modest, and so on. Presenting an unusual attitude can get you past the clichés inherent in the adoration of product.

## Consider irony

> All interesting attitudes are complex.
> —Walker Gibson[6]

Irony is an attitude toward one's subject; you are saying one thing about it, but you mean something else. We all use irony (and its cousin sarcasm) frequently. We will watch a Michael Jordan 360-degree slam dunk and say, "Not too bad." We'll look at our D in history and say, "I'm overjoyed with my success." We like those comments better than saying the obvious, exactly-what-I-mean phrases. Why? Basically because they allow us a more complicated attitude toward the subject and toward ourselves; we can create more than one meaning simultaneously, and we can create of ourselves someone smart enough to be of two minds about a single topic. With Michael Jordan we're saying "great shot," but we're adding other meanings: He is so good he should do that; we are so astounded that understatement better expresses our amazement; we intend to preserve some measure of our own integrity by jokingly withholding fawning endorsement from him.

The key to many funny and good ads is their ironically overstated or understated attitude toward the product. Such a voice is more arresting than a straightforward, positive attitude toward the product. For example, look at the Rockport ad, Figure 8.7, "Walk around topless," in which both tone and attitude are manipulated. The **tone**, the relationship to the audience, is apparent effrontery, an insult. Readers are being commanded in very slangy language to do something shocking; this tone, if taken seriously, would constitute sexual harassment. But the **attitude** (toward product, selling argument) is ironic. The voice says "go topless," but it doesn't mean it. It means, wear sandals.

[6]Gibson, *Persona*, p. 68.

**Figure 8.7** Here both the tone and attitude of the voice are pushed to an extreme to create attention and express the product benefit. Courtesy of Rockport/Reebok International Ltd.

The mismatch creates a humorous irony. Straightforward language might have been, "Wear the most comfortable sandals ever made. Enjoy work more." But those are clichés. Here the colloquialism works better; the attitude toward the sandals, while still positive, is now a joking one. This voice knows it's exaggerating, which makes us smile at its irony and respect its self-consciousness. Tone and attitude combine to create a more interesting voice.

Your attitude toward your product can never be negative—that the product is not good—but you can avoid a straightforward (and therefore often flat) endorsement by altering your attitude. You can intentionally exaggerate the product's virtues (hyperbole), like the Rockport ad, or understate them, as in this example (see Figure 8.8): By finding the man who *wouldn't* fit inside a VW Bug (seven-foot basketball player Wilt Chamber-

**They said it couldn't be done.
It couldn't.**

We tried. Lord knows we tried. But no amount of pivoting or faking could squeeze the Philadelphia 76ers' Wilt Chamberlain into the front seat of a Volkswagen.

So if you're 7'1" tall like Wilt, our car is not for you.

But maybe you're a mere 6'7".

In that case, you'd be small enough to appreciate what a big thing we've made of the Volkswagen.

There's more headroom than you'd expect. (Over 37½" from seat to roof.)

And there's more legroom in front than you'd get in a limousine. Because the engine's tucked over the rear wheels where it's out of the way (and where it can give the most traction).

You can put 2 medium-sized suitcases up front (where the engine isn't), and 3 fair-sized kids in the back seat. And you can sleep an enormous infant in back of the back seat.

Actually, there's only one part of a VW that you can't put much into.

The gas tank.

But you can get about 29 miles per gallon out of it.

**Figure 8.8** An example of attitude toward product that is intentionally self-mocking, understating product virtues rather than overstating them.
Courtesy of Volkswagen United States, Inc.

lain) and writing "They said it couldn't be done. It couldn't," VW mocked its product, but gently. Their attitude was jokingly modest—VWs *can't* do everything. Levi's develops a similar, jokingly negative attitude toward its product in this ad (Figure 8.9).

In an age inundated with hype and overstatement, you're wise to think about your copy's attitude toward its product. Can you find one more interesting than "This product is fabulous. Buy it now and be the happiest person alive."?

Remember, too, that with most advertising you're creating a relationship between words and pictures. So just like the ironic comment on Michael Jordan's basketball shot, you can make ironic comments about your ad's images. My comments in the

**Figure 8.9.** Another example of the attention-getting power and persuasiveness of voices that understate rather than overstate their endorsement of the product. Courtesy of Levi Strauss & Co. (Canada) Inc.

headline chapter about understatement and overstatement, mismatching what you show and say, are examples of ironic headlines (relative to their visuals). You create a more complex voice and your attitude toward your selling argument becomes subtler when the image is *more* than the usual, the comment *less* so (or vice versa). While we've been talking in this chapter about the words in an ad, remember that an ad's voice is really the entire rhetorical package: language + image. The whole ad has a voice, and you can use all the ad's elements to create it.

## Adopting the consumer's attitude and tone

Lifestyle and attitude advertising often doesn't project the tone and attitude of the corporation toward the consumers; rather it projects the tone and attitude of the consumers themselves. The ads, in effect, climb inside our heads and see things our way instead of making nice corporate talk. (See Figures 8.10 and 8.11.) What you'll usually manipulate here is tone. The Clarion car stereo ad creates a hip, assertive, inner voice. How close is this voice to us? It *is* us, that's how close it is. Our attitude toward the product is very positive: It gives us apparently everything; it doesn't waver, it works great, it *is* a state of mind. (In some ways, the rhetoric of the ad says, the stereo works better than we do.) While our attitude toward the product is positive, our attitude toward the selling argument itself is more "realistic," more ironic (that is, life's so bad it's good). In the Reebok shoe ad "we" are also talking, not the corporation. Here we see our own handwriting and its attitude toward life. (Our attitude toward the shoes is never stated, just implied.)

**YOUR JOB STINKS.**

**YOUR LOVE LIFE STINKS.**

**THE GUY IN THE CAR NEXT TO YOU STINKS.**

**IT DOESN'T GET ANY BETTER THAN THIS.**

This is escapism. This is accelerating as the road clears and the CD drops into the slot and U2's "Streets With No Name" begins. This is cranking it. This is leaving work early on Friday afternoon. This is the Clarion Car Radio 5770 CD AM/FM Stereo CD Player. This is a removable chassis, single DIN unit that fits almost every car that's been around since you've been around. This is no skipping CDs, regardless of how hot or cold it gets. This is 108 watts of power served up the most efficient way known to mankind: 4 channels each delivering 27 watts respectively. This is Clarion's Mag-Tune FM reception system that eliminates "picket-fencing" interference and locks in weak signals without crowding from stronger adjacent channels. This is it. This is purple haze. This is rock n' roll. Call Clarion at 1-800-487-9907, Dept. IN for more information. This is free.

**Clarion**

THERE IS NO SOUND BARRIER

**Figure 8.10** Attitude and lifestyle ads frequently adopt our point of view. They don't address us; they *become* us. We are, in effect, overhearing ourselves. Courtesy of Client: Clarion Sales Corporation , Gardena, CA and Agency: Stein Robaire Helm, Los Angeles, CA (1991-92).

5.29.92

Another summer spent bagging groceries, scanning bar codes, dusting canned goods.... When the manager asked if I'd be back next summer, I couldn't keep a straight face.

R.B.

There's a story in every Boks.

Boks™ Shoes that look good and feel good from the Reebok Design Group. Call 1-800-843-4444.

**Figure 8.11** Another example of an ad whose voice is ours, not the corporation's. Here a lifestyle is for sale; the implication is that the shoes either accompany it or help make it possible. Courtesy of Reebok International Ltd.

So you may want to get inside us. Don't address us, *become* us. What are we saying and thinking about life around us and the products in it? What shape are we in? How can products help us out and also help express our inner feelings?

## Exercises

1. Decide on the rhetorical triangle for the ad you're working on right now; that is, characterize its tone and attitude. Now change the product. (You can't talk about a Lexus the way you talk about Pepsi or the way you talk about HIV testing.) What changes in tone and attitude will you have to make when the subject (product) changes? Let's say you're selling the idea of a vacation, a big one, to your father, who's nearing retirement:

   *attitude toward vacation:* very serious, the reward for a life of service; the last, perhaps only, chance to reorient his value system

   *tone:* loving concern

   Now sell Dad on a day at a theme park, like King's Island or Disneyland. Notice that your previous attitude and tone just won't work. Here's how you might want to change them:

   *attitude:* casual, relaxed, kick away a day, no great insights; King's Island is a release, not a summation

   *tone:* maybe make fun of him, asking if he has the courage to take a walk in the park, can he "waste" a day?

2. Choose an ad you're working on, and holding the product constant, change the target audience. If you'd been selling men, sell women; if mature women, then switch to younger ones. If you've been selling thirtysomethings, sell to teenagers. How do you need to change the attitude and tone as a consequence?

3. Change the voice of an ad. Make a car ad friendlier, snootier, more finger-wagging. Take the copy and slant it toward another tone. Now change the attitude. If you've been praising the product, develop another attitude toward it—mock the product, or overexaggerate its benefits. Notice that changing any of the legs of your triangle usually necessitates changing the others.

## Keep your voice free of clichés

The best voices sound distinct, singular. One way they do so is by avoiding clichés, whether ones particular to advertising or general to the language. You remember from your freshman writing course that clichés—overused words, expressions, and ideas—are bad: They flatten the prose, numb the reader, and make your voice sound like borrowed clothes look. They are you at your least individual, least interesting, most plagiaristic. So if you find yourself writing a phrase that sounds too familiar, too slick, especially one that tumbles out too fast, cross it off and look for another way to say the same thing.

One problem with copywriting, however, is that the language that defines advertising's territory, the phrases which constitute its meanings, are themselves clichés: "buy now and save," "new and improved," "state of the art," "now with even more cleaning power," "take advantage of this special offer," "for a limited time," "be the first to," "introducing a revolutionary way to," "complete satisfaction or your money back," and so on.

Of course, we *do* want people to buy now and save, we *do* promise more power in this new formula, we *are* introducing a new product, and so forth. However, the language with which these arguments are made is itself so clichéd and corrupted that what we have to say and how we say it have merged into one big cliché in many consumers' minds. Indeed, advertising may have more and more overused clichés than any other field. We see advertising all the time, too, which only accelerates the speed at which fresh language decays into cliché.

It's a content and a form teetering on bankruptcy. The fact that as an advertiser you must go in there one more time, make the same argument but make it with enough originality to escape the dead zone of consumer disbelief, this is the great challenge of advertising writing.

## How to avoid clichés

Writing well with *so* many clichés around almost seems to require a new dictionary. And to the extent that your voice is un-adlike, to the extent that you can sound not like an ad but like a person, an *interesting* person, so much the better. However, sometimes you can avoid a cliché simply by inverting or otherwise modifying its expression: "at the touch of a finger" is really overused; "at a finger's touch" less so. You've slightly reinvigorated the phrase. Anything more original might be stronger still: "with a tap of your index finger." Lots of headlines and clever lines of copy result from twisting a cliché even harder, as Nike did before with the cliché "When the going gets tough, the tough get going": "When the going gets wet, the wet go Hawaiian." So don't shun clichés outright, but be certain that, if you do work with one, you've either tweaked or really twisted it.

My best advice is the same given in freshman composition courses for avoiding clichés: Recognize and replace them in your own writing, and read, read, read good prose (in this case body copy). Copywriters know how many land mines are buried in the fields they must traverse; read the good writers to see how they got across.

> Copywriters get only a couple of thousand common words to work with. Advertising has long ago burned the meaning out of most of them. Words like *service, value, quality* are impotent; part of the dead language of advertising. The best agencies today are creating a new language of words, pictures, techniques and personality to communicate product values.
> —Virgil Shutze, co-founder, HutchesonShutze, Atlanta.[7]

## Exercise:

Pick a product you're working on and write copy that invokes as many of the clichés of English and the product category as you can (every product has its own overworked language). Write as wrong, as laughably wrong, an ad as you can. Read several of these out loud to hear them. If you can imagine their exact opposites, then you've got an idea of what *to* do.

For example, an ad for the Peace Corps might sound like this:

> Become a Peace Corps volunteer and help those less fortunate than yourself. Bring your energy to an underprivileged nation and watch it bloom where there was desert. Bring smiles to the people as you teach them how to use modern methods of agriculture, develop better sanitation, and find hope in the future. Become your own best self by helping people help themselves....

By contrast, Figure 8.12 shows us a Peace Corps ad that knows about the clichés of volunteerism. So it gives us something else instead: ironic commentary about just how impossible the job may be. The **attitude** here is what hooks us: not overstated idealism but wise-guy cynicism (its first line of copy: "Look at it

---

[7]"Visit with Virgil," interview with Virgil Shutze, *Creative Leaders Advertising Program*, collected reprints of its advertising series, published by *The Wall Street Journal*, 1991, p. 45.

# There are no hammers.
# There are no nails.

# But that's okay.
# There's no lumber,
# either.

Look at it this way: at least you won't need a building permit. What you will need is plenty of determination.

Foresight. The ability to look beyond very real hardships and obstacles and discern a greater good: that of

empowering others, of helping them become self-reliant. It might mean

teaching people how to raise new shelters. Or how to raze old ones.

In every case, it will mean replenishing the most important resource a

person can have: their dignity. And you thought construction wasn't

a noble profession. **Peace Corps.** The toughest job you'll ever love.

**Figure 8.12** This ad knows the clichéd approaches to "cause" advertising—earnest pleas to our idealism—and avoids them, creating instead a voice that seems to smile through the apocalypse. Courtesy of Backer Spielvogel Bates.

this way, at least you won't need a building permit."). Thus the voice is richer than that of most ads because it's complicated, of two minds: Your Peace Corps experience may be both rewarding *and* nightmarish. There is a wisdom in this voice, and it wins us over by transcending clichés.

## How to find your voice

The two best ways to learn to write better are, simply enough, to read and write. As mentioned earlier, study the good copywriters like a fiend. Depending on where you live, you may not be getting consistently top-shelf copywriting. Especially in the smaller markets, local radio, TV, and newspaper advertising can be mediocre, and you are missing a good deal of work altogether. So reading the advertising annuals (and looking at ads in newspapers like *The New York Times* and *USA Today*) becomes doubly important. Read the brochure copy in the design annuals. Study the body copy in the advertising annuals. Subscribe to as many ways to read the good stuff as you can afford; seek out the rest in your library. [Recommended: the *Print* regional annual, *The One Show* (from the One Club for Art & Copy), the *Art Directors Annual, Communication Arts'* advertising and design annuals, and *Art Direction* magazine. *Adweek, Brandweek,* and *Advertising Age* cover the business side—trends, themes, issues—of advertising very well.]

> The larger one's repertoire of selves, the more wisely one can choose an effective voice in a given situation.
> —Walker Gibson[8]

Don't limit your reading to copywriting. The American voice—in all its variety—is the one you need to hear in your inner ear. Read E. B. White, Stephen King, Alice Walker, Tom Wolfe, Anna Quindlen. Read *Rolling Stone, Esquire, Glamour, The New Yorker.* Open Studs Terkel's books and hear us talk. You must assimilate American speech, from formal and literary down to funky and street-smart, because all copy comes out of these voices. You recreate the American vernacular when you write copy, becoming our voice, our human sound. The rhythms and words you need are out there in print (as well as in our music, our movies, our bumper stickers, and so on). Stock up.

Stylistically, the closest cousin to advertising copy is journalism, so attend especially to the voices of good journalists. Here, for example, is a little bit of Bob Greene, writing an obituary for the wrestler Buddy "Nature Boy" Rogers:

> Nature Boy had the greatest speaking voice. He sounded like confidence squared. He walked with a strut even when he walked with a cane. Two strokes last month killed him. The last time I was in south Florida, I took him and his wife to dinner at an Italian

---

[8]Gibson, *Persona,* p. 51.

restaurant called Casa Bella. He seemed to have a little trouble reading the menu. Maybe his eyes were going bad. I didn't mention it. Some things you just don't do.[9]

Greene's diction (word choice) is common, so he sounds real; he puts in details, so we see things; and his sentences are straight-line American vernacular, subject + verb + object, so they make reading easy. We simply follow someone talking out loud. There's an authenticity to it. You wouldn't want to sell a Cadillac with this voice, but there are plenty of no-nonsense products for which it would work. (And all you've got to do is open a copy of *Architectural Digest* to hear how you'd sell a Cadillac.)

Also you've got to write regularly yourself to get better; exercise that writing muscle. No one gets much better just by watching. Try to write every day. Begin copy assignments with **free writing**. As E. M. Forster said, "How do I know what I think until I see what I say?" You've got to get the words out there before you can do anything with them. Quick free writings push you past writer's block and begin to show you what you have to say.

**Remember:** The essence of good advertising language is its human sound. Your first job is to get our attention, and your next job is to convince us that this corporate announcement aimed at thousands, if not millions, is really a nudge of the elbow from one friend to another.

---

[9]Bob Greene, "Nature Boy Goes the Final Round," *Chicago Tribune,* July 6, 1992, sec. C, p. 1.

# CHAPTER 9

# BODY COPY II: Writing Well

*Many copywriters labor for endless hours to create and hone the headline and concept for an ad, only to dash off the body copy as an afterthought. This is a disservice to both the advertiser and the consumer. Seldom can a sale be closed, or a significant change in attitude be brought about, by a headline alone. A well-crafted, literate, and persuasive selling argument is at least as crucial to the ultimate success of an ad as any other element.*
—Rod Kilpatrick, copywriter, Fallon McElligott[1]

As we've seen, voice is critical to writing well, but it's not alone. Let's examine the other items from your English professor's list of principles:

1. **Voice.**

2. **Details:** The writing is full of specifics; it's particular, not vague.

3. **Thesis:** The writing has one central, unifying idea. It hangs together.

4. **Organization and structure:** The central idea is developed in some order; there is a beginning, middle, and end, and the writing coheres throughout.

5. **Style:** Form matches content: The prose is not overwritten. It's stylistically graceful, with strong, clear sentences, and well-chosen language.

---

[1] Rod Kilpatrick, quoted in Jack Haberstroh and Paul D. Wright, eds., *Copywriting Assignments from America's Best Advertising Copywriters* (Englewood Cliffs, NJ: Prentice Hall, 1989), p. 17.

## *DETAIL, DETAIL, DETAIL*

While no "rules" of writing are absolutely and always true, this one comes close: Good writing is concrete and specific; bad writing is abstract and general. Do you remember your freshman composition instructor always asking for more detail? You needed to point to things, put them in your writing, so that we knew what you were talking about. You had to hang your ideas on something besides thin air. This same obligation to support your generalities with specifics holds true in body copy. A well-chosen detail is more persuasive than a multitude of vague claims of superiority.

> The weight of an argument may often be multiplied by making it specific. Say that a tungsten lamp gives more light than a carbon and you leave some doubt. Say that it gives three and one-third times the light and people realize that you have made tests and comparisons.
> —Claude Hopkins[2]

## How to generate detail

### 1. Draw from your research

What works when you're researching your product also works when you're writing it up. Go back through the facts you discovered on the company and product—awards and honors won, the most intricate but essential part in the machine, the farthest place from which the company procures a part or the farthest flung user of the product, where, when, and how the CEO fell in love with the company's product, who he or she studied under, examples of corporate dedication. (Do the chefs grow their own spices outside the kitchen? Is the water recycled through filters every 20 minutes? Do the engineers—as Ogilvy discovered when researching Rolls-Royce—listen for axle whine with a stethoscope?) Look for particularities that you might use in the copy.

Which details you use depends on the purpose and scope of the copy you're writing. If it's a brochure, a lot of them might be useful; if it's a single ad, the headline/visual concept will obviously narrow and direct your writing. While you may mention additional selling points in such copy, focus only on the details that support that ad's concept; save the rest for other ads. Regard-

[2]Claude Hopkins, *My Life in Advertising & Scientific Advertising*, rpt. (Lincoln-wood, IL: NTC Business Books, 1991), p. 250.

less of which details you end up using, however, the point is always the same. Specifics give density to your copy—weight, realism, and reader interest. They make whatever story you're telling not only more *there*, but more believable.

Just as we look to the classic VW campaign from Doyle Dane Bernbach for other advertising virtues, we also see that it was a very specific campaign, citing fact after fact in its continuing argument for the Bug. (See Figure 9.1.) Good copy always shows that its writer did his or her homework. There are details in it that only come after someone has been immersed in the product for a while. Look at how vivid and convincing this is:

**After we paint the car we paint the paint.**

You should see what we do to a Volkswagen even before we paint it.

We bathe it in steam, we bathe it in alkali, we bathe it in phosphate. Then we bathe it in a neutralizing solution.

If it got any cleaner, there wouldn't be much left to paint.

Then we dunk the whole thing into a vat of slate gray primer until every square inch of metal is covered. Inside and out.

Only one domestic car maker does this. And his cars sell for 3 or 4 times as much as a Volkswagen.

(We think that the best way to make an economy car is expensively.)

After the dunking, we bake it and sand it by hand.

Then we paint it.

Then we bake it again, and sand it again by hand.

Then we paint it again.

And bake it again.

And sand it again by hand.

So after 3 times, you'd think we wouldn't bother to paint it again and bake it again. Right? Wrong.

**Figure 9.1** The persuasive power of this ad rests on its convincing assembly of selling facts. Detail, detail, detail. Courtesy of Volkswagen United States, Inc.

*Headline*:
After we paint the car we paint the paint.

*Copy*:
You should see what we do to a Volkswagen even before we
paint it.
We bathe it in steam, we bathe it in alkali, we bathe it in phos-
phate. Then we bathe it in a neutralizing solution.
If it got any cleaner, there wouldn't be much left to paint.
Then we dunk the whole thing into a vat of slate gray primer
until every square inch of metal is covered. Inside and out.
Only one domestic car maker does this. And his cars sell for 3
or 4 times as much as a Volkswagen.
(We think the best way to make an economy car is expensively.)
After the dunking, we bake it and sand it by hand.
Then we paint it.
Then we bake it again, and sand it again by hand.
Then we paint it again.
And bake it again.
And sand it again by hand.
So after 3 times, you'd think we wouldn't bother to paint it
again and bake it again. Right?
Wrong.

## 2. Use particular language

But "detail, detail, detail" doesn't simply mean bring in facts. It
also means be specific, not general, throughout the language.
Find particular verbs, precise adjectives and adverbs, the best
word, not just the most available one. Not "good" chocolate if
"seductive" chocolate does more. Not "fabric" if it's "wool."
Don't write "every zipper is well made," if instead you can write,
as Timberland did for one of its coats, "every zipper is milled and
tumbled smooth so as to not injure the leather."

In other words, don't float above your subject; get down into
its texture.

## 3. Find the right connotations

Connotation counts as much as denotation. We remember from
freshman composition that the denotation of a word is its strict
dictionary definition, and its connotations are the shades of
meaning that surround it. Thus *smile*, *grin*, and *smirk* all denote
the same thing, but each has a different shade of meaning, a
different connotation. There are no synonyms. *Childish* and *child-
like* denote the same state, but which would you rather be called?

The Timberland copywriters could have said their zipper
was "manufactured," but wisely they added the sense of old-
time, small company methods with the word "milled." They

could have said it was polished with "abrasives," but "tumbled smooth" sounds so nice I'd almost like it done to me. Both choices supply the right connotations to the same denotative facts.

This feeling for words, turning them over in your mind before using them, is central to writing good copy. A few bad words and you break the spell you're trying to cast. The pressure on word choice in the compressed space of body copy makes it similar to poetry—a high-wire act, grace along a narrow line.

### 4.  Create images

An image is anything that appeals to one or another of our senses: sight, touch, taste, hearing, smell. Good writing puts the reader somewhere and does so largely through its imagery. That's why "russet" is better than "potato" (we *see* more), "sandpaper" is better than "rough"(we *touch* more), and "simmer" beats "cook" (we *hear* and *smell* more). Appeals to our senses are also conduits to our emotions. The more we see, touch, and so on, the more we feel. Images reach us.

Read this Mitsubishi TV ad (Figure 9.2). It exemplifies both good copy and good concept. The creative problem was how to *show* in print the power of large-screen video. You can't really do that in print because you don't have the size and you don't have movement. So why not an all-copy ad that shows, through its vivid language, what dramatic pictures are like? One axiom of good writing is, "Show, don't tell." Look at how well this copy does that: Things are not referred to or labeled ("great," "terrible," "exciting,"); they're brought right in. We experience them; we've been shown, not told.

### 5.  Use metaphors

Whenever you choose to talk about one thing in terms of something dissimilar, you are using metaphor, and it's often a good idea—it makes writing more clear and more vivid. Here, for example, is a headline for a Porsche (Figure 9.3): "Imagine the stud fees we'd get if it was a race horse." And the copy develops this comparison between horse and car: "Since its introduction in 1974, the Porsche 911 Turbo has given birth to an entire generation of hopeful imitators. None of them even came close. Considering these bloodlines...." The metaphor here becomes a kind of detail; we see the car *as* a thoroughbred, which is more vivid than "widely imitated," "quality craftsmanship," or other nonmetaphorical equivalents would have been.

The danger with metaphors? Without thinking, you can add other metaphors to the current one and create what are called **mixed metaphors**, visual incongruities: "If he goes to the well

The sound of a single bullet buzzed straight past my ear. I didn't have to look at the rear-view mirror to know that Dubrov was back on our tail. Our only avenue of escape was through the street market up ahead.

The brightly colored patchwork of stalls rushed up to meet us as Johnson put his foot to the floor. A crate of watermelons exploded wetly against the car, the pink juice streaming across the windscreen.

I stole a quick glance in the mirror. Dubrov's gleaming black limo was getting closer by the second.

It was then that I sensed the first hints of acrid smoke. The stink of a grinding, dying engine.

Our car was going to go, and with it, all our chances.

And as the billowing smoke began to tear at my nostrils and burn my eyes, I realized that it was something much, much worse than an overheated engine. It was my

chicken pot pie burning in the kitchen, the charred, inedible victim of my engrossment in Mitsubishi's Home Theater with Dolby Surround Sound.

MITSUBISHI

**Figure 9.2** This ad demonstrates the vivid, involving power of language itself. There are virtually no pictures in the ad, just copy. But we see, hear, touch, taste, and smell a lot, don't we? Courtesy of Mitsubishi and Chiat/Day.

**Figure 9.3** An example of the power of metaphor. Copy of advertisement used by permission of Porsche Cars North America, Inc. Porsche, and the Porsche crest are registered trademarks of Dr. Ing. h.c. F Porsche AG.

one more time, he's going to get burned." That sort of thing. So comparing the Porsche to something else while also thinking of it as a horse—for example, saying "it's like a piece of sculpture"—would be a mistake; our minds prefer one picture system at a time. Also with any metaphor you're taking a chance: Maybe it's too weird, too cute, too clichéd, or—if overextended—too irritating. How many more times do you want the Porsche copywriters to mention horses in their copy? A few, but not too many, right?

## THESIS

Copy is not a random bunch of one-liners. It is not a Jay Leno or Stephen Wright routine full of clever sayings, catchy phrases, bizarre *non sequiturs.* (In this regard it differs from headlines, which often are like something out of a standup comedian's act.)

Just as an essay develops one main idea, or *thesis*, so too does copy. It follows from the advertisement's approach or thesis. Once you have figured out the strategy of the ad, the concept that underlies it, you will know what kind of copy to produce, and probably how much. Getting the copy right won't be easy—writing well is *always* hard—but you'll know what things ought to be there. If, for example, you have decided to sell children's toys because they help kids learn things, then the copy will sell the educational, imaginative benefits of the toys. If, however, you choose to emphasize the durability of the toys, then you will show an elephant standing on a truck and talk in the copy about the rugged plastic and tough wheels. Even though copy is, indeed, the place you cite additional selling points—that's part of its function, after all—the copy should have a dominant idea running through it, and that idea comes from the ad's strategy.

Write your sentences in a straight line. Ask of each one, does this follow the thesis? Is it firmly related to the central idea of the copy? If not, is there a good reason, or have you just digressed? Look back at that VW copy; it was all about the paint job and nothing else.

## ORGANIZATION AND STRUCTURE

"Begin at the beginning," the King said, very gravely,
"and go on till you come to the end: then stop."
—Lewis Carroll[3]

You can't just keep resaying the thesis, however; you've got to develop it. Like an essay, good copy has a beginning, a middle, and an end.

## Beginning

Think of the first line of body copy as the next sentence after the headline, or a reiteration of it in slightly different terms. That is, after all, the reason why people read copy—to seek further information, to finish what the headline/visual strategy has started—so give them what they expect. Follow directly from your lead. And pull hard. You either draw people down into the copy with a strong beginning—or you lose them.

[3]Lewis Carroll, *Alice's Adventures in Wonderland,* in *Alice in Wonderland,* ed. Donald J. Gray (New York: W. W. Norton & Company, Inc., 1971), p. 94.

## Middle

The middle is where you put the selling facts; after all, people don't want more jokes, more one-liners at the headline's level of generality. They have gone to the copy for the fine print, as it were; they want details. Give them these right here. Even though you're citing additional selling points, remember this: Whatever the ad's concept, don't drop it altogether in the copy. Use its dominant idea as occasional language or imagery, thus allowing the prose to flow with the ad's idea. In other words, *pull the ad's concept through the copy*—not only to make the copy cohere with itself but to unify it with the ad's Big Idea.

Notice in this ad for San Francisco (Figure 9.4) how its dominant idea reappears as language within the copy. The concept of the city as an amusement park full of activity is sustained throughout, especially by the command forms of the verbs. Notice also how the copy has its own unity and functions as a complete sales message, details included. Feel how everything pulls together?

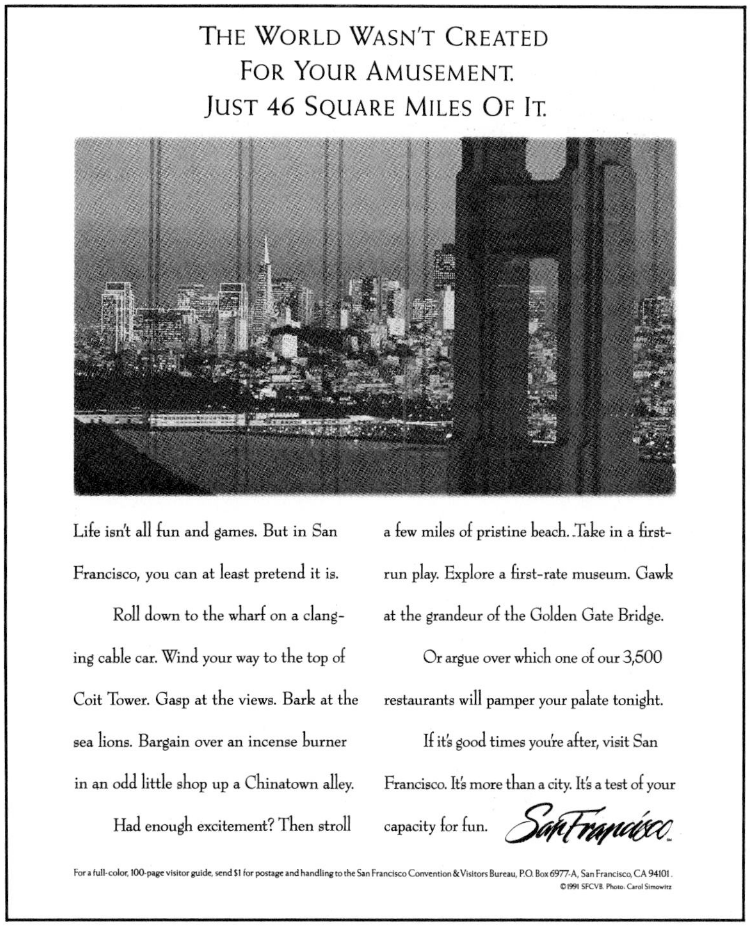

> THE WORLD WASN'T CREATED
> FOR YOUR AMUSEMENT.
> JUST 46 SQUARE MILES OF IT.
>
> Life isn't all fun and games. But in San Francisco, you can at least pretend it is.
>
> Roll down to the wharf on a clanging cable car. Wind your way to the top of Coit Tower. Gasp at the views. Bark at the sea lions. Bargain over an incense burner in an odd little shop up a Chinatown alley. Had enough excitement? Then stroll a few miles of pristine beach. Take in a first-run play. Explore a first-rate museum. Gawk at the grandeur of the Golden Gate Bridge.
>
> Or argue over which one of our 3,500 restaurants will pamper your palate tonight.
>
> If it's good times you're after, visit San Francisco. It's more than a city. It's a test of your capacity for fun. *San Francisco.*
>
> For a full-color, 100-page visitor guide, send $1 for postage and handling to the San Francisco Convention & Visitors Bureau, P.O. Box 6977-A, San Francisco, CA 94101.
> ©1991 SFCVB. Photo: Carol Simowitz

**Figure 9.4** Well-organized, well-structured copy, sustaining the headline's concept while delivering the specifics that complete its argument. Courtesy of San Francisco Convention & Visitors Bureau.

*Headline:*
The World Wasn't Created For Your Amusement. Just 46
Square Miles Of It.

*Copy:*
Life isn't all fun and games. But in San Francisco, you can at
least pretend it is.
Roll down to the wharf on a clanging cable car. Wind your way
to the top of Coit Tower. Gasp at the views. Bark at the sea
lions. Bargain over an incense burner in an odd little shop up a
Chinatown alley.
Had enough excitement? Then stroll a few miles of pristine
beach. Take in a first-run play. Explore a first-rate museum.
Gawk at the grandeur of the Golden Gate Bridge.
Or argue over which of our 3,500 restaurants will pamper your
palate tonight.
If it's good times you're after, visit San Francisco. It's more than
a city. It's a test of your capacity for fun.

For a full-color, 100-page visitor guide, send $1 for postage and handling to
the San Francisco Convention & Visitors Bureau, P.O. Box 6977-A, San
Francisco, CA 94101.

## End

The close is also the place where you put the **call to action**. Much
national brand advertising doesn't ask us to do anything more
than consider the product. But retail ads (and increasingly all
advertising) encourage a more active response: "Call today for
the latest price," "Act now; sale ends Tuesday," "Call 1-800... for
more information," and so on. In this ad we're invited to write
for a visitor guide. Whatever you want the consumer to *do*, put
it here, in the closing.

## Copy as a three-part structure

Body copy must also end rather than just stop. You want to create
a sense of completion, a verbal journey begun and satisfyingly
concluded. One way to do this is to think of your headline, first
line of body copy, and last line of body copy as a trinity—a
unified, frequently clever, almost syllogistic summary of the
selling idea. Here we see this classic closing strategy: "It's a test
of your capacity for fun," the copy's last line, reasserts the ad's

fundamental idea and relates both to the headline and to the first line of copy.

You don't have to write copy this way, but it can be effective. Such symmetry is itself a kind of persuasiveness: The argument is reiterated but not repeated; the case *feels* closed.

## Coherence

So far we've been saying that copy should have one central idea that everything hangs from; it should be unified. But it should also *appear* unified, which means it must **cohere**. In addition to hooking up with the big idea, the copy's words, phrases, sentences, and ideas must hook up with each other. One writer called good prose a "nest of hooks," and that's a fine image by which to understand coherence. You shouldn't be able to pull any sentence out of the copy without bringing others with it (or without tearing a hole in the copy's sense). Everything should depend on everything else. A nest of hooks. Thus, the relationship of the parts to the parts (**coherence**) is as important as the relationship of the parts to the whole (**unity**).

How to accomplish this? Lots of ways, but transitions are essential. They link one element to another: "first," "second," "another," "and," "but," "so," "however," "above," "under," "last," "therefore," and so on. Pronouns deftly stitch one part to another, too: "The driver walked away from his car unhurt. *Its* airbag saved *his* life." Prepositional phrases and other bits of language tie your meanings together for readers: "*In today's world,* who's safe? *As you know,* the police..." The repetition of a word or idea brings coherence, as we'll see with the following ad's repetition of "clock" and clock-related language. Put transitions up front in sentences so we know where we're going. In other words, let them steer how we read a sentence, as, for example, "in other words" just did.

Essentially, as you write each sentence, keep the previous sentence in mind. Write every line *in response* to the one before it. Keep stitching sentences together (or go back later and do so). Here's a whimsical, strongly-voiced ad for The Nature Company (Figure 9.5). Notice how each sentence is conscious of the one before it, and also how each sentence guides you through itself.

**Figure 9.5** This clever headline teases us into the well-written body copy, each sentence of which is nicely tied to those around it, thus demonstrating one virtue of good prose: coherence. Courtesy of The Nature Company.


## *STYLE*

Have something to say, and say it as clearly as you can.
That is the only secret of style.
—Matthew Arnold[4]

Copywriters shouldn't sound the same anymore than essayists or poets should. But this does not mean that all approaches to style are equal. Nor does it mean that style cannot be taught or

[4]Matthew Arnold, quoted in Joseph M. Williams, *Style*, 3rd ed. (Glenview, IL: Scott, Foresman and Company, 1989), p. 1.

that it has no rules. Here are some stylistic fundamentals that good writers observe, no matter what they're writing:

1. Tighten and sharpen ruthlessly; never waste words.
2. Write with nouns and verbs, not adjectives and adverbs.
3. Write grammatically straightforward sentences.
4. Use concrete subjects and verbs. Avoid nominalization.
5. Prefer the loose style.

Most stylistic advice boils down to one rule: Keep it simple. Use language and sentence structures no bigger than necessary to deliver your meaning (that is, never write to impress, write to say what you mean). Match form to content, language to idea.

In ways I hope to show you, all the preceding rules are interrelated; they're almost four ways of talking about the same problem.

## 1. Tighten and sharpen

> Omit needless words. Vigorous writing is concise. A sentence should contain no unnecessary words, a paragraph no unnecessary sentences, for the same reason that a drawing should have no unnecessary lines and a machine no unnecessary parts. This requires not that the writer make all his sentences short, or that he avoid all detail and treat his subjects only in outline, but that every word tell.
> —Will Strunk[5]

> You want to write a sentence as clean as a bone. That's the goal.
> —James Baldwin[6]

Don't waste words. One thing you can always hear in great copy is all the words its writer *didn't* use, all the words left out, pruned away. Great copy is lean and like an arrow: It goes right where it intends, no waste or wobble. Art directors (and readers) are in no mood for rambling discourses that leisurely visit the selling points.

[5]William Strunk Jr. and E. B. White, *The Elements of Style*, 3rd ed. (New York: Macmillan, 1979), p. 23.

[6]James Baldwin, quoted in George Plimpton, ed., *The Writer's Chapbook* (New York: Viking, 1989), p. 126.

As a working guideline, write your copy to the best of your ability...and then cut it in half. While you probably can't eliminate 50 percent without cutting into muscle tissue, you will be surprised by how much fat can go. When you strip your prose to its leanest, you'll notice a happy consequence: Your *voice* sounds better—sharper, smarter, more persuasive. One sure benefit of cutting into drafts is that you'll improve the sound of the writing in the process. The VW copy quoted earlier serves admirably as an example; it is so simple and unadorned, pure clear function, just like the car.

> When I see a paragraph shrinking under my eyes like a strip of bacon in a skillet, I know I'm on the right track.
> —Peter de Vries[7]

To tighten your work, reread it and ask of every word or phrase, do I need this?

1. Have I said the same thing elsewhere in the sentence?

2. Is there a word I can substitute for a phrase? (for example, "it will not be very long before" can become "soon.")

3. Am I using redundancies? (for example, "red in color," "visible to the eye," "new innovation," "final result," "completely and totally," and so on.)

4. Am I pompous, using more and bigger words than I need to?

5. Am I using the passive voice unnecessarily? ("After the car is painted, the paint is painted" is both wordy and do-er-less. Wisely VW wrote, "After we paint the car, we paint the paint.")

6. Do I make meaningless distinctions? ("Are you the sort of person who likes a recreational sport like golf?" might reduce to "Do you like golf?")

7. How many of my words are just along for the ride, words that look like they're doing something but aren't? ("Honesty is a rare human quality that very few individuals possess" says no more than "Honesty is rare.")

You can eliminate much wordiness simply by taking a pencil to it or hitting the delete button on your computer. You'll have to recast other sentences to tighten them. But either way, tight-

---

[7]Peter de Vries, quoted in Donald M. Murray, *Write to Learn*, 2nd ed. (New York: Holt, Rinehart and Winston, 1987), p. 210.

ening is a wondrous thing: Watch the sentences get quicker, the writing start standing up.

Scrutinize your sentences, too. How many of them can go? Are you taking two sentences to deliver an idea you could put in one? With body copy especially, check out your first few sentences. Are you taking too long to get started, just clearing your throat? Maybe your real first sentence is the third one. Mine often is.

Another piece of advice about editing yourself: The longer you can let a draft "cool," the more you can see the cracks in it. As time passes (an hour, a day, a month), the writing becomes less yours and more someone else's. Eventually it's just words on a page; you can hear and see them objectively. Editing can really get something done then. Try it.

## 2. Write with verbs and nouns, not adverbs and adjectives

At first this seems to counter common sense: If we're to be "descriptive" and "specific" in our body copy, what better way, we suppose, than by adding adjectives and adverbs. Don't they bring specificity to our nouns and verbs? Yes they do, and we need adjectives and adverbs, of course. But we can easily overindulge, clogging up the flow of our sentences with modifiers at every turn.

Nouns and verbs are the two big powers in our language. They run sentences, and you should let them run yours. Notice that strong writers, whose work "flows," write primarily with concrete nouns and verbs. They keep it simple, and don't let too much modification stall the movement or muddy up the meaning:

> On the day before Thanksgiving, toward the end of the afternoon, having motored all day, I arrived home, and lit a fire in the living room. The birch logs took hold briskly. About three minutes later, not to be outdone, the chimney itself caught fire.
> —E. B. White[8]

> A weasel is wild. Who knows what he thinks? He sleeps in his underground den, his tail draped over his nose. Sometimes he lives in his den for two days without leaving. Outside, he stalks rabbits, mice, muskrats, and birds, killing more bodies than he can eat warm, and often dragging his carcasses home.
> —Annie Dillard[9]

---

[8]E. B. White, "Home-Coming," *Essays of E. B. White* (New York: Harper & Row, Publishers, 1977), p. 7.

[9]Annie Dillard, "Living Like Weasels," *Teaching a Stone to Talk* (New York: Harper & Row, Publishers, 1982), p. 11.

You don't buy a car. The bank buys a car. Of course, if you had bought a Volvo two or three years ago, you'd have something today. You'd have a two or three year old Volvo. Which isn't bad to have. Because where three years is the beginning of the end for some cars, it's only the beginning for a Volvo.
—Ed McCabe, Volvo copy

In 1941 millions of Jews were looking for ways to escape Nazi death camps. Gandhi recommended suicide. The movie *Gandhi* portrays the Mahatma as a saint. But an original article in the July Reader's Digest shows the advice of a saint can be hard to live by.
—John A. Young, Jr., *Reader's Digest* copy

It would be easy to screw any of these up by throwing in adjectives and adverbs. Watch:

On the cold, snowy day before another turkey-filled Thanksgiving, toward the end of the long afternoon, having happily motored all day, I arrived home at last, and quickly lit a warm fire in the cozy living room. The very dry birch logs took hold briskly. About three minutes later, not to be vastly outdone, the red hearthstone chimney itself roaringly caught fire.
—E. B. White, ruined

We'd laugh and call this ridiculous exaggeration except that we realize how often we approximate it in our own writing. Find good nouns and verbs and then leave them alone.

## More about verbs

Don't praise the product. Just tell what it does, and how it does it, so that the reader will say: "I must try that." In short, go light on the adjectives and heavy on the verbs.
—James Webb Young[10]

Verbs hustle, weep, surprise, beam, tear, sear, shimmer, and shine; they can stick a finger right in your eye, split your heart open, or collapse into something you'd wedge in your hip pocket. Verbs (and verbals—words derived from verbs, like gerunds and participles) are the only words that *do* anything. Without them nothing happens, and with only general ones ("make," "do," "come," "go," "have"), not enough happens. So use strong verbs, and use them to express the action of an idea. In that one Timberland sentence earlier, we have "milled," "tumbled," and

---

[10]James Webb Young, *Diary of an Ad Man* (Chicago: Advertising Publications, Inc., 1944), p. 214.

"injure." A lot happens. In that determinedly simple VW paint-job copy, we get basic but vigorous verbs—"paint," "bathe," "dunk," "bake," "sand"—and they're repeated until we almost see the sweat of the workers.

### Is-ness

Track down and replace excessive "is-ness" in your writing, too many uses of "to be" as the *main verb* ("is," "are," "were," "will be," "has been,"and so on). "To be" is an odorless, colorless, actionless verb, just an equals sign really. It's the weakest verb; if it's running the sentence by itself, you risk the word pile, a sentence with a bunch of upright things in it, all tottering into one another but not going anywhere.

Remember that "to be" often functions as an auxiliary verb, a helper, and that's fine. Thus, the sentence "I am smiling because my hair is shining" really has two active verbs ("smile" and "shine"), so it moves, however quietly. "I am here but you are there and it is sad," that's is-ness. Try "I'm suffering here because you're living there" or "I wilt here because you bloom there." See?

You can't eliminate "to be," of course, nor do you want to. (I've been using it a lot in these sentences decrying its use.) We just rely on it too much. Verbs make sentences move; they animate the universe of things. Always examine your verbs to see if you've got your motor running.

## 3. Write grammatically straightforward sentences

This is perhaps the trickiest rule. Your sentences are your most complicated stylistic element. They're you. We can all locate a better verb and delete unnecessary words, but restructuring the way we use language is a larger matter. Nevertheless, we've seen that all my advice so far has centered on simplicity, and that all of it is interrelated. If you find the right verb, you'll avoid is-ness. If you keep from overdosing on adjectives and adverbs, your writing will be tighter and sharper. It'll move and be readable. Now let's take this same idea of simplicity and apply it to sentences.

If writing good sentences has one first principle, this is it: "State who's doing what in the subject of your sentence, and state what that who is doing in your verb."[11] This sounds easy and obvious, but it isn't. Remember that a sentence, any sentence, is

[11]Joseph M. Williams, *Style*, 2nd ed. (Glenview, IL: Scott Foresman, 1985), p. 8.

simply a way to say that some thing *does* something. Make sure that this thing (the real agent of action) is also your grammatical subject. And make sure that the real action is also the main verb. Lots of times we put the true agent of action elsewhere than in the grammatical subject, and stick the real action elsewhere than in the main verb. In other words, we hide what the sentence is really saying, and we end up with a fuzzy style that nobody likes, including us.

> The sensation of driving the Miata is pure enjoyment.

A bad sentence. Why? Its grammatical subject is "sensation," its main verb "is." Is the real meaning of the sentence "sensation is"? No. The real meaning is that you'll enjoy driving the car. You've hidden the true subject and verb. The real agent of action is either "you" or "driving," and the real action is "to enjoy" or to have sensation. So if that's the real meaning, then let's try to put it into the grammatical subject and main verb:

> Enjoy driving the Miata.
> Driving the Miata will thrill your senses.
> Recharge your senses in a Miata.

Although the last one is the freshest, any of these is better. Now the agent of action and the action run the sentence; they're not hidden. If you study one of your sentences that feels "blah," chances are good that you've got the wrong noun and verb in charge of what you're saying. Always ask yourself, what's the real do-er in my sentence and what's the real action? Then get those two things, the real subject and verb, in their grammatically correct spots:

> *Bad:*
> The use of a unique approach to outdoor gear by North Face has resulted in clothing that can be worn in any climate.

> "Use has resulted"?
> "clothing can be worn"?

> Are those the crucial meanings? Of course not.

> *Better:*
> North Face designs its gear so you can tackle any climate.

"North Face designs" and "you can tackle" carry your meaning more directly.

## 4. Avoid nominalization

We often fail to match agents and subjects, actions and verbs, because of something called **nominalization**. Nominalization means making nouns out of verbs, and it's the way we killed our Miata sentence previously. "Sensation" is a noun, but it comes from the verb "sense." Likewise, "enjoyment" comes from "enjoy." Somehow or other we learn to sound formal and pretentious and educated by writing in a style that's heavily nominalized:

> A determination of financial conditions facilitates re-evaluation of mortgage arrangements.

Do you mean that you should rethink your mortgage because rates have improved? Say so.

Much writing is deader than it needs to be simply because people fall in love with the pompous and the obscure. A nominalized style is like a crypt that entombs living speech. Let your nouns name real things, and turn your verbs loose. Don't lock them up in long, boring constructions. Get the real noun (often a concrete thing or a person) out there and give it the verb it deserves.

## 5. Prefer the "loose" style

Basically, you want to keep your sentences simple and conversational. You want to make them easy to read; you want them to "flow." How to do this?

Recast sentences that take too long to say. If you get tangled up in a sentence, back out and start over. It probably wants to become two sentences; you need to sequence what you're saying. Much of writing is simply starting into various constructions to see if they'll say what you want them to, like trying tunnel entrances.

Keep subjects and their verbs together. Put them early in the sentences, too, and add modifying material either to the ends of sentences, or in sentence fragments that follow the first sentence. In other words, don't layer your modification into the subject-verb mechanism, don't mess up the driveshaft.

Adding material to the *ends* of your sentences (rather than the beginning or between subjects and verbs) is called **the "loose" style**, and it's the American idiomatic voice. Simple, straightforward, and adding to itself as it goes. Sentences written in the "loose" style are called **cumulative sentences**; that is, they state their idea right up front, in straight subject and verb groupings, then accumulate additional meanings and modifications of that idea as they go. They're easy to read, and they sound like we're thinking as we go, which we are. We approximate speech with constructions like these because we just keep talking, and as we talk, we tack new ideas, like this one, onto the end of our last phrase, as they occur to us, so we can go on forever if we feel like it.... See what I mean?

The kinds of sentences you want to minimize are complex ones with too much modifying material either embedded in the main clause or preceding it. (Check your grammar book under **periodic sentences** or **compound-complex sentences** for constructions to use sparingly.) For example, a sentence like this becomes difficult on the mind:

> Although you seek a bank that has the sophistication with which to handle large accounts yet maintains the flexibility to manage smaller ones as well, you may think that without investing in two separate institutions you're asking too much.

This **periodic sentence** begins, not with the main clause, but with a subordinate clause, so the sentence is coiled, delivering its full meaning only at the end; thus we have to hold it all in our mind until the payoff. Some periodic sentences are great, of course, but if you use too many—especially too many with embedded modifications—then we flounder as readers.

Let's recast our periodic sentence as loose sentences instead (and use parallelism in the last two of them):

> You seek a bank sophisticated enough to handle large accounts yet flexible enough to manage small ones. But you think you'll have to invest in two separate institutions. You think you'll be asking too much of one.

See how this one is much easier to follow and sounds more like someone talking?

## How to use loose sentences for details

You will often use copy to cite product specs, to deliver the necessary detail, the rest of the product story. You can use loose structures to do this, simply adding your details to the ends of sentences. Here are two professional writers showing us how gracefully—and clearly—the loose structure handles details.

> Every so often I make an attempt to simplify my life, burning my books behind me, selling the occasional chair, discarding the accumulated miscellany.
> —E. B. White[12]

> He [Ken Kesey] wrote like he talked, antic, broad, big-breathed, the words flowing in a slangy, spermy, belt-of-bourbon surge, intimate and muscular, the rigors of the college wrestling mat somehow shaping his way of engaging the world in prose—you got a sense of a writer grappling with this subjects, pinning the story, the paranoia in his vision offset by the relish for the stage.
> —Chip Brown[13]

Each sentence is easy to follow: The first says "I attempt to simplify my life" and the second "He wrote like he talked," both straightforward subject-verb groupings, and then they pile up details off the end. Each sentence could have gone on almost forever and we wouldn't get lost.

In copy this approach works well, too. You can be specific but never let doing so overburden a sentence. Here's an example from the middle of some BMW body copy:

> The driver, meanwhile, sits not in a mere driver's seat, but a cockpit—behind a curved instrument panel replete with vital gauges and controls, all placed for optimum visibility and accessibility.

### Sentence fragments as the copy version of the loose style

But since copy sentences tend to be shorter than other prose sentences, often you will want to hang your modifications off the end of a sentence as **fragments**. You punctuate them as separate sentences, but they're really part of the main thought that preceded them. Here's an example:

> So you need shoes and apparel that don't give up either. A shoe like the Air Cross Trainer Low from Nike, with the cushioning you need for running. The flexibility you need for aerobics. The stability required for court sports. And the fit and comfort your feet beg for regardless of where you tell them to go.

See how all these punctuated sentences are really fragments off the main assertion?

[12]White, "Will Strunk," *Essays of E. B. White*, p. 258.

[13]Chip Brown, "Ken Kesey Kisses No Ass," *Esquire* (September 1992), p. 160.

So you need shoes and apparel that don't give up either.
A shoe like the Air Cross Trainer Low from Nike,
with the cushioning you need for running.
The flexibility you need for aerobics.
The stability required for court sports.
And the fit and comfort your feet beg for
regardless of where you tell them to go.

### Fragments are almost essential to good copy

Copy is like one side of an intimate, friendly conversation, written down. Like the personal letter, it pulls the reader close. That's why sentence fragments (and short sentences) are so important to copy. Cutting off snippets of a sentence and writing sentences that are themselves snippets can give you the speed and openness you want. Well used, they become almost a hallmark of good copy. They focus the eye and mind. They're quick. They simplify issues and make things seem easy and convenient. Plus they sound intimate and conversational.

But don't go too far. If you chop up prose too much, it gets unclear and jumpy, too fragmented to make sense. So like all good writers, use sentence fragments but only *on purpose*, when doing so helps the prose.

## Study style

> The lyf so short, the craft so long to lerne.
> —Chaucer[14]

This discussion of style gets us back, as it should, to writing well in general. I've been telling you all along that copy is simply good prose and that you've already had a course in that. But none of us ever graduates, once and for all, from composition class. We're lifelong students of well-made sentences. Since you're a writer now, cultivate a writer's habits. In addition to learning by osmosis—reading good copy and good prose—study style systematically. One book you should always keep around is your grammar handbook from freshman composition. Handbooks vary; some are short, others are more complete, but they're all road maps of the English language, and you can't drive long or far without consulting one. Here are five other books that I recommend if you're serious about getting someplace with your writing style:

---

[14]Chaucer, quoted in Murray, *Write to Learn*, p. 264.

1. Joseph M. Williams, *Style: Ten Lessons in Clarity & Grace*, 3rd ed. (Glenview, IL: Scott Foresman, 1989). A wonderful book that repays the time you spend with it. If you really want to study the engine of style, this book opens the hood.

2. Chris Anderson, *Free/Style: A Direct Approach to Writing* (Boston: Houghton Mifflin, 1992). A book that encourages free writing and teaches the "loose" style. Gracefully written, very readable.

3. William Strunk, Jr. and E. B. White, *The Elements of Style*, 3rd ed. (New York: Macmillan, 1979). A little book that's authoritative and eccentric at the same time. But it remains a classic, a must read; especially invaluable is White's closing chapter, "An Approach to Style."

4. William Zinsser, *On Writing Well*, 4th ed. (New York: HarperCollins, 1990). A much-admired book full of practical, sound advice.

5. Ken Macrorie, *Telling Writing*, 4th ed. (Portsmouth, NH: Boynton/Cook, 1985). This book will set you free. If you read it, you'll never write stiff, awkward "engfish," ever again.

## How long should copy be?

One caveat, however. In the rush to cut into your copy and keep it simple, never forget that your goal is *effective* prose, not quick prose. How long is long? How short is short? As advertising copywriter Alastair Crompton has pointed out:

> The question, "How long should an advertisement be?" is the same question as "How long is a piece of string?" There is no *rule*. An ad is too short if it ends without saying the right things to make a sale. An ad is too long if it repeats itself, gets boring, stops giving facts and information, or uses two words when one would do.[15]

Since there is no "rule" about copy length, you must decide for yourself when that string is long enough. Determine how much more information the reader of your ad needs and wants to know. Look to both your product and your ad's concept for guides to the amount of copy you should write. If your strategy uses rational argumentation and your product is a complicated durable good—a car, a $1,000 racing bike—then a lot of copy may make sense. If, however, your ad appeals to emotions with a

[15]Alastair Crompton, *The Craft of Copywriting* (Englewood Cliffs, NJ: Prentice Hall, 1979), p. 152.

brand-image strategy, and the product is one we *feel* rather than explain—a diamond, a cologne, clothing—then almost any copy may be too much. You must decide for yourself how much of the story is left to tell after you've found the concept and written the headline. There are no firm rules—I have in my office a fascinating diamond ad with several hundred words in it. On the other hand, a bike or car ad may use few words, relying instead on a feeling or image and counting on other mechanisms to tell the rest of the story (brochures and salespeople at the dealers', for instance).

## Copywriters versus art directors

As a copywriter, you'll engage in an eternal struggle with art directors. Since they design the ads and brochures, often they'll just consider your copy a design element—so many gray shapes to integrate gracefully into the piece, usually the fewer and shorter the better. You, however, have bloodied yourself writing all those words, and each one is crucial. Also, if you'll admit it, you often write long because you get interested in the product's story and can't stop. This crossroads between your long copy and other people's short inclinations is one you'll come to constantly. You and your art director partner will both make the best decision, we hope, but one piece of advice: If you think you've written well and it's tight, too, then argue that because it's interesting, people will want to read it. Here are some other copywriters who've stood at the crossroads:

> A letter from a client, commenting on a successful advertisement, says his only objection is that the copy is too long. I verily believe that if a good advertisement were shown to a newborn babe in his crib this would be his first comment on it. In short, the fear of long copy seems to be congenital—and persistent. This in spite of the facts (a) that people buy publications solely for the purpose of reading; and (b) that every direct mail advertiser has proved over and over again that the more you tell the quicker you sell.
> —James Webb Young[16]

> The experts say people won't read long copy about common products; for example, beer. But we keep writing long copy about beer, and people keep reading it. You *can* entertain people in print. You *can* make print emotional. And you can *sell* your product.

---

[16]Young, *Diary of an Ad Man*, p. 66.

Print copy can cover all the small differences that add up to a big reason for buying a specific brand.
—Hal Riney, founder, Hal Riney & Partners[17]

## On overwriting

One reason writing well is difficult is that it never reduces to formula; every good rule can be taken to a bad extreme. You can tighten too much and sound clipped and inhuman. You can sharpen too much and sound fussy. Your search for the precise expression can lead to thesaurus-writing—trading in your natural words for artificial ones—short for long, idiomatic for Latinate, real for bookish. Never write out of a thesaurus; in fact, try never to use one at all and you'll be a better writer. Only the words you own and know will work for you; you can't substitute elegant variations and still sound real. That's why reading a lot helps you as a writer; you come into possession of a larger, more supple vocabulary the natural way.

Good prose must be particular enough to carry meaning but not so overwrought that it sounds like our ruination of E. B. White: every noun with an adjective, every verb with an adverb, the whole thing overqualified until its voice lies buried under baroque ornamentation. And copy is especially easy to overwrite: You're making a case for something, you're persuading, and it's easy to push too hard, to *hype* instead of communicate. Plus you're often writing description. Adjectives and adverbs pop up, as they must, and verbs wither, since you're drawing a picture rather than telling a story. The prose overgrows into a thicket, strangling both your voice and reader interest.

How do you know when you've overdone it? By ear. Good prose is finally a matter of sound. Read your work out loud, *hear* it, especially with your target audience's ear. Would they like what you're saying and the way you're saying it? Are the sentence lengths varied? Long mixed with short, a good **rhythm** among them? While sentences are generally shorter in copy than in essays—ease of reading being such a priority—you don't want sentences so short as to sound staccato. Nor do you want them all the same length—one after another, they'll drone. Is your **diction** (word choice) precise enough to serve the argument but common enough to sound real? These balances are things you can hear; they're also things that improve with practice.

[17]"How Now, Hal?," interview with Hal Riney, *Creative Leaders Advertising Program,* collected reprints of its advertising series, published by *The Wall Street Journal,* 1991, p. 42.

## *HOW BODY COPY IS NOT LIKE FRESHMAN COMPOSITION*

As you've seen, most of what makes an essay good also makes body copy good. Good copy is simply a variant of good writing. There are important distinctions in the variant, however, and here they are:

### Sell, don't just describe

Copy is always selling something, a fact too many beginning copywriters forget. In researching the product and in employing the rules of freshman English, too many writers merely describe product specs. Description and analysis are fine purposes for many essays, but they are never the *purpose* of copy. You are making the case for a product, talking someone into wanting it or wanting more of it or trying it again after all those years ("Have you driven a Ford lately?"). Even when you are describing or analyzing something, you're doing so to make it seem more appealing, or less complicated, or so well made that it must be bought. No matter what the prose's task seems to be at the moment, you are always a salesperson.

### State the benefits, not just the features

If you slide into product specs and forget that you should be selling instead, you will often write about *features* instead of translating those features into *benefits*. We've been here before. Remember, features belong to the product, but benefits belong to the people. Your copy will be "so what?" stuff until you show the advantages to be gained from all those features.

### Brand-image copy has its own rules

Remember, however, that brand-image, lifestyle, and attitude copy describes and sells consumer *feelings,* not hardware. Many ads don't talk about products at all. Instead they resemble short stories, character sketches, or psychological counseling. So don't lock into thinking that ads must talk hardware. Body copy really sells the *idea* of the ad in words. So if the idea is the romance of the sea or the lifestyle of the clothes wearer, then write that as well as you can.

Here, for example, is a Honda ad in which the station wagon is not described at all; the owner's lifestyle is (Figure 9.6). Instead of detailing product features, the copy narrates the changes in circumstance which the vehicle serves. (Notice the use of "you" to pull us in as readers.) In following a life and its humorous, endearing complications, we not only identify with the owner but also appreciate, by implication, the capabilities of the Honda. Well written lifestyle copy.

One day you get married, have kids, get a dog and buy a wagon. So you start driving to day care. You drive to the baby-sitter's place. You drive to your parents'. And, according to your grandparents, you don't drive over to their house as often as you should. Then you start taking the children to preschool. Then to kindergarten. Then to grade school. You drop the kids off at swimming lessons, ballet lessons, trombone lessons and ice skating lessons. A week later, they drop the trombone lessons. You go to the beach one summer and to the lake up in the mountains the next. And you finally decide to go see the Grand Canyon. Your dog barks at all the gas station attendants along the way. You pick the kids up from soccer practices, which soon turn into basketball practices, which soon turn into baseball practices. Then come the football games, which they don't play in, but still need a ride to. And just when you're starting to feel a little like a taxi service, one of your little darlings walks up to you, smiles sweetly, and asks for the keys to the car. You might as well enjoy the trip. The Accord Wagon [HONDA]

**Figure 9.6** Good copy serves the ad's concept, whatever that may be. Here rather than detailing the features of the product, this copy details the lifestyle of its owner, demonstrating the wagon's utility in the process. Courtesy of American Honda Motor Co., Inc.

## Lay out the language to work visually

ing writing doesn't look like an essay either. Glance back, for instance, at the VW paint job ad (Figure 9.1). Notice that this copy of only about 160 words contains 14 paragraphs. That's a paragraph break every 12 words or so. Such abbreviated "paragraphs" not only make reading easy, they add meaning and rhythm to the copy itself. Note how the breaks create dramatic pauses, accentuate the parallelism and repetition in the copy, and help—by surrounding the assertions with emptiness—to reinforce the main idea: that many separate operations are performed on the car.

What you should learn from this is not necessarily to make breaks that often, but to make breaks more often than you would in an essay and to realize that the line in copy functions like the line in poetry: as a way to make meaning. In copy, you must accomplish a lot in a little space, so remember the power of the line itself and use it.

And if you're writing long copy, in addition to making frequent paragraph breaks, make it equally accessible by writing **subheads**. That way we can scan our way through it, if we wish. Subheads, in larger, bolder type than the copy, really open up a page for readers and invite them in.

While all the language of an ad is its copy, we use more specific terms to label its various functions. Some of these you already know, of course. But here they are:

**display type:** the copy in large point sizes meant to attract attention

**headline:** the dominant type of the ad, its major verbal statement; the visual's complement

**subhead:** secondary headlines; display type used to help explain headlines; sometimes more specifically used to denote the larger type headlines within body copy

**overline:** a subhead above the headline that leads into it

**underline:** a subhead below the headline that leads into the copy

**body copy:** the small type-size explanations, the text portion of an ad

**logotype:** the name of the corporation or product, usually in a special typeface, often accompanied by the corporate symbol (For example, the word "Prudential" in its distinctive typeface is the logotype; the graphic Rock of Gilbralter is the symbol.)

**slogan** or **tag line:** the phrase or sentence which, often cleverly, identifies the product or corporation; it often appears at ad's end next to the logotype

**captions:** little explanations that appear beneath pictures

**call-outs:** body copy that surrounds a visual and is keyed to various parts of it

## *A FINAL WORD: ON REWRITING*

> There is no writing, just rewriting.
> —John Updike[18]

> Who casts a living line, must sweat.
> —Ben Jonson[19]

I could have put this in the headline chapter, too, because you can rewrite a headline all day long. But with body copy there are even more words to get right. Rewriting is not a curse visited on bad writers. Writing *is* rewriting. I often wish it were otherwise, but it isn't. I must write lots of drafts, go through a process every time, from fumbling and stupid and incoherent prose to something less so, until sometimes I arrive at good work. Occasionally I can write a headline or short copy block that comes out okay right off. Or sometimes it has to be okay because it's going out the door, no time to fiddle. But most things take me a few drafts. They'll probably take you a few drafts too: A couple just to get the territory of it out, then a few more to tighten and make it make sense, then a couple more to give it some grace. But even that "sequence" isn't true. Every piece develops differently, few come easily. So learn to accept this process as natural. Rewriting is the way of writing, and eventually it becomes the fun of it, too. Honest.

> Say, it is Monday, and you write a very bad draft, but if you keep on trying, on Friday, words, phrases, appear almost unexpectedly. I don't know why you can't do it on Monday, or why I can't. I'm the same person, no smarter, I have nothing more at hand. I think it's true of a lot of writers. It's one of the things writing students don't understand. They write a first draft and are quite disappointed, or often should be disappointed. They don't understand that they have merely begun, and that they may be merely beginning even in the second or third draft.
> —Elizabeth Hardwick[20]

---

[18]John Updike, address, Evenings with Authors, The Thurber House, Columbus, Ohio, October 14, 1989.

[19]Ben Jonson, quoted in Plimpton, ed., *The Writer's Chapbook,* p. 101.

[20]Elizabeth Hardwick, quoted in Plimpton, ed., *The Writer's Chapbook,* p. 111.

## Exercises

The basic writing exercise is simple and unvarying: You write a draft, read it aloud, and get criticism; or you put it on the overhead projector, read that aloud, and get criticism; or you make copies of it, pass them around, and get criticism. Keep rewriting until it sounds right, until it works. That's the method. No tricks, no shortcuts.

During that process here are some things you can do:

1. Circle the verbs in your copy. How strong are they?

2. Examine subjects and verbs and align them with the agents of action and the action.

3. Circle transitions. Are there enough? Are they up front in the flow? Are there too many?

4. Tighten and sharpen the piece: Get as many words out of it as you can without drawing blood.

5. The lead: Does it pull hard enough, make a quick enough and strong enough transition out of the headline/visual?

6. The middle: How specific is it? How complete? Are there details and images? Almost always copy is thinner and more vague than it should be.

7. The close: Do you pull things together, relate back to the concept of the ad? Provide a call to action?

8. Do you sustain the idea you're developing in the copy (for example, Porsche's horse metaphor, San Francisco as an amusement park, or Nike's tone of voice)? Copy must sound like a continuation of the ad's concept, whatever yours is.

9. The sentences. Are they graceful? Varied? Rhythmic? Strong? Simple? How do they sound, not one by one, but all together?

10. Does this copy persuade or just describe? How convincing and motivating is it?

Tough questions—and the reason we read aloud, solicit commentary, and then, invariably, rewrite.

# CHAPTER 10

# GRAPHIC DESIGN

*... tell me of anything more difficult than taking a white piece of paper and using that as your sole device to reach out and convince someone of an argument. It is a very difficult proposition.*
—Bill Westbrook, chief creative officer, Earle Palmer Brown/Bethesda[1]

The most important thing an ad can have is a selling idea. No combination of design, layout, and typography, no amount of sheer graphic handsomeness, can overcome a bad strategy—a concept that's unclear, off base, or non-existent. Yet we see such "beautiful-but-dumb" ads (to use Ogilvy's characterization) all the time. Adman Stavros Cosmopulos puts the issue this way:

> Concept is all important. Good ideas shine through poor layouts but beautiful layouts can't help poor ideas. That's the cosmetic school of advertising: the use of makeup to create the illusion of beauty. But no matter how much pancake makeup you use, it can't disguise the lack of a real idea. Focus on the concept. Make your layouts rough; make your ideas fancy.[2]

Both men rightly stress the centrality of concept. But neither man means that if an idea is great, its graphic execution doesn't matter. While you can't save a bad idea with good design, and you have to try to ruin a good one, it nonetheless can be done. Typography and layout, the two topics of this chapter, are the graphic means by which you either do—or don't—deliver that great idea of yours. They are the means by which you create ads both smart *and* beautiful.

---

[1]Bill Westbrook, quoted in Tracy Lynn, "Southern Crossing," *Creativity* supplement, *Advertising Age,* October 1, 1990, p. 21.

[2]"The Cosmos of Stavros," interview with Stavros Cosmopulos, one from a series of *The Wall Street Journal* ads, *Advertising Age,* April 22, 1991, pp. 6–7.

## *TYPOGRAPHY*

## Type and you

The technical aspects of type—whether you execute it by hand, with dry transfer letters, or on a Macintosh or other computer, and how deeply you're involved with it in your projects—all those things will be determined by your course, instructor, facilities, and so forth. What's important is that you know the essentials of typography. There are, however, lots of essentials—so many, in fact, that I have colleagues here at the art college who have dedicated their professional lives to them. I know people who can talk about the varieties of emotional experience possible with Gill Sans, at each weight and point size, in uppercase, lowercase, and small caps. Who will spend seven hours kerning, leading, and ragging a five-word headline, and then rekern it for use in a smaller format. Who can discuss the sweet balance created by mixing Serif Gothic Heavy headlines with Souvenir Demi Italic subheads and Souvenir Light Italic body copy. And they're neither kidding nor engaging in oversensitive self-indulgence.

You and I don't need to go that far, but we do need to see their point. Many of us look at type, however, and see only words. We understand that *they* matter, obviously, but the differences between those words in one typeface or another, one point size or another, placed in this layout or that one, seem minor. In short, we are initially blind to type itself as part of the idea.

Acquiring a sensitivity to type takes time; for a while you'll hardly distinguish one face from another, beyond noting whether it's serif or sans serif. (Even type veterans have trouble recognizing many typefaces on sight, beyond noting certain family resemblances.) But if you keep looking, type's variety will finally open to you, and you'll begin, in a rush, to acquire that sensitivity you need. Although you'll probably never become as incessantly preoccupied with typographical nuance as are art directors and designers, you will learn just how crucial good type is to powerful communication.

## How much to know?

In a theoretical sense, you can never know too much, but in a practical sense, if you become a copywriter, you'll never need to know too much because type decisions will be made by art directors, those visual sorts with the felt-tip markers who got

BFA degrees from graphics departments and art colleges. In fact, more and more American ad agencies, following the lead of their European counterparts, are adding a typographer to the traditional art director/copywriter team in the belief that even art directors, visual thinkers though they are, can't be expected to know enough about type. Hence, Chiat/Day/Mojo in New York has created the position of in-house typographer (at this writing, Englishman Graham Clifford) to oversee typography in all their advertising.[3]

## Lesson # 1

Here's perhaps the fundamental lesson in typography—simple enough, but profound.[4] It demonstrates how the type, like the words themselves, is part of an ad's meaning:

# Fresh Eggs
# Fresh Eggs

If you saw these two signs along the road, whose eggs would you stop for? Obviously those from the hand-lettered sign. Why? Because you're certain they're the freshest. How do you know that? Because the sign communicates all the right things: Here's a man or woman so plain and honest he or she just hand letters the message. No art director tinkers with the type, no ad agency middlemen slow down delivery. You sense that these are eggs still warm from nearby hens. The other sign, by contrast, is just too neat, too slick: it stands *between* you and the eggs. While the farmer worried about type, the eggs cooled off. The henhouse might even be in another state. Your choice is a no-brainer.

[3]A typographer's typographer, Graham Clifford nevertheless said in a presentation to the Columbus Society of Communicating Arts, Columbus, Ohio, March 15, 1990: "Good typography never helped a bad ad. Bad typography never hurt a good ad." He exaggerated, of course, but he did so to reiterate the point that Ogilvy and Cosmopulos made.

[4]The original source of this anecdote is probably uncertain. I heard it from Robert Bender, Creative VP at Lord Sullivan and Yoder Advertising in Columbus, Ohio, who heard it from an adman in Chicago. A variant appears in Pentagram's *Living by design*, rev. ed. (London: Lund Humphries, 1979), p. 131.

This simple little example embodies the whole point of typography: Match your idea with its physical expression. Allow the connotations of the type to reinforce the denotation of the message itself. Every good ad invokes this egg principle, just in more complicated settings, by using the type that's right for the product, audience, and purpose. Type is thus part of the **voice** of an ad; its *look* is its sound. Make the look of your ad sound right:

$$\text{Taste the High Life}$$

# TASTE THE HIGH LIFE

If one line were asking us to spend a week at an Aspen resort and the other to have a blue-collar beer, you could choose the right type for each, couldn't you?

## The anatomy of type

Making distinctions that broad is easy enough, but subtler discriminations require better eyes, and educating yours depends on knowing where to look. Here's a brief anatomy lesson in letterforms.

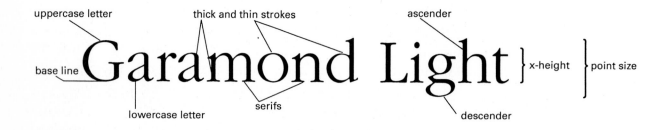

## Some terms

Type size is measured in points, 72 points to the inch. The preceding example (measured from top of an ascender to bottom of a descender, plus a little shoulder on each end) is 48 point. The type of this line of text is 12-point Palatino. Body copy is often set in the 10–14 point range; anything smaller than 10 points is tough to read. Type larger than 14 points is usually called **display type** or **headline type**. Because of the varying lengths of ascenders and descenders in different typefaces, type nominally the same size often isn't. For example:

This is 14-point Times Roman.

This Century Schoolbook is also 14 point.

A type's **x-height** is the height of its lowercase letter x and thus of that typeface's body size. Some typefaces have large x-heights and some have small ones; they contribute to character and to readability; a large x-height, like Helvetica's, for example, makes a typeface more readily legible.

**Leading** (pronounced "ledding") is the measure, also in points, of the space between lines, so a typographer's notation "14/16 Palatino" signifies 14-point type with 2 points of leading between each line. Lots of leading opens up the lines, too little makes reading tough. Leading is adjusted as line length, point size, typeface, and weight change. Line length and depth are measured in picas, 12 points to a pica, 6 picas to the inch.

Typographers also spend lots of energy on letterspacing and word spacing. **Kerning** is their term for adjusting the spaces between letters, getting exactly the right optical fit between them.

## Typefaces

There seem to be about a million typefaces, and there are literally thousands, more every day, but they divide into categories quickly enough, and besides, a relative handful do much of the work. Learn the categories, recognize the handful. The big fork in the typographical road is **serif** versus **sans serif**; that is, whether the type has little lines or strokes (serifs) at the ends of its main strokes, or is without (sans) them. Thus, the face I've been writing in (Palatino) has serifs, as you see, but this face I've just jumped into (Futura book) doesn't.

So what? Well, it gets back to feel again. Serif faces tend to feel more traditional and classical than do sans serif, perhaps because the bulk of the last 500 years of our literary tradition has been set in serif type. Many people find sans serif faces more modern, especially so since the Bauhaus, the influential German design school of the 1920s and 1930s whose aesthetic ideas still dominate much graphic thinking, decreed that sans serif typography *was* the future, enough of the decorative chaos of serifed faces. Although sans serifs sometimes seem too impersonal, too severe an equation of form and function, type designer Sumner Stone has said of the sans serif form, "It holds a major place in our visual vocabulary, linked with no-nonsense functionality, lack of adornment, and practicality. Its use connotes a detachment or even a disengagement from traditional culture. The 20th century is arguably the century of the sans serif."[5]

It's an oversimplification, however, to assume that a typeface's character is entirely a consequence of its state of serifhood. Like personality in people, the personality of a typeface is a complicated affair, the result of a number of features. When we respond to a face, we do so with an admixture of feelings about its general cut, the sense of self it creates. As designer Philip B. Meggs points out, "Typographic resonance is generated by the cultural, stylistic, and connotative properties that typefaces possess in addition to their function as alphabet signs."[6] Here are some of the most widely used faces. Try to feel their resonance as you read them:

**Garamond** is an "old-style roman." "Roman" means that the letters have serifs and contrast between thick and thin strokes. In "old style" romans the contrast between thick and thin strokes is less pronounced and the serifs less mechanical than in the "modern romans," the best-known of which is Bodoni. (As if to confuse us, typographers also use "roman" to mean the opposite of "italic"; that is, upright letters, not *slanted* or *oblique* ones.)

**Bodoni is a very elegant face, as you can see. It and the other modern romans feel more mechanical, more regularized, less handmade than do Garamond, Caslon, and the other old-style romans. Their classicism bears the imprint of the mechanical age.**

"Transitional" romans lie somewhere between the handmade and mechanical, like the **Times Roman** you are reading now. Although originally created for newspapers and considered by some to be both

[5]Sumner Stone, "Type Style," *HOW* (January/February 1991), p. 41.

[6]Philip B. Meggs, *Type and Image* (New York: Van Nostrand Reinhold, 1989), p. 120.

too abundantly applied and too generic, Times has its admirers. World-class designer Milton Glaser, asked what typeface he'd take to a desert island if allowed only one, chose Times Roman because it "has classical proportions and it is readable."[7]

Roger Black, who has designed such magazines as *Rolling Stone and New York*, chose **Caslon,** which you are reading now, "because English is my native language and Caslon is the core typeface of the English language. Every language has its basic typeface. For example French would be Garamond, Italian would be Bodoni, Dutch is Jansen.... Caslon goes perfectly with everything, from Shakespeare to Martin Amis. And it's funky enough to never get tiresome."

This line is presented in **Avant Garde,** which shows the evenly weighted lines characteristic of most sans serif faces. Notice how big an x-height this type has.

**Futura,** which comes to us from the Bauhaus, is a sans serif like Avant Garde, but you can see that even though it's written in the same point size, its larger ascenders and descenders and correspondingly smaller x-height make it seem smaller. By the way, designer Louise Fili would take Futura with her to that desert isle as her one typeface because "it's the typographical equivalent of the basic black dress."

**Helvetica,** one of the Swiss gothics, is less geometric than Futura; note the "a," for example. Helvetica might be the most widely used sans serif face—a blessing and a curse, in that it threatens to become a cliché through overuse, yet it's so well designed that we forgive its ubiquity.

## Type's tremendous variety

In addition to typeface and point size, there are different weights of a face, its italic forms, small capitals, and all the extensions, condensations, and other manipulations that can be made to the basic face. Together these constitute the type **family,** offering a multitude of possible looks within what we might consider just one face. Here, for example, is just some of the available variety at one point size in the Futura family:

[7]All desert island quotes from "One Type to Spec," *HOW* (January/February 1991), pp. 48–49.

Futura Book
*Futura Book Oblique*
**Futura Bold**
***Futura Bold Oblique***
**Futura Extra Bold**
Futura Condensed Light
**Futura Condensed Bold**
***Futura Condensed Bold Oblique***
**Futura Condensed Extra Bold**

By the way, a **typeface**, a **family**, and a **font** all used to mean distinctly different and fixed things, but since the advent of computers and desktop publishing, the terms are sliding around some. A **typeface** used to mean one particular style of type, as, for example, Garamond Light or Helvetica Medium. A **family** was all the variations of a given face—for example, all the Futuras, some of which you saw earlier. A **font** meant one specific point size of a particular typeface (a 12-point Futura Condensed Extra Bold font, for example). Now, however, to many computer users font means what family used to, that is, all point sizes and variations of a typeface. Thus, all the Futuras are now called, loosely, a font; sometimes more particularly a **font family**.

## Some rules of thumb

**1.** When mixing type in an ad, restraint is best. Don't be the kid in the candy store, splurging on three or more type styles for the same page. Nothing marks someone more quickly as a visually-impaired typographical amateur than the indiscriminate mixing of faces. Stick to either variations within one type family or just two different faces. And if you're mixing, prefer bold contrasts (sans serif headlines with serif body copy, or vice versa) to wimpy ones. Two serif faces that are close to each other, for example Times Roman and Baskerville, would mesh badly. The same is true with sans serif faces. There's no point in mixing Univers with Futura. Mix Univers with Baskerville, Futura with Palatino. Get a clear contrast between your faces, not some muddy mesh that's neither here nor there.

**2.** Because serifs make reading lengthy text easier (guiding the eye along the letterforms and lines), many designers prefer serif faces for body copy and use sans serif faces, with their speed and power, for headlines and other display text. This is certainly not a rule, and lots of great ads work otherwise, but it is a common tendency.

**3.** Similar advice: Don't run long headlines in all caps; they're hard to read. However, this rule, like all others, is often broken. You can gain power with an all-cap headline, especially if the line is short. And even long headlines can be set in caps, as many of the examples in this book show. Customarily, however, if you're going after sheer ease of readability, use upper and lowercase letters or try "down-style" heads, that is, headlines only the first word of which is capitalized. Here are different versions of a Parker pen ad's headline:

> It's wrought from pure silver and writes like pure silk.
> (Downstyle—and the one Parker used.)

> It's Wrought From Pure Silver And Writes Like Pure Silk.
> (Upper and lowercase letters. Note that when this is used, most art directors set *every* word in an initial cap.)

> IT'S WROUGHT FROM PURE SILVER AND WRITES LIKE PURE SILK.
> (Caps and small caps.)

> IT'S WROUGHT FROM PURE SILVER AND WRITES LIKE PURE SILK.
> (All caps.)

**4.** While often dramatic, **reversed type** (that is, white type on a dark field) is harder to read than normal type and also requires a typeface that holds up; the thins in Bodoni, for example, are so thin that they often fragment when reversed.

**5.** Break headlines sensibly. That is, if you've got a headline that takes up more than one line, break it at coherent junctures—at the ends of phrases, not in the middle. For example, a Honda CRX headline,"Around the world in 50 tanks." can be broken into two lines easily enough:

> Around the world
> in 50 tanks.

But breaking it into three lines is trickier. Here, for example, are bad line breaks. They obscure meaning by making each part incoherent:

> Around the
> world in 50
> tanks.

Honda actually broke the three lines this way, and we can see how sensibly it reads:

Around
the world
in 50 tanks.

**6.** Your typographical choices will always have to balance two goals: what Edward Gottschall calls "clarity" versus "vitality."[8] (Sometimes art directors call this a conflict between "legibility" and "readability.") In other words, the fundamental typographical obligation is legibility—type is meant to be read, after all, and yours must be readable and accessible. In short, it must have "clarity." But serving the god of legibility alone courts a kind of tedium. How visually interesting are you making the reader's trip? Is your type serving any graphic purpose? We readers want to enjoy the visual experience as well as the linguistic one, so you also want "vital" typography. But this often threatens that first goal, legibility.

Gottschall likens the dilemma to a continuum, along which you must find a balance point every time. Too safely legible, and you might just as well lay the type out like a textbook page. Too wild and creative, and you'll hear howls from readers who claim you're *defying* them to read it. Designers are now and will forever be at war with themselves, writers, and readers on this issue. There is no easy answer, especially since pursuing one goal often means fleeing the other. Thinking in terms of a "balance point" rather than in terms of "either-or" is probably the best advice.

## Type as rhetoric

Let's see how some of the principles of this chapter operate out there in the real world of advertising. As I mentioned earlier, if you think of type as part of the voice of an ad, it then becomes part of that ad's argument—one more means by which you make your case persuasive to us. This is nowhere more apparent than in corporate typography, which is meant to symbolize by its physical appearance the sensibility and mission, the *character* of the company or brand. Apple, for example, employs a "corporate font" that is a condensed version of Garamond. The distinctive headline typeface that Volvo uses was developed by John Danza

[8]Edward M. Gottschall, *Typographic Communications Today* (Cambridge, MA: MIT, 1989), pp. 2–3 and throughout.

at Scali, McCabe, Sloves, who drew inspiration from well-established Swedish and German typefaces.[9] Though derived from others, Volvo's typeface is clearly and immediately its own self, and all of us recognize it at a glance. The same holds true for Apple's face. The advantage is obvious: a consistent (and they hope appropriate) persona—a sensibility and ethos—is projected for the corporation.

What does Volvo believe in? In subtle but distinctive ways, the typography of their headlines tells us. The sans serif face implies simplicity, its bold weight suggests solidity and durability, and the curved edges add spirit, all of them combining to create our sense of Volvo cars themselves and the corporation behind them. (See Figure 10.1.) Who is Apple? Their logotype answers for them. An old-style roman, Garamond transfers its elegance and simplicity to Apple and its products. The classical, serifed face helps allay any anxieties we might have about the newness of the company and the complexities of computers, while condensing the face adds a contemporary, information-age pace to it. We reason that if Apple itself functions like these words look, then truth and beauty, utility and grace, must reside together in their machines. (See Figure 10.2.)

Such a consistent typographical approach is essential to projecting and then reinforcing a brand's image. Our only acquaintance with lots of corporations is through their logotypes and advertising typography, but we feel that we know much about them already, don't we? If, however, first one week and then the next week, first this ad and then that one, were given different type treatments, our sense of the corporation or brand would dissolve into confusion. Consistent usage of type is not only crucial to a good advertising campaign, it's fundamental to the corporation itself—part of the edifice, not mere ornament. Brands and companies that are in trouble often reveal that conflict by changing too much of their corporate identity too often. If we have a fuzzy rather than firm sense of a brand, it might be partly because typography isn't being allowed to do its part.

## Some last words

Most of what's been discussed here and much, if not all, of the nitty-gritty of type specifications will be handled by typogra-

[9]Roy Paul Nelson, *The Design of Advertising*, 6th ed. (Dubuque, IA: Wm. C. Brown, 1989), p. 180.

**Figure 10.1** With a few, unsettling exceptions, the distinctive Volvo typeface has been used for over 20 years of headlines—quietly, consistently, incrementally adding to our sense of the corporation and its cars. Courtesy of Volvo.

**Figure 10.2** Apple's logotype (with symbol) and an ad, both showing the characteristic, condensed Garamond typeface. Through sustained use of this face, Apple has built equity: We consumers have imprinted on it as their typographic voice. Garamond's resonance transfers to the corporation. Courtesy of Apple Computer, Inc.

phers and art directors. But learn the lingo, develop a nodding acquaintance with the terms of type, and understand essential distinctions among faces and families. See and feel how type operates in ads you admire. You gain nothing by remaining an uninformed bystander, and besides, the more you understand type, the more your advertising ideas become enriched by that understanding. A common misconception is that you have ideas and then sheath them in the skin of type, but type lends substance to ideas; it is part of their body. It can even transform the ideas you do have into better ones and give you ideas you would never have had otherwise.

## *LAYOUT*

Like choosing type, laying out the art and copy of a print ad is a visual skill. In fact, my colleagues here at the art college approach advertising itself from a design point of view. They regard a print ad as essentially a problem in two-dimensional design: The task is to pull a variety of elements into an interesting, unified relationship, creating from the components a design of the page itself. They apply certain aesthetic principles associated with fine art (color theories and principles of composition like balance, contrast, proportion, and so on) to the elements of an ad. From this point of view, the illustration, headline, subhead, copy, logotype, and any other elements—taglines, symbols, borders, coupons, and the like become, not pieces of an argument, but pieces of a design.

Is a print ad persuasion, or is it the interrelationship of line, shape, and chroma? The correct answer is that it's both, of course, and that's why art-oriented designers and marketing-oriented concept people are needed to make ads great. If you regard an ad as just an argument for buying something, a commercial proposition, then you'll stunt that argument by missing the graphic opportunities to enhance it. If, however, you see an ad as just a design, you'll create something nice to look at but persuasively inert or irrelevant. You need to do both.

Copywriters see their words as inspired argument, but designers see them as blocks of tonal grays, elements in the overall design. And readers do, too. We all respond to the *look* of type, its density, shape, and placement, as well as to its content. That multiple perspective is what we're talking about here. We are simply looking beyond type itself to include the other visual elements, as well.

## Some first principles

> Graphics need to reflect the nature and purpose of the proposition.
> Design is not merely a matter of "taste," it is an understanding of
> the problem.
> —John McConell, Pentagram[10]

**1.** If design is indeed understanding the problem, then the first
step in solving it is to assemble the parts of your ad. You can't
create a great layout until you know what it is you're laying out.
The usual components are:

- Headline, subheads, and other display type

- Major illustration, plus any other visuals

- Body copy

- Logotype (and symbol), plus tagline

- Any other elements, like coupons or borders

These will, of course, vary from ad to ad. Some may even be
absent or almost absent in a given ad. Since layouts aren't forced
down from above like giant presses but rather emerge from the
material, assembling one helps you see what visual arrangement
best expresses your idea. You want to fit the ad's graphic style to
its content. That's the key. Are you laying out *the idea* well or not?
And are you observing the fundamental aesthetic principles that
underlie any effective layout?[11]

**2.** Next establish a **visual hierarchy** among those components.
What's most important, less important, least important? Express
what's most important rhetorically by making it most important
visually. One rule of thumb is to decide whether your ad should
be type-dominant or image-dominant. Is your selling proposition rational, dependent on the wit of the headline, a verbal idea
more than a visual one? If so, create a type-heavy layout. If,
however, what you *show* us is most important, if we're essentially
*seeing* something (with verbal annotations), then give the image
or images dominance.

    As a graphics maxim puts it, "If you emphasize everything,
you emphasize nothing." We viewers cannot look everywhere at
once, nor should we be asked to. A page with several equally
dominant areas just confuses our eyes and mind. What *is* important

---

[10]John McConnell, quoted in *Living by design,* p. 131.

[11]This discussion of design principles draws from Nelson, *The Design of
Advertising,* pp. 50–66, and Meggs, *Type and Image,* pp. 69–116.

here, we wonder, as our gaze oscillates among the competing things shown and said. Decide for us what's most important, give it control of the page, then let the secondary elements follow from it.

The most obvious way to establish visual hierarchy is by scale: using size to tell us what matters. We viewers will work our way down from biggest to littlest, associating relative size with importance. But there are other ways to control hierarchy, too. Some things have more **optical weight**—visual strength—than others, and we ascribe more importance to them. Thus, color has more weight than black and white; irregular shapes more weight than regular ones; dark, dense areas more strength than light or empty ones; certain positions on the page more impact than others, and so forth. A complete understanding of such issues is what we have graphic designers for, but you should realize that creating dominance, essential to a well-expressed idea, is more than a matter of manipulating size.

**3.** Closely related to dominance is the idea of pushing our eye through the page, controlling the **sequence**, or visual flow. By tradition and habit, our eyes want to read pages from top to bottom and from left to right, so you can take advantage of that inclination by putting items in the areas we naturally scan (and leaving other items out of the flow, as do cigarette advertisers, for example, by placing the warnings in areas of least visual interest). Sometimes this eye pattern is called a Z-shape or a backwards S-shape, indicating the path our eyes customarily describe when moving through a page. (See Figure 10.3.)

You can, however, violate our visual habits with big shapes in wrong places, unusual placement of chroma, and so on, *making* us deal with the page in a certain fashion. Either way, you want to be in charge. The order in which you deliver information is part of getting its meaning right. We can look at an ad wrong or right, and that depends on you.

**4.** Your layout should be balanced, that is, contain within itself a sense that its elements are in equilibrium. One kind of balance is **symmetrical balance,** a very obvious kind of order in which one half of the page mirrors the other—both are balanced around an invisible center line or vertical axis. (See Figure 10.4.) Symmetrically balanced ads are very stable and orderly, working well to communicate the essence of some products, but less well for others; for example, insurance and bank ads may seek balance; skateboard ads may shun it. The other kind of balance, **asymmetrical balance**, lays things out in a less obviously ordered way, but achieves a resolution of the various forces nonetheless. Its

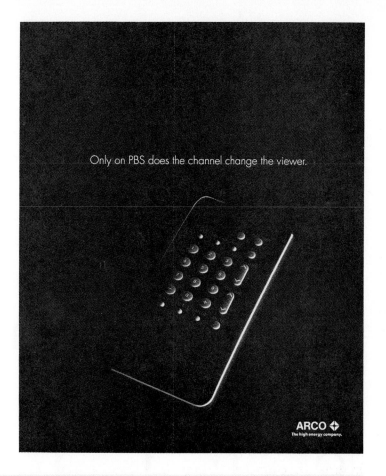

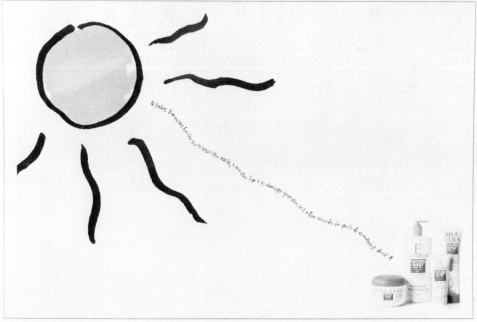

**Figure 10.3** Two layouts that take advantage of our habit of reading from upper left to lower right. The cleverly placed headline in the skin care ad reads, "It takes 8 minutes for the sun to reach the earth, 3 minutes for it to damage your skin, and a few seconds for you to do something about it." In reading the ARCO ad, our eyes almost perfectly describe a Z. Courtesy of ARCO and DEP Corporation.

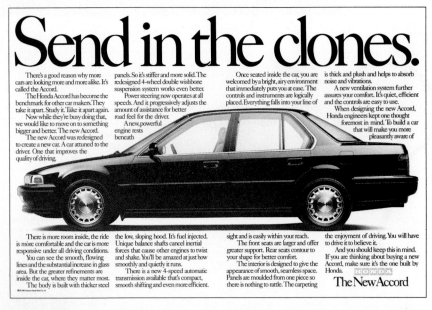

**Figure 10.4** Examples of formal, or symmetrical, balance. Notice the sense of order and stability it communicates. Grey Poupon ad copyright and trademark owned by Nabisco, Inc., used with permission; courtesy of American Honda Motor Co., Inc.

elements, too, are balanced around an invisible central axis or point, but the ad's halves are not mirror images. (See Figure 10.5.)

Asymmetrical balance is where art directors earn their money. They need a good feel for the optical weights of various lines, colors, and shapes so that they can bring them into a

**Figure 10.5** Here, rather than order, the ads seek to communicate activity, so they use informal, or asymmetrical, balance to add dynamism to the products. The white space in the Nike ad assumes various shapes, helping invigorate the spread. The beautifully designed apple ad balances placement and weight of the apple with those of the headline and girl, the peel gracefully interrelating the elements of both pages. Both layouts deliver more energy than would formally balanced arrangements. Courtesy of Nike, Inc. and Washington Apple Commission.

balanced relationship, whether you and I looking at the page recognize that or not. We can *see* symmetrical balance, but we usually just *sense* asymmetrical balance. Again, some ads and products are best served by the dynamism of asymmetry as, for example, youth fashion or athletic products—anything requiring a sense of the new or the energetic. Neither kind of balance is right or wrong by itself; whether it matches the concept, product, and audience is what makes it so.

**5. Proportion** is the relationship of the various elements in an ad *to each other*. The key idea is variety: Avoid the monotony of evenly repeated, evenly spaced, evenly sized shapes. Contrasts of all sorts are visually exciting. So don't let the type take up exactly half the page, the visual the other half. Seek different sizes and shapes for the ad's elements—visual rhythms, like written ones, profit from a changing vocabulary and stress pattern. Monotonous writing doesn't change its word choice or sentence structure or stress pattern. One short (or long) sentence follows another, *ad nauseam*. An analogous repetition can occur in visual work: Think, for example, of the tedium of a checkerboard table. Instead of repeat and repeat, repeat and vary.

For example, the space itself can be too regularized. Try not to place things right in the middle of the page, and avoid breaking it into halves or quarters or some too-obvious relationship—use thirds or fifths instead. One definition of pleasing aesthetics is "unity with variety." Proportion is the term by which you ask yourself if you've got enough variety.

**6.** But the other half of that definition is **unity**, and as you might expect, it asks you to consider opposing virtues. Does your ad hang together? Do you have harmony, coherence, a good relationship of the parts to the parts, of the parts to the whole?

How do you make a page hang together? Lots of ways. Throw the white space (the **negative space**) to the outside. If you get too much negative space between your elements, the page starts to fall apart because you are literally pushing things away from one another. We perceive things placed together as belonging together (the visual principle of **proximity**), so you want to make the parts of the ad hang together, not break apart. **Alignment** of objects (letting their edges correspond with each other) visually relates them, too. For example, if the left edge of the copy leads down into the left edge of the dominant image, then the alignment moves readers clearly from one element to the other. Similar axes can be created through the layout, aligning other elements and moving readers gracefully through the material. Similarity of shape, texture, or size (the principle of **correspondence**) also tells the eye that the items are related. (See Figures 10.6 and 10.7.)

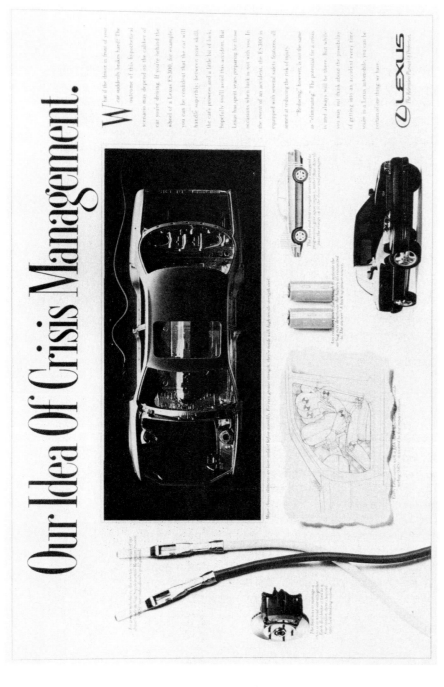

**Figure 10.6** Handsome design that does what it should: provide unity with variety. There is enough obvious organization of the space that we readily comprehend the ad *and* enough variety that we enjoy the process. **Alignment** of shapes along vertical and horizontal axes establishes order. The **proximity** and typographic **correspondence** of the body copy's initial cap leads us easily from the headline; the correspondence in visual weight between the drop cap and Lexus logotype at the bottom of the copy block pulls us through it visually. Similarly, the twisting electrical cords on the left side pull the eyes down into the illustrations, where the **proximity** of each caption to its illustration tells us at a glance what language belongs with what image. But there is variety, too: the **proportions** of the ad's elements change; no two are the same size or configuration, so there's no visual monotony. The dissimilar shapes and sizes of the illustrations make the surrounding **negative space** irregular and "activate" it; without quite realizing it, we enjoy moving among those illustrations and captions. Altogether, a very effective layout. Courtesy of Team One Advertising: Photography © Michael Ruppert Studios, Illustration © Richard Leech, Illustration © Jonathan Wright.

**Figure 10.7** Do you see how readily we can "read" this ad's design? The helmet shape and the ellipse of the headline block exemplify **correspondence** and **alignment:** We see the helmet, then immediately read the headline, and accept them as two halves of the same thought. Meanwhile, the **contrast** of the two pages (one dark, one light; one visual, one verbal) reinforces the "two-halves," right brain/left brain feeling of the ad. The decreasing **proportions** among the three vertically aligned shapes on the right-hand page relate them to each other and lead us inescapably to the logotype; their irregularity of shape activates the page and gives visual interest to the surrounding body copy. This ad's argument is both a feeling and an idea, and its design helps express this dual appeal. The design synthesizes the argument, and we are led unerringly through it, never missing a step. Courtesy of Specialized Bicycle Components.

## Kinds of layouts

In theory, every layout ought to be unique; after all, this exact combination of image and language has never—or should have never—come together before. But in practice, layouts do fall into general categories—a lot or a few, depending on who's counting. This list isn't testimony to the lack of imagination of art directors; rather such a relative handful of basic layouts testify to their own inevitability: They are found and refound whenever visual and verbal material is brought together on a page.

After all, layouts organize graphic space, and since most ads contain the same few elements, possible organizations are themselves limited. But just as we saw the multiple looks within just one type family, so too can one general layout support a multitude of manipulations. Here, then, are some of the basic themes within which art directors constantly create variations.

## 1. Type-Dominant Layout

In the beginning was the Word, and lots of great ads don't go any further. Big, sensuous, well-chosen type has great graphic impact. Why not take advantage of it? Such ads may be all type, without any visuals, or they may use visuals, though clearly in a subordinate position.

Especially here and in the image-dominant ads, the proportional relationship between headline and image is crucial. Beyond determining which element should dominate (not always easy), you must decide *how* dominant it should be. The perfect fit between the two explodes the ad's idea. A bad fit fizzles it. (See Figures 10.8 and 10.9.)

## 2. Image-Dominant Layout

Sometimes called the picture-window layout, this is probably the most common format. The classic DDB VW Beetle ads scattered through this text constitute Exhibit A: big picture occupying most of the page, headline and body copy picking up what's left. Although DDB's format was also symmetrically balanced, that's just an option. Layouts vary, as my examples indicate, but in all instances you're featuring image over language. (See Figure 10.10.)

## 3. Multi-Element Layout

A number of ads just won't distill into two primary elements—headline and visual (with copy)—one of which you let dominate the page. You're committed to saying and showing several different things, so layouts must become more complicated. How then to organize? By deft employment of the aesthetic principles we've already discussed: emphasis, sequence, balance, proportion, unity. The complexities of graphic design are beyond the limits of this necessarily brief discussion, of course, but with some oversimplification we can place multi-element ads into categories:

*Visual Parallelism.*

"Two-fer" ads usually repeat verbal and visual structures from page to page, using such repetition of shapes to create unity and balance—and then violating the repetition to emphasize the ad's

**Some people inherit athletic ability.
Some people inherit musical talent.
Some people inherit mechanical skill.**

**I got awnings.**

I'm a 4th generation awning man. You should see
what I learned growing up in their shadow. Call 841-0507.

**SOMMER AWNING COMPANY**

**In 1941, millions of Jews were looking for ways to escape Nazi death camps. Gandhi recommended suicide.**

The movie *Gandhi* portrays the Mahatma as a saint. But an original article in the July Reader's Digest shows the advice of a saint can be hard to live by.

Certain that his non-violence would work miracles, Gandhi told his countrymen to let Japan conquer India — but make the conquerors feel unwelcome. He suggested the English surrender their country to Germany — but not their souls. And to European Jews he counseled mass suicide, promising their martyrdom would leave humanity "a rich heritage."

Reporting that dispels myths behind men: For 39 million readers, that spells The Digest.®

**PICTURES DEVELOPED WHILE YOU WAIT.**

**BERNIE'S TATTOOING**
2924 West Avenue, Bristol, PA, 788-6496

**Figure 10.8** Examples of all-type ads, in which the entire interest and power derive from language, well written and then pumped at us effectively. Such all-type ads are sometimes termed either big-type ads or copy-heavy ads (as, for example, *Reader's Digest*), depending on their approach. Courtesy of Young & Laramore; Reader's Digest Association/Posey Parry & Quest; and The Martin Agency.

# QUIT.
# OR DIE
# TRYING.

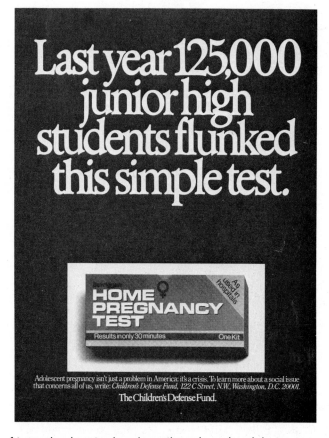

# If Our Coffee Were Any Richer It Would Vote Republican.

*Cityscape Deli*

# THIS BUILDING IS FILLED WITH MAD SCIENTISTS.

They're some of the most respected scientific minds in the country.

They're also mad.

You would be too if you had to teach and conduct critical research in Cal's Life Sciences building.

There are cracks in the ceilings and cracks in the walls.

And leaks in all the cracks.

Because of the rotten plumbing.

Which may be what's causing those terrible odors.

The ones that won't go away, on account of all the ventilation problems.

And it won't be long before we'll have to put laboratories in the lavatories. (We've just about filled up the halls.)

Despite these and other hardships, our Biosciences departments continue to achieve world acclaim for breakthrough research in cancer prevention, brain development, and many other areas.

But the fact remains, Nobel Prize winners and Guggenheim Fellows don't grow on trees. In order to hang on to those we have—and continue to attract top faculty—we need more than a few new beakers and Bunsen burners.

We need your support.

Because largely through private contributions, we hope to begin building a Biological Sciences facility befitting a world class university.

So please call the number below.

And help us put a stop to this madness.

## U.C. BERKELEY

It's not the same without you.

U.C. Berkeley Foundation, 2440 Bancroft Way, Rm. 301, Berkeley, California 94720.
Call the Donor Line, collect, Mon.-Fri., 9-5: (415) 642-4379.

# Last year 125,000 junior high students flunked this simple test.

Adolescent pregnancy isn't just a problem in America: it's a crisis. To learn more about a social issue that concerns all of us, write: *Children's Defense Fund, 122 C Street, N.W., Washington, D.C. 20001.*

The Children's Defense Fund.

**Figure 10.9** Examples of type-dominant ads, where there is a visual, but it's clearly secondary to the type, which carries the ad. The visual usually completes or clarifies a headline's concept, but it may simply decorate it (as does the coffee cup in the deli ad). Courtesy of Cole & Weber, Inc.; Cityscape Deli; Goldberg Moser O'Neill, UC Berkeley Foundation; and the Children's Defense Fund.

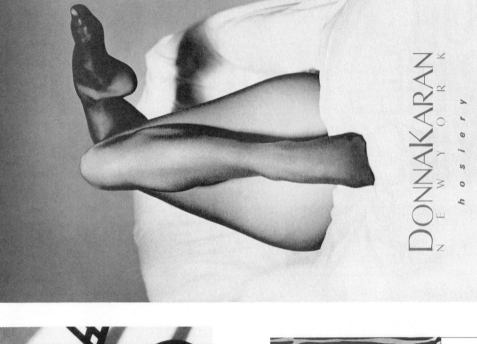

**Figure 10.10** Image-dominant ads (also called picture-window ads) constitute a large category. Type can be included or excluded from the visual, which may be contained within the page or bleed to its edges. Layouts vary tremendously. In all instances, however, the visual is more important and so dominates the page. [The Wamsutta sheet campaign employs *trompe-l'oeil* ("trick of the eye"), making us think we're looking at something other than a bed sheet. This ad's tiny headline reads, "This is not an avant-garde mobile. It's a sheet."] Courtesy of Wamsutta, American International Group, Inc., and The Donna Karan Company (© 1989 The Donna Karan Company).

# DL DH
# DOMES
# DAYS OFF
# DETOX AND
# DIBBLE

[WHAT IT IS]                                [WHAT IT WAS]

If you prefer baseball the way it was, call us. We have the largest selection of authentic Mitchell and Ness wools and flannels available. In jerseys and jackets for every major league team from 1890 to 1969. ALL-STAR SPORTS 503.659.3099. Milwaukie, OR.

**Figure 10.11** "Two-fer" ads usually repeat and vary elements across the two pages in order to maintain a unity but create enough diversity to draw our attention. Here the similarity of shapes unifies the two pages while the dissimilarity of texture (type versus image) creates visual and conceptual interest. Courtesy of Birdsall Voss & Kloppenburg, Inc.

point. In other words, whatever does change from page to page becomes the focus of the argument. So, for example, the earlier Macintosh ad (Figure 10.2) empties out the right-hand page to indicate ease of operation. Figure 10.11 shows how similarities of shape (but dissimilarities of texture: image versus type) creates both the repetition that organizes the space and the variation that makes it interesting and drives the concept.

## *The Grid*

A fundamental way to arrange multiple elements on a page is with a grid. Any layout that organizes itself into squares and/or rectangles, that divides its own space into modules, and then fills them with headline, visual, and so on, is using a grid. One kind of grid is called the **Mondrian layout**. If you've ever seen any of this Dutch painter's work, you'll know why. It's entirely geometric: rectilinear shapes of primary color with black borders divide

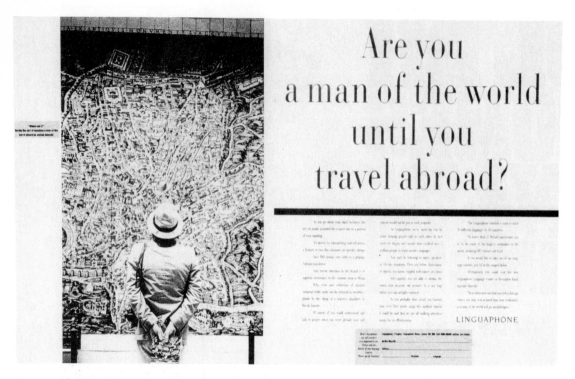

**Figure 10.12** A Mondrian layout, a series of interlocking rectangles, within which the ad's information is placed. Courtesy of Linguaphone.

the canvas horizontally and vertically. An ad organized via squares and rectangles is thus called a Mondrian layout. Here proportion becomes the dominant aesthetic principle. This layout guides the eye among lots of images and copy blocks. (See Figure 10.12.)

Other grids are more uniform than a Mondrian layout, employing evenly sized squares or rectangles and then using only multiples of them to place elements. Magazines, newspapers, annual reports, catalogs, and other multipage formats require such grids to achieve the continuity of visual flow from page to page that you expect as a reader. (See Figure 10.13.)

Many ads, while not organized strictly on a grid, nevertheless do have a highly regularized structure. For example, in the multi-element BMW ad (Figure 10.14) you can see that the many elements on the page align with each other, edge to edge. An invisible, **informal grid** is holding the elements together, establishing a strong sense of balance and order.

### Hierarchy of Elements

We talk here at the art college about dominance, subdominance, and subordinance—a specialized way of saying that a page often achieves unity by having one central, dominant feature, a less dominant one, and a supporting one. Why? Besides establishing

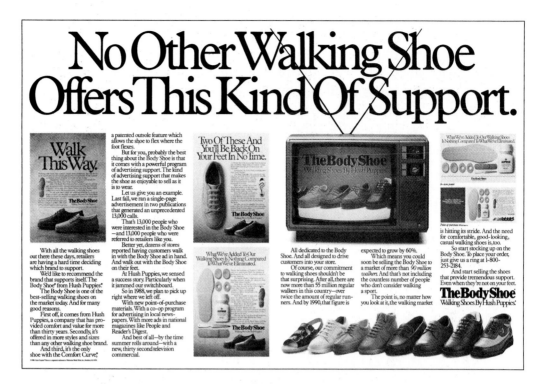

**Figure 10.13** A grid layout. Here you see the material divided to fit six vertical columns, with enough variety of placement to avoid monotony. Courtesy of Wolverine Worldwide, Inc.

**Figure 10.14** This BMW ad has a less obvious structural scheme, but it feels very balanced and ordered nonetheless. There are a number of axes cutting through this page with which the items are aligned. An example of an informal grid. Courtesy of BMW of North America, Inc.

emphasis and visual flow, such visual triangulation pulls the page together, allowing the eye to relate the parts to the whole. Many ads use a three-point structure, moving the eye, 1–2–3, through their elements. Frequently, however, you don't need precise triangulation, simply a clear hierarchy among elements. So, for example, with multiple things to show, you can let one image dominate, and use the others in subordinate positions on the page, often inserting them into the copy to break it up. (See Figure 10.15.) Multiple images can also be configured so as to create one larger image, in effect turning a multitude of things into one shape.

## Field of Tension

Used more in poster and other graphic design than in straight advertising, **field of tension layouts**[12] rely less on grids or dominant-subdominant relationships than they do on tight interrela-

**Figure 10.15** These ads are organized along a hierarchy of scale. Our eyes move from the dominant element to the subdominant element to a subordinate one, and so on. Thus, proportional relationships among the elements, combined with their placement, organize the space. Courtesy of California Prune Board and The Museum of Science and Arnold, Fortuna, Lawner & Cabot.

[12]I'm using Philip Meggs's term, *Type and Image*, p. 94.

tionships among their elements. Shape, color, texture, placement, overlap, and other aesthetic principles are used to bind the elements of the page into a dynamic tension with each other. This is another place where good designers separate themselves from the rest. Because such layouts are less formal than many, with no one obvious organizing principle, these are sometimes called **circus layouts**. (See Figure 10.16.)

While we might list even more approaches, any catalog of layouts is in a sense an illusion. Art directors will tell you that basically they push the shapes around until they "feel right." What works best for one product and audience may not work for another. What feels best for this group of elements won't ever organize that other group. And what works in any instance can only be given a name after the fact. Good design, like good writing, is a sophisticated enough art form that it won't fit into labeled boxes, nor can it really be pulled out of one. Nevertheless, the boxes do help us. Although too large and too illusory, they give language—where none would exist otherwise—to some of the basic themes in advertising design.

## In summary

The point to remember about both typography and layout is that what you seek with each is, in Philip B. Meggs's term, **graphic resonance**. You want not only to embody some specific advertising argument, but you want to make every element of that embodiment contribute to the total effect, add intensity and expressiveness to it. As Meggs says, "Every visual nuance and every decision made by the designer contributes to the overall resonance of the design. Typeface selection, scale and cropping of images, the denotative and connotative properties, color, and spatial organization all play roles."[13]

Great ads live on the borderline between word and image. They are right brain/left brain wonders, and although each of us is probably more gifted in one than the other—more verbal than visual, or vice versa—work to muscle up the weaker half of your brain. If you tend to think in words, study design, layout, and typography. If you're visual, write headlines and copy. The more you know, the better the synergy between you and your team, and the more impact you'll have on the look and feel of your ideas, on the whole project itself. Ad agencies want writers who can think visually and art directors who can write headlines. Practice peering over the transom of your own skills. You'll find that the exercise will help you rise in other ways, too.

[13]Meggs, *Type and Image*, p. 118.

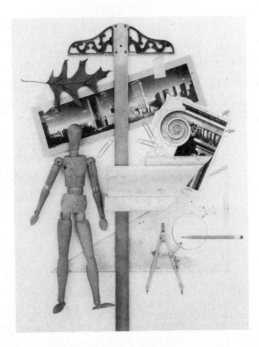

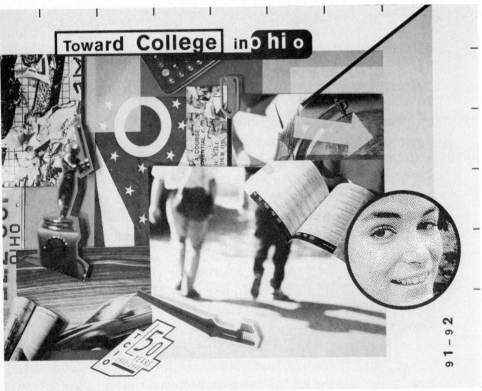

**Figure 10.16** These field of tension layouts are good examples of designers demonstrating their chops. Here tight interrelationships among the elements organize the space. "Toward College in Ohio" is the cover of a brochure; the other piece is a poster for the Columbus Landmarks Foundation. Courtesy of Columbus Landmarks Foundation and Crit Warren and Catherine Schmeltz (Schmeltz + Warren).

# CHAPTER 11

# TV

## *SOME BASIC TRUTHS*

Several things are true about TV advertising and the undergraduate advertising major:

**1.** You can't really do it. It's too complicated.

**2.** If your work is aimed at creating portfolio pieces by which to get a job, then you may not need any TV ads. Art directors and creative directors looking at your book often will not take the time to examine, frame by frame, your storyboards. Nor will they always read typed radio copy. Would you? It can be way too tedious. Besides, they can determine whether you can think and sell by looking at your print ads.[1]

**3.** TV ads are really little films created, in large measure, by film makers. As a senior vice president at DDB Needham, Chicago, recently noted, "The two disciplines—feature films and commercial films—have blended together to the point now where it's just film-making."[2] As an ad major, you're not supposed to be able to do this. You will never do it yourself anyway. Agencies hire film makers to make their TV spots. Two of the most famous names in TV advertising, Leslie Dektor (Levi's 501s) and Joe Sedelmaier (Wendy's, Federal Express, Sprint), two men who have helped define TV advertising in the 1980s and 1990s, aren't with agencies, but have their own film production companies.

Cross-overs have become routine between advertising and film making. Ad-makers who have become film makers include Ridley Scott (*Alien, Blade Runner,* and *Black Rain,* director of the celebrated Macintosh "1984" ad), Alan Parker (*Midnight Express,*

---

[1]See Ken Musto, *Breaking Into Advertising* (New York: Van Nostrand Reinhold, 1988), p. 52 and throughout; Maxine Paetro, *How to Put Your Book Together and Get a Job in Advertising* (Chicago: Copy Workshop, 1990), pp. 39–41.

[2]Quoted in Mark Crispin Miller, "Hollywood: The Ad," *The Atlantic* (April 1990), p. 50.

*Mississippi Burning*), and Adrian Lyne (*Flashdance, 91/2 Weeks, Fatal Attraction*), whose rapid cut, very sensual spots for Jovan Musk, "What Is Sexy?," attracted much comment. Film makers themselves no longer scorn advertising as a genre; directors who have made ads include Robert Altman, Martin Scorcese, Federico Fellini, Francis Ford Coppola, David Lynch, Spike Lee, and many others.[3] And not only do filmmakers themselves make the spots (often only loosely based on agency storyboards), but frequently editors are hired separately to create the commercial itself from the filmmakers' footage.[4] As you can see, all this gets a long way from you and your Ad-Art sketch pad.

**4.** A storyboard does not bear the same relationship to a TV ad that an ad rough does to a print ad. A rough of a print ad *is* that ad, more or less. A storyboard, however, is only a map of the TV spot. It simply refers to it, the way a map of Colorado refers to the state itself. This is an important distinction. You realize it every time you look at reproductions of TV advertising in textbooks and annuals: four or five isolated stills from the video are accompanied by copy providing the voice-over and some explanatory comment. Good luck trying to recreate it. Unless you have seen the spot, you usually cannot recover it, or sufficiently imagine it, from such a map. The same is true of any storyboard you'll make. You cannot really express your vision, whatever it is, in such a manner.

## WHAT TO DO

All this said, should you just forget about TV storyboards and leave them to the pros? Of course not. But you do need to realize these practical limitations on your TV thinking. You will never have the control over TV advertising that you will have over print advertising, unless you go to film school and learn how to make movies. But you can participate in the process. You can sell by making things move, by unfolding your advertising idea, not in the space of a print ad, but in the time of a TV spot.

Don't feel intimidated by all the sophisticated trickery, all the technical inside knowledge, involved in making TV commercials. Even though I just finished telling you that, indeed, filmmaking pros are the ones making the TV ads, this does not mean that you are ignorant about TV advertising. Far from it. You

[3]Miller, "Hollywood: The Ad," p. 49.

[4]Roy Paul Nelson, *The Design of Advertising*, 6th ed. (Dubuque, IA: Wm. C. Brown, 1989), p. 320.

know more about TV advertising than any generation in history. By the time you've graduated from high school, you have spent 11,000 hours in school but over 15,000 hours in front of the TV.[5] By age 20 you have seen 800,000 TV commercials, about 800 a week.[6] It can be stated, without exaggeration, that TV is the thing you have studied the most. If you or your family has a camcorder, if you've been filming birthday parties and trips to Disney World, your own rock band, summer vacations, and the like, you have also been acquiring tricks of the trade, some sense for pacing, framing, zooming, and so forth. In short, you know so much about TV that it's almost your native tongue. Remember that.

## FUNDAMENTALS OF TV ADVERTISING AND STORYBOARD MAKING

### Begin at the beginning

Ads dramatize the benefit, so start with your strategy: What is the problem that your product solves? What benefit does it deliver? Show that problem being solved. Dramatize that benefit.

### Choose an appropriate format

TV can accommodate any of the kinds of strategies we examined in Chapter 6: generic claim, product feature, unique selling proposition, positioning, brand image, lifestyle, and attitude. Use a format that best executes your strategy, that best dramatizes the benefit you've decided to express. Here are some, but by no means all, of the forms that TV ads take.[7]

### TV Formats:

TV's dramatic possibilities are nearly limitless, but you won't go wrong if you start by considering the two techniques that TV handles so much better than print: **demonstrations,** the testing

---

[5]V. C. Strasburger, *Pediatrician* (Spring/Summer 1986), cited in "Vital Statistics," *In Health*, 4, no. 4 (July/August 1990), 12.

[6]Neil Postman, "She Wants Her TV! He Wants His Book!," *Harper's* (March 1991), p. 48.

[7]See Huntley Baldwin, *How to Create Effective TV Commercials*, 2nd ed. (Lincolnwood, IL: NTC Business Books, 1989), pp. 95–121.

of your product's selling point, and **narratives,** the telling of stories. Many, if not most, TV spots can be considered some combination of demonstration and story.

## 1. Demonstrations

Show us how your product works, demonstrate its benefits. You can do this several ways:

### A straight product-in-use ad

Show us what the product is and how it works: how the can opener opens cans, how the kitchen knife cuts tomatoes, and so on. Demonstrate its benefits, straight-up. (See Figure 11.1.)

### A torture test

A dramatic, extreme (but truthful) demonstration of just what the product will do, what abuse it can take: Demonstrate that can opener by opening, not one can, but several, each bigger and tougher than the last; demonstrate the virtues of the knife by slicing, not simply a tomato, but something more substantial, like a pipe, then something more delicate, like a piece of paper. (See Figure 11.2.)

### A comparison with a competitor

Side by side pouring of spaghetti sauces to show which is thicker, and so forth. (See Figure 11.3.)

### Before and after

Show the person's gray hair before using the product, darker hair after using it; or show the stained necktie before being shaken in a tumbler with Cheer and cold water, the stain-free necktie afterwards, and so on.

### A whimsical demonstration

An intentional exaggeration of the product's effects can take the form of what goes wrong without the product or with the wrong product; or it can humorously exaggerate what goes right with it. Here you're using hyperbole for comic effect rather than telling strict, literal truths. As long as we know they're whimsical, such spots can be very effective. You can make your point, memorably, without asking us to "believe" the spot. (See Figure 11.4.)

Since demonstrations are so widely used a format, they can become clichés unless reinvigorated, given unexpected treatments. For a longer discussion of demonstrations and torture tests, see The Toolbox.

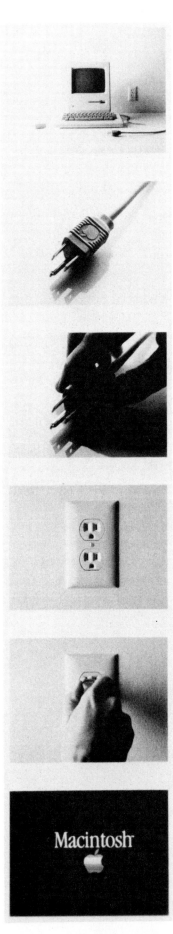

ANNCR VO: Using Apple's new
Macintosh.
OPEN ON BEAUTY SHOT OF
MACINTOSH COMPUTER.
ANNCR VO: does require some…
CUT TO SHOT OF PLUG.
ANNCR VO:…technical skill.
CUT TO SHOT OF SOCKET. HAND
PUTS PLUG IN SOCKET.
DISSOLVE TO LOGO.
ANNCR VO: Macintosh.

**Figure 11.1** Notice how the voice-over's ironic overstatement gives this product-in-use demonstration its power. Had the ad said, "Using Apple's new Macintosh is easy," with the same visual of a person plugging in the Mac, all would be lost. Courtesy of Apple Computer.

(MUSIC THROUGHOUT)
(SFX: CLICK)
ANNCR VO: How well does your car stand up to heavy traffic?
(MUSIC OUT)

**Figure 11.2** A torture test. Here, notice the voice-over's ironic understatement (and pun). Courtesy of Volvo.

**Figure 11.3** Side-by-side comparisons with competitors need not be dull. This ad humorously twists comparison and dog food clichés—asking people, not dogs, to judge which brand is better, and to do so simply on the basis of good looks. Courtesy of Heinz Pet Products.

## 2. Narratives

You can tell a *story* on TV that you can only suggest in print, so lots of ads are driven by little stories—funny, serious, all cut up or in one long sequence, families around the table, kids ambling down streets, you name it, but stories and partial stories and stories with products helping lives out abound. Narratives can be of several kinds.

### The demonstration as a story

Often instead of simply a bare-bones, tabletop demonstration of product virtues, you can show them within a narrative context, wrap the demo up inside a storyline. (See Figure 11.5.)

### Slice of life

This is a more pronounced, hard-sell approach to demonstrating within a story context. Sometimes it's called **problem/solution,** and we've all seen a million such ads: The spot opens with a problem (dirty clothes, bad odor, streaked windows). Our surrogate wonders what can be done. Enter product, often at a friend's advice. Problem solved. Moment of verification. Thanks be to product. Close.

This, of course, is a cliché. At some level, however, the structure continues to work, as witnessed by the abundance of such ads in this formula for household products and package goods, most of which do express the product benefit and make their cases clearly. Done well, this format may not only work but be reinvigorated. You can use it without being enslaved by it. (See Figure 11.6.)

# maxell®

## "BLOWN AWAY NEW/ NO STRETCH"

COMM'L NO.: QMDL 1315                                    LENGTH: 30 SECONDS

(SFX: FOOTSTEPS)

BUTLER: Something new, sir?
CHAIRMAN: Please.

ANNCR VO: Maxell releases a new
higher performance tape.

(MUSIC UP: MOZART "REQUIEM")

(MUSIC)

(MUSIC)

(MUSIC)

(MUSIC)

(MUSIC)

(MUSIC)

(MUSIC)

ANNCR VO: Maxell. Take Your Music To
The Max.

**Figure 11.4** Many demonstrations aren't literal, but metaphorical, casting
their product's advantage into other terms to clarify, simplify, or make more
memorable. This famous ad equates sound quality with wind velocity. It's
also a visual pun: The sound "blows him away." Courtesy of Maxell
Corporation of America.

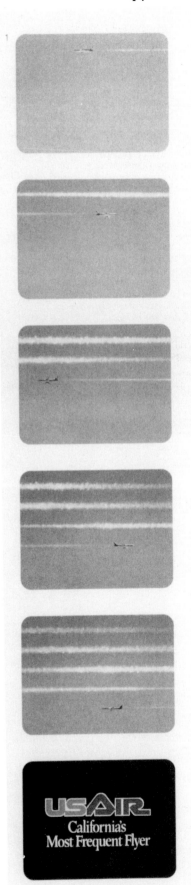

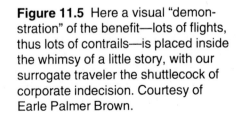

"Mr. Big"
(Open on empty, blue sky)
Secretary (VO): Mr. Big wants you here at 9 a.m.
(Plane enters the frame on the right. Moves across
screen. Contrail follows)
SFX: Jet engine.
Anncr. (VO): In business, when you have to be there,
you have to be there.
Secretary (VO): Mr. Big cancelled the meeting.
(Plane flies from left to right)
SFX: Jet engine.
Anncr. (VO): That's why USAir has more jet
departures in California than any other airline.
Secretary (VO): Mr. Big changed his mind again.
(Plane flies from right to left)
SFX: Jet engine.
Anncr. (VO): With convenient schedules to
fifteen California airports.
Secretary (VO): Mr. Big says the deal's off,
forget it.
(Plane flies left to right)
SFX: Jet engines.
Anncr. (VO): So you can get out and back in
the same day.
Secretary (VO): Guess what? The deal's on.
(Plane flies right to left)
SFX: Jet engines.
Anncr. (VO): And maybe even out again.
Super: USAir. California's Most Frequent Flyer.

**Figure 11.5** Here a visual "demonstration" of the benefit—lots of flights,
thus lots of contrails—is placed inside
the whimsy of a little story, with our
surrogate traveler the shuttlecock of
corporate indecision. Courtesy of
Earle Palmer Brown.

"Puddles"
Music: Upbeat jazz throughout.
(Open on woman frantically trying to hail cab)
Anncr. (VO): At the Baskin Spring wardrobe sale
almost every suit and tailored outfit in the store
is under $400 when you buy two.
(Cut to the man across street watching the woman
He notices apuddle in front of her. Close-up of his
face as he considers the problem)
Anncr. (VO): (continuing) Not two from last year.
Not two that nobody else wanted. And not two
that only come in two sizes.
(Cut to man crossing street, lays suit coat over
puddle in front of woman. She glances away
and steps into cab that has just pulled up,
running over man's jacket)

Anncr. (VO): So, now you're probably asking
yourself do I really need two suits.
Super: Baskin Wardrobe Sale

**Figure 11.6** Creative variant of the
problem/solution format. Courtesy of
Baskin Clothing Co.

## Vignette

Here quick little stories, onerightaftertheother, combine to verify a selling idea. We get snatches, moments, from a variety of winsome lives, that reveal the fun or strength or whatever of the product. So, for example, we see lots of kids chewing their way around urban settings for Trident gum. Or we see lots of women bouncing their curly heads for a curling iron. The key to this format is that it's not one story, it's not a lot of stories, it's vignettes—repeated *moments* verifying the product's value.

## Brand image montage

Somewhere beyond vignettes and slice-of-life ads are the brand-image montages of Life With the Product, the TV versions of brand-image and attitude advertising. They're not quite narratives, though they have narrative elements. They frequently take the form of a visual collage of scenes, often of hip product users, having fun or being moody. There may be some superimposed type, with music, and a minimal voice-over. One difficulty here is to create a new enough feel that the spot separates itself from all the others. Another difficulty, of course, is to give meaning to the spot, to do more than evoke a vaguely positive feeling toward the brand, provided the viewer can remember it.

A frequent dilemma with such montage advertising is choosing between product specifications and brand image. It's hard to sell a key item or product spec *and* a brand image: If we see the moody kids, we usually don't see the product very well. If we see the product well, we usually don't see much of the mood. To resolve this problem, go back to your strategy: What one thing *do* you want to accomplish? And study good TV work to see how it finds a balance between image and hardware. Usually image dominates, but product is worked in, often with a quick cut to the tag on the jeans, or a close-up flash of its distinctive buttons. (See Figure 11.7.)

## Little movie

One complete story with a short but strong plot, developed characters, and honest dialogue, often an emotion-tugging celebration of the American life: for example, the old man on his first day on the job at McDonald's, uncertain but fitting in with the kids, finding his sense of self-worth returning; Michael J. Fox sliding down the fire escape and dashing through the rain to buy a Pepsi for his beautiful visitor, only to discover himself locked out of his own apartment. And so on. Obviously the shorter the spot, the more difficult it is to establish such a movie.

Music: "You always hurt the one you love."
Anncr. (VO): People have a love-hate relationship
with their cars.
(Woman slams door with her foot. Car with sofa
on roof. Man tries to get inflated boat in trunk.
Car bumping on train tracks)
Anncr. (VO): They love them, but don't always
treat them right.
(Man gets out of car and slams the door, so does the
woman)
Anncr. (VO): Yet with all the abuse they get, over
90% of all the Subarus registered since 1974 are
still on the road.
(Cut back to man and woman still slamming doors)
Anncr. (VO): Now imagine how much longer they would
last...
(Car pushes another up a snowy hill)
Anncr. (VO):...if people didn't "love" them so much.
(Car backs down driveway, hits garbage cans, backs
across road, hits neighbor's garbage cans)
Anncr: (VO): Subaru. Inexpensive. And built to
stay that way.

**Figure 11.7** Vignette and brand-
image advertising, as these frames
indicate, can be difficult to communicate in storyboard form, so dependent
are they on the feel of the finished
piece. Nevertheless, we do gain
some sense of the spot's character.
Courtesy of Subaru of America, Inc.

*Satire of the nonuser*

Like demonstrations of the failures of Brand X, these ads are whimsically overblown accounts of what happens if you buy the wrong product: Your family's trip through the fast-food drive-in window comes to 62 dollars, the buttons pop off your too-tight jeans and ricochet around the house, frightening the kids, and so forth. Here the tone is often humorous, the situation intentionally exaggerated, and the characters grotesques. Joe Sedelmaier's work with Federal Express is an example. In one ad corporate types are reduced to simpletons making hand-shadow presentations at the big meeting because they failed to send the needed props via Federal Express. (See Figure 11.8.)

### 3. Product as hero

This format relies less on stories and people and more on our simple interest in the product itself. The Taster's Choice ad that made a coffee pot (that poured) from the instant coffee jar itself was pure product as hero. The Safeguard soap campaign (always the smallest bar in the house) in which we watched the bar disappear before our eyes was, too. Any campaign in which the product or some manipulation of it forms the visual and selling interest can be said to be product as hero.

### 4. Testimonials

Talking heads, although once more prevalent than today, remain a durable technique. Pick someone and have him or her or it (Charlie the Tuna, Morris the cat, Elsie, and others) deliver the ad. Thus, you can have celebrity endorsers, authority spokespeople, the common man or common woman testifying, and so on. If these spokespeople are good enough, they can become continuing characters and carriers of brand image as Bartles and Jaymes were for the wine cooler. (Since testimonials, unaltered, are such a cliché, usually they need to be twisted to be effective. See "Testimonials" in The Toolbox for a longer discussion.)

### 5. Special-effects exotica

This category, largely beyond your reach in a storyboard, includes all the special-effects-driven ads—those employing animation, claymation, music and choreography extravaganzas, image manipulations (in which, for example, James Cagney dances in a fusion of time and space with Paula Abdul). All of these are dreams that only the big budgets of Hollywood make

"Slide" :30
SFX: Insect humming noise of very hot day.
Open on a boy on a slide as he attempts to go down)
SFX: Squeak of sweaty legs sticking on the slide.
Anncr: (VO): It's gonna be a long summer.
Boy: Mommmm.
Super: Water Country USA
Anncr: (VO): Take the kids to Water Country USA.

**Figure 11.8** Satires of the nonuser get their power by inviting us to imagine the scenario's *opposite.* Courtesy of Earle Palmer Brown.

possible. Unless you have special abilities here or access to equipment that can perform such video wizardry, it's best to bypass these approaches.

REMEMBER: These categories are really empty slots until you fill them with something interesting, and most ads are, in truth, a combination of several of these categories. As with all lists, use them; don't let them use you.

## Visual advice

### Keep it simple

In creating storyboards, especially ones for your portfolio, ones that stand a good chance of being "read" by art directors, make them short and simple. Twenty frames with a paragraph of copy/explanation per frame just won't get it. Reduce your concept, or rather think up a concept, that can be expressed in no more than six to nine frames. And try to make it clever. Short is no good if it's ordinary. You've got to jump out of the portfolio, leap up off those frames and into the mind. You've got to create a TV idea so strong that it even looks good in print. It must hold together when disassembled into frames and copy. Look at how astoundingly simple these ads are (see Figures 11.9 and 11.10).

### Start strong, close strong, don't waste anything

The same obligations of economy and speed that we've discussed with print advertising operate even more so in TV. Whatever your idea, get to it fast. The first few seconds are critical. Don't segue toward something interesting; start with it. What's your hook? What's your lead?

Traditional wisdom has been to show the product early, feature it—often in close-up—throughout the spot, and end with a tight shot of the product, followed by a superimposed campaign theme line and logotype. This is reasonable advice, and the argument for following it is obvious: You make the product and point of the ad clear to even the least attentive viewer. Through repetition you punch home the brand's selling idea.

However, it's best to create a spot that we *want* to watch—inserting the product into the storyline, making it, if not indispensable, then a supporting player to the concept. Following "rules" does you no good if you just hit us over the head with unrealistic, forced, product hard-sell.

"Sophisticated"
(Open on bottle cap of Perrier being removed)
SFX: Bottle opening
Music: Laid back jazz under throughout.
(Hand starts to pour…into yellow dog dish)
SFX: Gurgling.
(Zoom out to reveal dog watching pour. Fade
up "Sophisticated Hush Puppies")
SFX: Dog lapping

**Figure 11.9** A TV ad so simple that it
even looks good in print. Courtesy of
Wolverine Worldwide, Inc.

"Wrench" :30
(Open on super of a green wrench logo. Wrench
appears between each statement)
SFX: Mechanical music.
Supers. This means your copier
needs maintenance.
If you've seen it
a lot lately,
maybe the person who
sold you your copier
needs fixing.
SFX: Rock music up under.
Super: Savin. The copier that comes with a human being.
(dissolve)

**Figure 11.10** Here's another TV spot
(the campaign featured one indicator
button in each ad) that's visually
powerful without being complicated.
The brightly colored symbols, the
reversed type, and the soundtrack
combine to dramatize the unique
selling proposition of Savin copiers.
Courtesy of Savin Corporation.

## Make it move

With TV you rely not only on our sophisticated ability to unpack symbols and images in microseconds, but also on our demand that you keep those images coming. If your spot doesn't move, forget it—you've probably been zapped.[8] Notice that even when someone is being interviewed in a spot or the product is being shown, something is moving—the camera is wobbling up or down, moving from left to right, sliding in or out, and so forth. Nothing is still, even what "ought to be." In a series of images the camera frequently slides right for the first image, left for the second, comes down into the third, pulls back and out into the fourth, and so on. The segues between shots are a kind of choreographed visual dance, a subliminal design element. Part of what's exciting about TV advertising is that it moves so much: There is the illusion of great energy, all of which transfers to the product and makes it seem energy-giving.

How much of this you indicate in your storyboards will depend on your skills and your particular course and problem. But realize just how much movement is a part of TV ads, even the simple ones.

## If it doesn't move,
## make things associated with it move

One virtue of stories and demonstrations is that things move by definition. But even if you're working on an idea that's neither, try to find a way to get movement into the spot. Ask yourself simply: What part of my product story moves? What motion is inherent in my product? Does it go around like a can opener, splash through water like a car or a bike, squirt like a tube of toothpaste? If your product doesn't move, then consider creating movement by changing camera angles, or by finding things associated with your product that move. This TV spot (Figure 11.11) understands that copiers don't move but repairmen do. It dramatizes reliability by emphasizing the omnipresence of the repairman if your firm buys the wrong brand—an example of finding movement *associated* with the product.

---

[8]Miller in "Hollywood: The Ad" argues that advertisers want their commercials to look like movies precisely so that viewers will be less likely to zap them (p. 49). He calls quick cuts, the staple of advertising, a "subvisual" device that stuns viewers, providing a "serial rush" that is itself mesmerizing: "The mere contrast stuns us pleasantly"(p. 50).

**VO:** This man is not a company President. He's not a Vice President. While his face is well known to everyone from the security guard to the summer intern his name doesn't appear on the company phone list. Yet he controls the productivity of the office...down to the last sheet of paper. And we think that's a serious problem. Because business should depend on a copier that works. Not a repairman. Ricoh Copiers built to work. And work. And work.

**Figure 11.11** If the product doesn't move, something associated with it probably does. Courtesy of Ricoh Corp.

Here's another example of how to get motion in a spot whose product doesn't naturally suggest any. An ad for Target stores, advertising its "family" orientation, showed us an adorable 4-year-old girl playing with the things she was pulling out of a Target shopping bag, while the voice-over talked about Target's family values and something-for-everyone selection. We were mesmerized watching the girl happily trying on sunglasses and the too-big hat, dusting the toilet paper with a feather duster, peeking in a mirror, scooting items around, throwing them in the air, and so forth. She ended up laughing, head first, inside the bag. Was this a demonstration? Not really. Do items at Target move? No. But "family shopping" was dramatized by finding movement associated with the store: her charming moments with a bag of shopping goods. A good visual idea, and a simple one.

Sometimes, of course, it's possible to be very attention-getting by moving nothing. In a TV world jammed with motion, color, and visual extravagance, a quiet, motionless, or nearly motionless spot can be arresting. (See Figure 11.12.)

## Remember your MTV lessons

You've been watching MTV for ten years. Recall its lessons:

Hyperkinetic imagery

Visual speed and sophistication

Ironic, wise guy attitudes

Unexpected humor

Quick, suggestive cuts rather than slow, sensible segues

Narrative implications rather than whole stories

Attitudes, not explanations

Tightly cropped, partial images instead of whole ones

Odd mixtures of live action, newsreel footage, animation, typography, film speeds, film quality

Unexpected soundtrack/audio relationships to video

All these techniques, at first unique to MTV, have become common to TV advertising. They are now its visual "rules." While many of them are obviously more the province of film makers than your immediate concern, you do want to make ads that fit the visual expectations of today's TV viewer. Proposing a two-minute spot with an announcer reciting product specs may have worked in the 1950s but not anymore (unless perhaps it's a

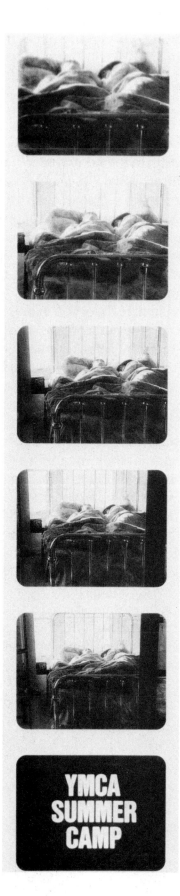

"Sleeping In"
(Open on a man and woman asleep in a bed. sunlight streaming through the window)
SFX: Birds chirping, man snoring, clock ticking.
Anncr. (VO): Remember what life was like before you had kids?
Camera card: YMCA Summer Camp
Minneapolis 822-CAMP   St. Paul 292-4100

**Figure 11.12**  Rise above TV's clutter by breaking one of our expectations—here that TV ads should move. This also very cleverly and simply dramatizes the benefit for its target audience. Courtesy of YMCA of Metropolitan Minneapolis.

direct-response infomercial). A long spot with lots of characters and a leisurely lead-in won't get it either. And remember the power of cropping and the virtue of suggestion: If you can intrigue us more by showing just feet instead of whole people, as in Figure 11.13, then do it.

## Be visually precise

Don't just decide that a woman is standing in the doorway. What kind of person is she? How is she standing? What's the angle and tightness of the shot? What part of her are we supposed to focus on? Are we far enough away that it's a study in body language? Are we tight enough that it's the expression on her face? Are her surroundings important? How much of them are we to see? Make sure that the pictures in your head are as precise as possible. Fuzzy is easy, but it will get you in trouble later.

How *much* of your ad can you visualize? Do you want it grainy or black and white with only the product in color? High chroma with garish close-ups? Will there be a lot of cuts? Or perhaps just two sets of scenes, intercut? (For example, close-ups of a fellow getting ready for a date, close-ups of a woman also getting ready—their scenes intercut to suggest the approaching event, your spot ending perhaps with the moment they meet.) How *busy* do you think your camera ought to be?

The look of your ads is as much a part of their meaning as is their plot. It creates a distinct "feel" for your product, isolating it in a context, an environment. If, for example, you envision ads with a "raw" look—odd, chopped angles; wobbly, unfocused, handheld camera shots; grainy film; a blending of black and white footage with color or blanched color throughout—then you can make your product seem more *real* than others, since the immediacy and nonprofessionalism of your ads induce the feeling that the presentation of these products is unmediated.

Or you may want to use quick cuts that never let us catch up visually, unfinished but clearly implied storylines (both of which generate excitement and longing, the sense that more is here in this product than the screen can contain).

In other words, beyond the literal here's-what-happens of your spot, try to *see* as much of it as you can.

## Use type

Creative use of typography in TV advertising is very much with us: the sliding type in recent Subaru ads (see Figure 11.14); Nike's ads with type that telescopes to the beat of a John Lennon song, intercut with athletic images; GAP's simple but elegant type

"Toe to Toe/Women" :15

SFX: A heavy rainstorm, accentuated by deep back-woods blues music.
(Open on a lonely road. A woman and man approach each other at ankle camera level in some kind of duel. Only at the end do her feet go tiptoe, telling you their encounter isn't manacing but passionate)
Anncr. (VO): Finally, the only women's shoe on earth that can go toe-to-toe with a Timberland boot.

**Figure 11.13** The power of visual cropping and narrative truncation. We see neither complete people nor complete story. Courtesy of Timberland Corporation.

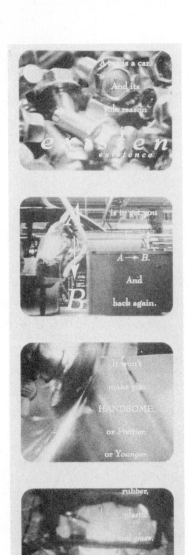

"Factory" :60
SFX: Music up and under
(Open on an automobile factory)
Anncr. (VO): A car is a car. And its sole reason for existence is to get you from Point A to Point B. And back again.
(Camera pans down assembly lines)
Anncr. (VO): It won't make you handsome. Or prettier. Or younger. And if it improves your standing with your neighbors, then you live among snobs with distorted values.
(Camera continues to show cars being built)
Anncr. (VO): A car is steel, electronics, rubber, plastic and glass. A machine. And in choosing one the questions should be: How long will it last? How well will it do the job? Could I get a comparable one for less? And do I like the way this machine feels and looks? And in the end, with an absence of marketing glamour about the automobile. May the best machine win.
(Finished car comes off the line)
Anncr. Subaru. What to drive.

**Figure 11.14** A handsome and trend-setting use of type as a design element. Courtesy of Subaru of America, Inc.

superimposed over black and white film of the human parade. Take what you know about typography and consider using it as part of the visual design of your spot.

No matter what your idea, it makes sense to put type on the screen—at some point or points—in addition to the images and the voice-over. The most sensible, safe, and customary location is at the end, with a super of the product's slogan and logotype, so that you close by telling who just brought us the spot and what it was about.

## Soundtrack advice

**1.** Be sure that you **synchronize** the audio with the video; whatever is being said or sung or sounded had better relate to what we're looking at. Just as in print ad, however, don't be redundant. If we can see it, don't say it, too. Say something else. If you show a car splashing through the mud, don't say, "Built for the worst weather." We can see that. Instead say how it endures what we're witnessing, talk about features or the emotional benefits to the driver.
**2.** The only exception to this don't-repeat-yourself advice—and it's an important one—is that when you put type on the screen, either say nothing or have the voice-over say exactly those words. You never want to say words and show words that aren't exactly the same. We can't process separate sets of language simultaneously, and we learn better when you imprint the message visually as well as aurally.

**3.** Remember that TV is visual. Most student storyboards talk too much and move too little. *Listen* to some TV spots. Notice that in the soundtrack there's less language—and more music and sound effects—than you supposed. (And visually, of course, there is almost always some dramatic movement.) A working rule of thumb is no more than two words per second, so a 30-second spot can manage only 60 spoken words—or fewer.

**4.** The tension between headline and visual, so frequently the essence of print advertising, has its analog in TV advertising: the tension between what is shown and what is said. Interesting tones are created by running one sort of language on top of another sort of imagery.

Do you remember the ad in which a monkey stands in water listening to a Sony Walkman? If you saw it, you do. Part of its memorability is that arresting image, but the ad elevates it by running opera music on the soundtrack. The monkey is, apparently, listening to opera and being uplifted by it—we can see by his expression, as he stares out to sea, that it enraptures him. Thus, we get the idea that music and technology combine to help man evolve. The ad almost plants the idea, whimsically, that Sony has helped make evolution possible—as deft an example as I've ever seen of claiming the highest possible benefit for a product.

Opera music has been run over many different visuals, often ironically: sandwich making, in one instance, thus elevating the spreading of mayonnaise into an art in the process. Another TV spot runs a soprano's aria over the slow-motion, attempted smashings of locks—sledge hammers bang on them, cars try to drive through locked fences, and so forth. The ad, for Masterlock, includes the memorable image of a rifle shot failing to crack the lock, but the soundtrack and slow-mo violence themselves create an odd, ironic tone—almost the orchestration of violence—and it's this tone, really, that raises the spot, that announces a new feeling. We get absorbed in the pleasure of destruction, nicely accompanied, and the beauty of the music also tells us that everything is finally secure, thanks to Masterlock.

Rock music is everywhere, frequently run over something not immediately associated with it: mid-life luxury cars for one thing, American Express card ads for another. As the 1960s rock generation has moved into its mid-life, ads for many products once thought too staid for rock have adapted their soundtracks to the demands of their target markets. So consider your audience's favorite music and see if that can be fitted to the concept.

You don't have to think music, either. In Reebok's controversial "UBU" TV ads, old scratched recordings of epigrams from Ralph Waldo Emerson were run over bizarre visual imagery, creating a nicely unsettling mix. It was as though Emerson's voice itself had been resurrected, throwing us into the American past as the imagery launched us into a bizarre American future, an Outland of Individuality. That campaign showed just how rich a mix you can create by placing soundtrack and imagery into creative tension. So think about juxtaposition and irony. Try running something over the images that is neither redundant nor too safe. See what effects you can create.

And remember the tremendous power of audio to alter our response to video. In a simple TV spot, a mud-splattered Range Rover in a studio was washed off with torrents of water. A flat idea, right? But the advertisers replaced the sound of the rushing water with jungle noises—shrieking animals, rhythmic African drums, and so on—adding novelty and excitement to the spot.

Now the off-road thrills of driving the vehicle were dramatized through the wild sounds we heard as the mud was washed off. From no idea to a great idea—by simply altering the soundtrack.

## TV VOCABULARY

### Camera shots

**CU**—Close-up: the chosen image fills the screen; no background or context visible. If it's a close-up of the gleaming, beautiful product right there looking at us, the shot that establishes what it looks like and how pretty, it's often called a **beauty shot,** like a studio photographer's 8 x 10 glossy of a celebrity.

**ECU**—Extreme close-up: visual cropping; the chosen image is so close that we see only part of it.

**MS**—Medium shot: exactly what it sounds like. When two people are in it, it's sometimes called a **two shot**.

**LS**—Long shot: a wide shot that sets the scene, establishes locale, and so forth. Much TV imagery exists in the close-up, extreme-close-up range because, unlike movies, television is on a small screen in an intimate relationship with the viewer, plus it's representing products to us, ones we need to identify.

### Transitional devices

**Cuts**—Abrupt change from one thing to another; cuts are by far the most common transitional device.

**Dissolves**—The fading from one scene to another.

**Wipes**—One scene is pushed off by another.

### Other

**VO**—Voice-over (MVO: male voice-over; FVO: female voice-over).

**SFX**—Sound Effects (or Special Effects).

**VFX**—Video Effects.

**Mortise**—A hole cut inside the frame of the ad that contains something else, often a small image of the product or product line.

**Super**—Superimpose, used both as a noun and a verb. A *super* is something, frequently language, superimposed, placed, on the screen's image. Contrary to print, most TV language is *reversed*, that is, white or light-colored type on a black or dark background.

**Fade**—Audio drops in volume to inaudibility; *fade to black* is the video version of this.

Use these terms as you need them. But don't get hung up in all the technology of a TV spot or in the terminology of its presentation. A storyboard with a lot of stage-directions—MSs, ECUs, SFXs, dissolves, cuts, and so on—will do you no good if the spot itself is a loser. All it tells someone looking at your book is that you learned a lot of terms and are anxious to show them off. Terminology serves only to augment an idea, not substitute for it.

Prospective employers know you're an amateur, fresh out of college. They also know that you're not a film school graduate, and that you'll never actually make the commercials yourself. Finally, they know that you're going to be a copywriter: Words and ideas, not visual sophistication or storyboard rendering skills, are your strengths. What they're looking for is someone who understands advertising. Show them that you do. Show them good selling ideas. Strong and simple.

## HOW TO PRESENT TV ADS

## 1. Storyboard

The usual way is via the **storyboard,** a convention with which we're all familiar: a series of little TV frames with copy blocks beneath them. You (or your art director partner) sketch in the major moments of the spot and write in the voice-over and any other stage directions below the images. Usually the copy itself is upper and lowercase, but all other explanations are in all caps. This lets the viewer see, at a glance, what is spoken and what is simply a direction.

However, you may instead want to present your ideas in the following ways:

## 2. Script format

Here, rather than drawing pictures, you describe them. Create two columns on a sheet of paper. In the left column, describe each key visual in a few sentences. Across from each entry, in the right column, write down whatever directions or voice-over accompanies that visual. It's like a storyboard sequence, except that it's all in words. This format is useful if you don't draw, and your idea can be visualized by readers surprisingly well.

## 3. Scenario

You can also write up your idea without blocking it out. This is called the **scenario.** You simply write your TV spot in a paragraph. Explain your ad in synopsis. What do you see happening? How does the spot start? How does it end? What is the narrative, the demo, the twist? Say it out.

One piece of advice: If you can tell your story without mentioning the product, you've too loosely tied your drama to it. Try to create a story in which the product is indispensable. The trick here is not to be so blatant about product as hero that the spot becomes a sledge hammer.

Another piece of advice is to write a scenario *before* blocking out a storyboard to ascertain whether you've got an idea at all.

## 4. Key frame

Generate a **key frame,** one central visual that sums up the ad's idea and the spot itself. What is the central moment? For example, Tropicana orange juice created a TV campaign that showed people trying to stick a straw in an orange. It was funny and absurd and dramatized the product's freshness. That was each ad's key visual: a person trying to stick a straw in an orange. Here's another example: A pin dropping in slow motion in front of a telephone receiver has become the key frame as well as a visual slogan for Sprint. What began as a visualization of the quality of Sprint's optic fiber network ("so quiet you can hear a pin drop") evolved into an ad-closing visual slogan. The key frame became a mnemonic device. (Most recently the receiver has been eliminated, the pin simply dropping behind the Sprint logo—an example of the ability to keep graphically shortening an idea once it's been established.)

The key frame technique is a handy way to present ideas. Rather than showing a whole storyboard, you draw just one major visual and write the paragraph explaining your idea beneath it. Key frames are thus easier to consume, since we're looking at and reading only one thing. Provided that your copy is clear and specific, we can get a strong enough sense of your ad.

Even if you don't present your ideas this way, ask yourself, of every TV spot you create, is there a key frame? Can I reduce my idea to one central visual? If you can't, maybe you haven't yet created a spot that's simple enough.

## THE NEW VIEWER

Zipping, zapping, and muting TV commercials via remote control units have become so widespread that they've altered the ground rules for television advertising. Various pressures are now placed on commercials: that the visuals work alone (for those who mute spots), that the sound work alone (for those browsing in the kitchen), and that the spots themselves survive the quick triggers of TV "grazers" (those who cruise the channels in search of something that will stop them). The new viewers simply will not be interrupted by a commercial if they don't want to be anymore. Ads must have inherent watchability, or people will slide elsewhere on the system, zip past them on tape, or mute them if live. TV ads face enormous obligations now. Hence the movement toward *film making* as commercial. We'll still watch a movie, however short.

## BEST ADVICE

The demands of the new viewer have pushed much TV advertising into such elaborate technology that expressing it via the flat work in your portfolio just isn't possible. While all the hyperkinetic complexity we see on TV can make for great finished commercials, it often makes for chaotic storyboards in your book, so for ads in search of a job, simple and sweet may be best. Unless you're taking a TV course that lets you put your ideas on video, I'd recommend that all storyboards follow the advice of TV copywriter Bruce Bildsten, of Fallon McElligott, who wrote the Timex "Psychic" spot (Figure 11.15) and likes simplicity and clarity:

> I see a lot of commercials where there is a good idea, but it's buried in production values or too many benefits. The spot can still be beautiful and richly produced, but it's more the simplicity of the idea itself. You have to make it work so that the idea comes through.[9]

All the spots I include as examples for this chapter share a simplicity of idea and execution. They work well and fast. Try to create a storyboard that works as economically, wittily, and powerfully. Architect Mies van der Rohe's "less is more" dictum can apply just as well to storyboards as to buildings.

[9]Bruce Bildsten, quoted in *Adweek*, February 4, 1991, p. C.R. 14.

PSYCHIC
30 seconds
SFX: Eerie background music
VO: Timex. It takes a lickin' and keeps on tickin'.

**Figure 11.15** Tongue-in-cheek return to Timex's "It takes a lickin' and keeps on tickin'" slogan. Here the psychic tries to break the watch through his power of concentration. Courtesy of Timex.

# CHAPTER 12

# RADIO

*When I sign off my television newscasts by saying, "See you on the radio," it's my way of saying that radio is like television, but with better pictures.*
—Charles Osgood, CBS News[1]

Osgood's insight is essential to understanding radio. He invokes the "theater of the mind" quality that you have probably heard your grandparents tell you about, from the days when listening to the radio, rather than watching TV, was the national living-room pastime. The most fundamental distinction between radio and any other medium (except reading) is its demand—an inescapable invitation, really—that you, not the medium, create the pictures in your head. This unique-to-each-listener imagery, especially its extravagant possibilities, ought to dominate your thinking about how to advertise on the radio.

## HOW WE USE RADIO

Some interesting facts about radio: We usually listen to it by ourselves, and, given the universality of car radios and portable headsets, we're frequently mobile when doing so. In 1988 there were 5.6 radios per household,[2] so everybody has them, everywhere—they're on joggers, at the shopping center, on the hiking trail, in the classroom, perhaps even on the ears of the person sitting next to you right now. Thus, we bond with radio in a very personal way—it's a one-on-one medium—but since we're almost always doing something else when listening, we're inattentive to it. Radio is far more likely to be a background presence than the focus of our awareness. These facts suggest how to use it.

---

[1] Charles Osgood, quoted in Bob Schulberg, *Radio Advertising: The Authoritative Handbook* (Lincolnwood, IL: NTC Business Books, 1989), p. ix.

[2] Schulberg, *Radio Advertising*, p. 2.

## *CONSTRAINTS OF RADIO ADS*

Since we aren't listening closely, you've got to try pretty hard to catch our attention, keep your message simple, and then repeat yourself—within each spot and in the number of spots themselves—to counteract this persistent problem of inattention. Direct-response advertising can be difficult because we can't cut out coupons from a radio ad or write down numbers, especially while driving. In fact, we can't remember much, which is another reason that you'll have to keep it simple and repeat yourself. If getting one point across is good advice for a print ad, it's great advice for a radio ad. One Big Idea, hammered home, sweetly. Get us to notice your spot, understand your point, remember it.

## *VIRTUES OF RADIO ADS*

Since our relationship with radio is personal and local, it's a terrific medium for retail advertising. We listen, often, to stations in our area, so you can change your spot (or part of it) readily, adjusting to different targets, different offers, changing retail circumstance. Radio has immediacy and can work while we're mobile, so it's often close to the point of sale, perhaps even the last thing we hear before buying something, or we have the radio on *while* buying something, as at fairs and outdoor events. McDonald's, for example, uses radio heavily. Statistics indicate that 40 percent of its customers decided to eat there within two minutes of arrival (80 percent within two hours), over 85 percent came by car, 81 percent of whom had their radios on.[3] I'd advertise on radio, too, wouldn't you?

If the mass market is indeed vanishing, markets are fragmenting, and target marketing is a 1990s way of life, radio is ideal for the times. Because there are so many radio stations and formats, you can reach out and touch almost any audience you target. Dream up a demographic/psychographic segment or niche, and you can literally dial that audience on the radio. You can target precisely and not go broke doing it. Also lots of people who are light users of other media are heavy users of radio. There is an invisible audience out there, almost unreachable except by radio; it thus becomes a good supplement to TV and print campaigns, extending their reach. Radio is also a great daytime medium, the morning and late afternoon being its prime times, before America turns on its TV sets for good. In fact, radio

---

[3]Schulberg, *Radio Advertising,* p. 145.

listening is greater than TV watching from 5 A.M. to 5 P.M.[4] Overnight radio has become a huge phenomenon, as Larry King, Tom Snyder, and others can testify.

## HOW TO CREATE RADIO ADVERTISING

You create a radio spot by manipulating no more than three things: words, sounds, music. With them, and only them, you create entire worlds, the miniature auditory universes that are radio ads.

> Radio is really the most intimate medium of all, which is why you have to be so careful in how you create it. It's so intimate because the listener is actually the art director....all the listener has is the words and the sound effects, so in effect the listener becomes a collaborator.
> —Joy Golden[5]

## Words, words, words

It's a copywriter's medium, obviously, since your words become everything. Almost. The talent cast to deliver those words adds a lot to a spot, of course, as reading the radio typescripts in this chapter will show you. You sense how much better they'd be if you could hear them as produced, with the great voices and their rhythms. But good radio spots are still good—funny, imaginative, persuasive, memorable—simply sitting there in type.

What words to use? The most fundamental and most common radio ad language is simply that of an announcer, someone who gets our attention and then delivers a specific offer, complete with copy points, much like someone reading the headline and body copy from a print ad. Although sometimes effective, especially when read by well-known radio personalities, the genre of announcers-reading-copy often fails to prove distinctive or memorable. "Radio falls apart when people try to make it newspaper advertising on the air," says Bill West, Vice-President, Radio Works, Houston, by which he means that good radio should construct images in our heads, not just be data read aloud.[6]

[4]J. Thomas Russell and W. Ronald Lane, *Kleppner's Advertising Procedure,* 11th ed. (Englewood Cliffs, NJ: Prentice Hall, 1990), p. 209.

[5]Joy Golden, quoted in Mill Roseman, "Joy Radio," *Communication Arts* (January/February 1989), p. 69.

[6]Bill West, Address, *Advertising Age* Creative Workshop, Chicago, August 10, 1990.

# Characters, scenes, dialogue

Think, therefore, in terms of characters and scenes. This can be as simple as creating an unusual persona for the announcer. I once drove to work, nodding along to a warm woman's voice on the radio telling me all about the equally warm and wonderful things at Borden. The voice was supposedly Elsie's—I was listening to a cow and feeling good about it. The award-winning Motel 6 ads (see Figure 12.1) rely on the charm of Tom Bodett's folksy persona: He embeds the motel's selling points in his whimsical monologue, and by spot's end his character and values have become the motel's. This is really testimonial advertising, in that the *who* of the message becomes part of the *what*. And it makes sense: Why should we listen to Mr. or Ms. Straight Announcer when we can listen better and be sold harder by hearing an unexpected character make the announcements?

The next step is adding a character or characters to the announcer, either by creating interaction between the announcer and others or by establishing characters-in-dialogue, and using announcer commentary to supplement it. In Figure 12.2, for

Music: Under throughout.
Tom: Hi. Tom Bodett for Motel 6 and I'm here to wax a little philosophic. You know at Motel 6 we have a philosophy: People sleep, therefore, we are. And the way we figure it, since you don't appreciate artwork when you're sleepin', why hang it in the rooms. I guess if you wanted to be technical though, our walls can be considered art. Abstract art. You know, nothing to get in the way of individual interpretation. Sort of like an empty canvas to be painted on with the mind. Holy smokes, that's deep. I'd just better do the commercial. At Motel 6, you get just what you need. A clean, comfortable room and a good night's sleep for around 22 bucks in most places. A little more in some, and a lot less in others, but always the lowest prices of any national chain and always a heck of a deal. It's a simple philosophy, but it just makes good sense. Sort of like a rolling stone not gatherin' any moss. Or that bird in the hand stuff. Ah, I think you get the drift. I'm Tom Bodett, art critic, for Motel 6 and we'll leave the walls bare for you.

Music: Under throughout.
Tom: Hi. Tom Bodett for Motel 6 with a few thoughts about fiscal responsibility. You know this bein' an election year and all, I got a suggestion. If you're runnin' for office and you're out there on the campaign trail, why not stay at Motel 6 and save a few bucks. What with money bein' too tight to mention and government tools costin' millions, it'll be refreshing to get a clean, comfortable room for the lowest prices of any national chain. And while stayin' at Motel 6 may not win you the election, it'll sure make you popular with us regular folks. And don't forget with the free local phone calls you can rally support from some of those local constituents right from the comfort of your room. And with the free color TV, you can sit back, watch the headlines, and see how you're doin' in the polls. Well give it some thought. For the rest of you not runnin' for office, well, Motel 6 is still a heck of a deal, and who knows, you just might run into your next elected official. I'm Tom Bodett for Motel 6 with America's future on my mind.

Music: Under throughout.
Tom: Hi. Tom Bodett for Motel 6. A lot of you have written lately and said, Tom, we'd sure like to make reservations at Motel 6, but you say the phone number so doggone fast, we don't have a chance to write it down let alone remember it. Well the folks at Motel 6 thought a jingle would help you remember it a little better. I told 'em I could just say it slower and you'd get it, but they said no, they want a jingle. I even told em I wasn't very good at that sort of thing, but they said that's OK. So get your pencils ready. Here goes. (Sing very off-key) 505-891-6161 Ah, I told you I wasn't any good at that. I hope it worked. I'm Tom Bodett for Motel 6 and boy am I embarassed.

**Figure 12.1** Think in terms of character: Who is telling us the spot? Here the folksy persona of Tom Bodett delivers, whimsically, the selling points of these motels. Radio scripts were provided compliments of Motel 6 and The Richards Group.

"Rat"
SFX: Eerie music under
Man: I can chew through glass,
cinderblock, aluminum and lead. I'm a
carrier of Black Plague and food
poisoning. And every year, I bite more
than 45,000 people, mostly children and
infants.
SFX: Music stops.
Anncr.: Pests don't mess around. Why
should you? Call Rose Termite and Pest
Control. We've been getting rid of pests
in this country longer than anybody.
Effectively, cleanly and quickly.
Guaranteed.
SFX: Music starts.
Man: I start thousands of unexplained
fires. And I love to swim in your sewer.
SFX: Music stops.
Anncr.: Just call
1-800-R-O-S-E-M-A-N. We'll get 'em.
Because if we don't, we'll come back
and get 'em for free.
SFX: Music starts.
Man: I can get into your house through
a pipe as small as an inch and a half.
SFX: Music stops.
Anncr.: Rose. The Pest Pros.
1-800-R-O-S-E-M-A-N.
Man: Yesss, I think a rat like me could
get used to a home…like yours.

**Figure 12.2** Anyone can talk to us—here it's a rat—and you can add an announcer to deliver the straight material, the core proposition. Courtesy of Rose Termite and Pest Control.

example, a rat is speaking to us, and his disturbing testimony is punctuated by the announcer, who makes the specific service pitch. The Memorex spot (Figure 12.3) lets us in on the confession of an apparently deranged man, in the process demonstrating product superiority, as explained by our announcer's brief appearance at spot's end. In Figure 12.4, we witness a hilarious language barrier in action while the announcer informs us of the newspaper's increased world coverage.

In all the examples—the press conference, the self-important rat, the man who hears things—as well as in any other good-but-crazy spot, the wild premise doesn't hook us at the expense of the product benefit; rather, it dramatizes it. This, as we've discussed, is fundamental to effective advertising. Can you think up a scene or a character who engages our interest *while* dramatizing the product benefit? You can if you try. Look at the *Crain's New York Business* spot (Figure 12.5) for an obsessively simple approach to selling its product's benefit.

"Hearing Things"
Man: (Takes a breath) Well, I've
been…I've been a…I've been
hearin' things lately.
SFX: Music.
Man: Things that, um, well, no one else
can hear.
SFX: Music.
Man: Sometimes, I'll, I'll hear voices,
voices…
SFX: Scream.
Man: It's like they're right inside my
head. I also hear, I hear music…
SFX: Music.
Man: I think other people must hear, but
when I look in their faces I know they
can't. They can't hear it.
SFX: Music under.
Anncr.: New Memorex headphones
sound so powerful and feel so
comfortable you might forget you're
wearing headphones.
Music down.
Man: I don't know, man, is it me?
Anncr.: Or was it Memorex?

**Figure 12.3** Another example of a bizarre character who gains our
attention and interest, then is augmented by an announcer at spot's end.
Courtesy of Tandy Corporation.

Anncr.: Choy Mun Jern, visiting dignitary
from the People's Republic of China.
(Man speaking Chinese under throughout)
Translator: (a woman's voice with hint of
British accent) I'd like please to thank
you…for this shiny opportunity… to
become plastic fruit. Your country is
happy…like a sheep…with its
head…stuck in a fence. For sure…it is
a monkey wrench. The people fill me…with
a great…reluctance. We are all…we are all perculators.
Anncr.: What's Mr. Choy really saying?
Cross-cultural confusion is just one of
many reasons why the *San Francisco Examiner*
will soon open three news bureaus in the
Pacific Rim. Prize winning journalists
will be dispatched to Tokyo, Seoul and
Beijing, from there to report news of the
Far East clearly, concisely and
comprehensively. From the next generation
at the Examiner. (Chinese-speaking man resumes)
Translator: Finally, I would like to
say…I admire…your stupid haircut…
Thank you many buckets.
SFX: Applause.

**Figure 12.4** This spot uses a dialogue between two characters to
demonstrate the product's benefit. Developed by Goodby, Berlin &
Silverstein, advertising agency for the *San Francisco Examiner*.

SFX: SOFT COCKTAIL PARTY MUSIC WITH CLAMOR OF VOICES
Man:   Do you have my card?
           Do you have my card?
           Do you have my card?
           Do you have my card?
           Do you have my card?
           Do you have my card?
           Do you have my card?
           Do you have my card?
           Do you have my card?
           Do you have my card?
           Do you have my card?
           Do you have my card?
           Do you have my card?
           Do you have my card?
Anncr: Thankfully, there is another way to
        pick up leads. *Crains New York Business*.

**Figure 12.5** Gaining attention and dramatizing the product benefit need not conflict, as this oh-so-simple spot proves. Courtesy of *Crain's New York Business*.

## Ears only prose

Remember that you're writing for our ears only. We listeners will not have the chance to go back and look at what you've said, so keep it simple and readily consumable (no more than two words per second). Use a tape recorder to play your work back to yourself. Let your ears tell you what to do, not the look of the words on the page. And don't neglect the white space of radio advertising—silence. By rushing to cram lots of copy points into a small space, far too many ads yell at us with breathless announcers. Unless you're satirizing that tradition, avoid it:

> Just as an art director achieves contrast in a print ad or sets off an important graphic element by framing it in white space, so can the radio writer give words and sounds room to breathe.[7]

## Sound as sights

Sound effects (SFX), your second tool as a radio writer, offer unlimited possibilities—libraries of sounds are available, and with minimal equipment you can, of course, create your own sound effects. Think how readily and completely sounds evoke whole places and things. They become parts standing for wholes. Rain drumming on a tin roof, the rhythmic slapping of waves, and we're suddenly somewhere exotic, in the Caribbean or South

[7]Huntley Baldwin, *How To Create Effective TV Commercials*, 2nd ed. (Lincolnwood, IL: NTC Business Books, 1989), p. 267.

Seas. A howl of wind, dry crunchings, one after another, and we could be walking across the Antarctic. An echo to a droning voice, and we find ourselves in a large hall, listening to a speech. Dogs barking, and we're in a kennel. Dogs barking with an echo, and suddenly *they're* in the hall—*not* listening to the speech. It's all possible. On the radio.

Not only are sounds rapid transits to almost any scene or situation, however outlandish, but they're emotional triggers, too. Hearing is our first sense—babies can hear sounds outside the womb—and our association of feelings with sounds is almost instinctive. For this reason "sound becomes a lexicon of emotions."[8] Think of how readily we associate feelings with sounds. Take, for example, that Caribbean rain. If it's a hard rain, with lightning and thunder, we edge toward fear. If it's soft, we feel cocooned, dreamy, wet with wondering. As rain slows to a drizzle, we grow restless, expectant of change. Almost all sounds "mean" something to us, so consider using sound not only to establish place and mood in a spot, but also to forge emotional linkages to products. The two radio spots for the Church of Latter-day Saints (Figure 12.6) most obviously use SFX to establish setting, but the sounds also suggest the brevity and poignancy of our everyday moments, thus reinforcing the ads' theme.

One of the most obvious ways we bond with products is through the **music** associated with them. From the jingles we can't get out of our heads though we try, to whole ads sung, music serves as graphic shorthand, often becoming a kind of logotype or slogan. Hearing only bits of certain music, we can often identify the brand itself, the notes having staked out that brand's aural territory. And as each of us who hears a certain pop song and finds a flood of summer memories attached to it knows, music, emotion, and memory form almost molecular bonds with each other. Songs sung for products can thus build emotional bridges similar to those we associate with any music.

## *RADIO ADVERTISING, IN A NUTSHELL*

Winston Churchill may have said everything worth knowing about radio copy when he stated these five rules for effective speechwriting:[9]

[8]Jeanne Chinard, Senior VP, Creative Services, NW Ayer, New York, *Advertising Age* Creative Workshop, Chicago, August 11, 1990.

[9]Winston Churchill, quoted in Schulberg, *Radio Advertising,* p. 110.

Anncr.: The average family talks less than five minutes a day. You don't believe it, do you? 7 a.m.
SFX: Alarm clock rings. A mother calls.
Mom: Hurry up, Scott. Breakfast.
Anncr.: 7:25.
SFX: Milk pouring. Toast pops up.
Mom: 'Kay now, don't forget your vitamins.
Scott: Okay.
Mom: You're going to miss the bus, now hurry. Have a good day…
Scott: Bye.
Mom: You got your homework?
Scott: Yeah.
SFX: Screen door slams.
Anncr.: 3:40 p.m.
SFX: Dinner sounds.
Scott: Mom, I'm home.
Mom: Hi sweetie, how was school?
Scott: Okay.
Mom: Good. Any homework?
Scott: No, I'm going to go outside, okay?
Mom: All right. Be back for dinner.
Anncr.: 5:45
SFX: Dinner table sounds.
Mom: Take your elbow off the table.
Dad: So, how was school?
Mom: Take your elbow off the table.
Dad: So, how was school?
Anncr.: 8 p.m.
SFX: Cowboy TV show.
Anncr: NFL Football.
Anncr.: 9.
SFX: Police TV show.
Mom: Come on Scotty. Upstairs. Get your P.J.'s on…
Anncr.: The average family talks less than five minutes a day. Unbelievable, isn't it?
Dad: Good night.
Anncr.: Why not talk it over with your family? From the Church of Jesus Christ of Latter-day Saints.
Mom: Good night.

Anncr.: This is what a day sounds like.
SFX: Rooster crowing. Alarm clock ringing. Traffic. Walking on pavement. Phones ringing. Typing. Jackhammer. Someone yelling for a taxi. Bus door opening. School bell. Thunder. Traffic. Crickets.
Anncr.: Today, the average American family will spend less than five minutes talking to one another.
SFX: Car door slams.
Anncr.: The average father will talk to his kids less than three minutes…
SFX: Screen door opens.
Man: (yells to his wife) Hi, hon, what's for dinner?
Anncr.: The average couple, less than seven minutes…
Wife: Lasagna.
Anncr.: Hard to believe, isn't it?
Man: Newspaper?
Wife: Den.
Anncr.: Why not talk it over with your family?
Man: Kids?
Wife: Outside.
Anncr.: From the Church of Jesus Christ of Latter-day Saints.
Man: Any calls?
Wife: Uh uh.

**Figure 12.6** Sound effects play important roles in these two spots, emphasizing the value of life and, thus, the ads' message. Used by permission of Bonneville Communications.

1. Begin strongly.
2. Have one theme.
3. Use simple language.
4. Leave a picture in the listener's mind.
5. End dramatically.

While I have seen discussions that prescribe various structures for radio spots—and these can be helpful—it seems to me that the great spots don't subscribe to any short list of structural features beyond Churchill's. Besides, radio is such a singular medium—demanding a great ear for dialogue and the rhythms of speech, as well as an ability to create scenes both funny and dramatically sure—that becoming a great radio writer may be more a matter of innate feel than of diligent effort; radio writers are perhaps born, not made, the way playwrights are. Do some work in radio writing, and you'll appreciate its unique properties, as well as discover if it's the best medium for you.

# CHAPTER 13

# OTHER ADVERTISING GENRES

*In simpler times, advertising people had two concerns: what to say and how to say it. Now the issue is where, when and how can advertising reach receptive prospects. The average American can receive 22 television channels, choose from 11,000 publications; add vcrs, direct mail, news retrieval by computers—the options are staggering. Today's toughest question is how to find your customers at the most strategic time—that's why media is the new creative frontier.*
—Keith Reinhard, chairman, DDB Needham[1]

As an advertiser, you will never be asked simply to create visual/verbal relationships in the abstract. Nor will you always be asked to create a magazine ad or radio or TV spot. Your work will encompass a variety of tasks—from naming things (products, promotions, exhibitions, collections of pots and pans) to writing, editing, and/or designing brochures, point-of-purchase displays, catalogs, packaging, outdoor advertising, and so on. And as Keith Reinhard notes in the opening quote, media multiply so rapidly in this era of exploding information that it's hard to predict all the advertising forms you will work with.

One thing is certain, however. Each medium contains its own particularities, and you can't solve all advertising problems by invoking some variant of the mythic trinity of headline, visual, body copy. Here are a few such cases: often encountered advertising genres whose characteristics strongly influence how you approach them.

---

[1] "Keith's Beliefs," interview with Keith Reinhard, *Creative Leaders Advertising Program,* collected reprints of its advertising series, published by *The Wall Street Journal,* 1991, p. 40.

# *DIRECT-RESPONSE ADVERTISING*

This is a burgeoning field. Last week I got catalogs from J. Crew, Lands' End, and the Art Institute of Chicago, plus a piece selling various options from TIAA Teacher's Retirement (are they trying to tell me something?). My phone bill from Ohio Bell had inserts encouraging me to consider call-waiting, call-forwarding, and other exotica. Last class my aerobics instructor handed out coupons for a yogurt shop; today, fluttering on my car windshield, was an invitation to get a free car sponge with a BP fillup; and last night on TV I watched too much of a half-hour, "long-form" infomercial for Soloflex body-building machines. Grazing along the cable, I found myself pausing on the home shopping club channels, just to watch their hyper-enthusiastic sales pitches. Tonight I was interrupted writing this paragraph by a phone call from a telemarketer offering me a free ten-day preview of something called the *Time-Life Book Digest.*

As different as these scenarios seem, they're really all the same: direct-response advertising. *Direct* because no retailers or wholesalers stand between me and the product: I am hooked up, one to one, with the advertiser—through a phone call, a letter, or a print, TV, or radio ad. And *response* in that each instance is a two-way interaction: I'm asked to use a response device—an 800 number, a reply card, something—that connects me to the advertiser and completes the transaction. There is a call for direct action, usually buying the product or requesting more information. This interaction, unmediated by retailers, is what is meant by direct response.

## The direct-mail piece

Even though, as a week in my life shows, direct-response advertising uses many media, let's choose the direct-mail piece as our working example. You will probably get several versions of it today, and the chances of your writing or designing a direct-mail piece are high, since it's the third biggest advertising medium, after TV and newspapers. The direct-mail piece also serves as a template for the rhetoric of direct-response copywriting, regardless of medium.

What approach should you take?

### 1. Be attention-getting

While this is an obligation of all advertising, of course, it operates with a vengeance in direct mail. Americans receive almost four tons of "junk mail" every year, and 44 percent of it is never opened. Obviously, you want to be in the 56 percent, yet far too much direct mail looks alike, talks alike, and has the whiff of the "pretend-personal." So it's a tough genre to work within yet still be original enough to transcend the stereotypes.

How to do so? Put some language or design or both on the envelope to get it opened. Your envelope (or whatever part of your piece first confronts the target audience) functions like a print ad's headline or dominant visual as the grabber. (See Figure 13.1.)

## 2.  Think of the copy as a letter to a friend

Since direct-mail advertising has become increasingly targeted over the years, chances are you'll have a specific audience to write to: current Porsche owners, women who have previously bought expensive lingerie, men 35–50 who have dyed their hair, and so on. And as computerized technology and data base tracking grow in the 1990s—along with our reliance on credit-card assisted, push-button, stay-at-home shopping—such accuracy will only increase. You will know, to a greater degree than with mass-media advertising, just who you're talking to.

This knowledge not only helps you figure out what to say to get your mail noticed, but it also helps you understand your rhetorical relationship with the audience: it's one-to-one sales; you're speaking directly to one consumer. Be as warm and informal as the situation allows, use the language of the consumer, share his or her mindset. Although the offer itself will have the greatest effect on sales, how you phrase that offer, the **voice** of your copy, will go a long way toward separating your piece from "junk mail."

## 3. Cover *all* aspects of the transaction

Unlike traditional national-brand advertising, direct advertising functions as a *complete sales message*. You're not just piquing interest, tinkering with an attitude, or laying down one more stratum in the geological structure of a brand image. You're conducting the whole deal, from getting your target audience to open the envelope to closing the sale.

Your copy must do a lot: catch attention; stimulate desire and belief by stating, then proving, the benefit(s); overcome general skepticism and specific objections; make the product tangible in the face of its intangibility (there's usually no store we can walk into to check out the product); and close with a strong enough call-to-action that an immediate, positive response becomes not only convenient but inescapable.

Remember: Since you're addressing someone already interested in the product, once your prospect begins to read, he or she

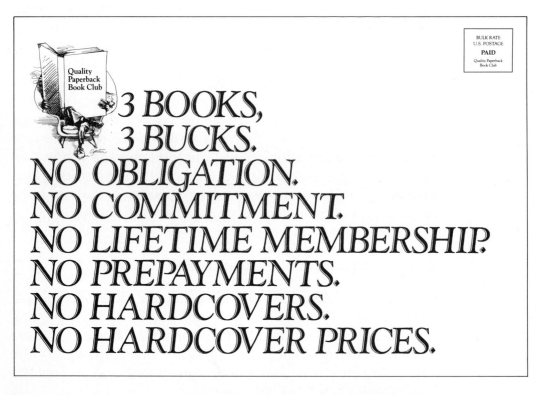

**Figure 13.1** Notice that the copy on these envelopes, like all good "headlines,"
piques our interest *as* it expresses benefits. These aren't blind headlines or
borrowed interest headlines. The book club language, with its strong use of
parallelism, is both the attention-getter *and* the complete selling promise.
Microsoft's "shortcut to work" is computer software, and on the outside back
of the envelope, the "subhead" elaborates, "Introducing Microsoft Word 5.1
for the Mac with an all-new, customizable toolbar. It's the fastest way to work."
Reprinted with permission from Microsoft Corporation and Quality Paperback Book Club.

is likely to stay with you. So write longer, with more selling facts. Sell harder and straighter. If at the end of your copy, the prospect decides only to "think about it," you've probably failed. If some aspect of the persuasive sequence doesn't happen, then the sale doesn't happen. You're it or nobody is.

Bob Stone, one of the best of the direct marketers, advises following a seven-step formula, one open enough to let you steer past clichés but still sequenced well enough to cover the arc of persuasion (see Figure 13.2).

1. Promise a benefit in your headline or first paragraph—your most important benefit. [You may want to start with the *problem* your target has, in order to set up the benefit your product delivers, the way it solves the problem.]

2. Immediately enlarge on your most important benefit.

3. Tell the reader specifically what he or she is going to get.

4. Back up your statements with proof and endorsements [testimonials].

5. Tell the reader what he or she might lose if he or she doesn't act.

6. Rephrase your prominent benefits in your closing offer.

7. Incite action. Now.[2]

## 4. Use multiple pieces within the mailing

While your assignment may ask for a brochure alone, typically a direct-mail piece contains several items: a letter; a brochure; a separate reply envelope (often with an "involvement" device, like a punch-out tab or perforated tear-slip); sometimes an accompanying gift offer for ordering immediately; and a final, shorter letter to try one last time to catch prospects if they've been unmoved by everything else. The exact contents of a direct-mail piece vary, but many direct advertisers feel that several items, in concert, carry the selling argument more effectively than does one element alone.

## 5. Analyze your own mail

Direct mail, unlike most advertising, can be so readily measured that it's the ultimate testing ground for what works. Advertisers can adjust all aspects of headline, copy, promise, and so on and then exactly determine the results of those changes. Consequently, your mail is an experimental laboratory of the art and science of persuasion. Study it to discover what techniques do

---

[2]Bob Stone, *Successful Direct Marketing Methods*, 4th ed. (Lincolnwood, IL: NTC Business Books, 1988), pp. 334–335.

QUALITY PAPERBACK BOOK CLUB® Camp Hill, Pa. 17012

Dear Book Lover,

How would you like to save up to 65% on the books you want to read?

That's just what you can do when you become a member of QPB.

So if you would normally pay as much as $20 for a book, thanks to QPB you might read the same book for as little as $7. At those prices you can buy two books for the price of one and still have $6 in your pocket.

One reason for our low prices is simple: we replace the hard cover on today's most popular books with a soft cover. But except for that difference a QPB softcover book is very

(over, please)

**Figure 13.2** Here is the beginning of the book club's letter, following from the envelope's lead. Note how many of Stone's suggestions it covers. Courtesy of Quality Paperback Book Club.

and don't work on you. What makes you throw something away unopened? What compels you to open it? How much of it do you read? What makes you keep going or stop?

## Direct-response catalogs

The trouble with many copywriters is that they think their job is to write copy. That is equivalent to a salesperson saying, "My job is to talk." The job is not to "talk." For a writer, the job is not to "write." For both the job is to sell.

—Don Kanter, vice president, Stone & Adler, direct marketers[3]

## The art of catalog copy

Your obligation to create the complete argument is the defining characteristic of direct-response copy, and it's nowhere more evident than in catalogs, one of the most durable of direct-mail forms, and also one of the best places to study the art of persuasion. (See Figure 13.3.) Lands' End writes catalog copy as well as anyone, and since this year's fat, December issue just thumped into my life, let's turn to a page, almost at random, and read this headline beside a picture of a man and woman in similar sweaters:

> New hand-framed 4-ply Merino Cardigans that could last
> a couple of lifetimes.

All their headlines sell; they say, straightforwardly but energetically, what this product is and why we should buy it. Here's the copy:

> Though these beautiful sweaters have a full hand, they are soft.
> After all, Merino is one of the world's finest wools. And our
> 100% Merino is worsted-spun (in Italy, no less) for extra soft-
> ness and smoothness. Our new cardigans are double-breasted.
> And have fully fashioned "j" armholes, which have a comfort-
> able modified drop to them. Men's has a shawl collar for snug-
> ging around the neck. Women's, a classic reverse (or notched)
> collar. Both sweaters are hand-framed by an intimate, painstak-
> ing firm located near the headwaters of the Clyde. And won't
> both make a very comfortable alternative to a classic blue
> blazer? Dry clean. Made in Scotland. Navy (with Plum tipping
> on cuffs and waistband)." [sizes and price]

## Copy is specific, complete, persuasive

This is not even a featured item; it's one of two items on one of 259 pages. Yet even here, in a catalog filled with entries, in a section stuffed with sweaters, I know the peg on which this item is hung. I know this sweater's story. In fact, every sweater, every piece of clothing in Lands' End has a story, and the copywriters tell it: The Lands' End Expedition Parka was designed by Ant-arctic explorer Will Steger; the Matterhorn Parka is three layers warm; their locker bag was actually designed to fit lockers; even their cotton socks are "knit with a special blind-loop process that eliminates the bulky toe-seam found on ordinary crews." You leave even the most mundane item with a stronger sense of its individuality, its material distinctions and their benefits to you.

---

[3]Don Kanter, quoted in Stone, *Successful Direct Marketing Methods*, p. 324.

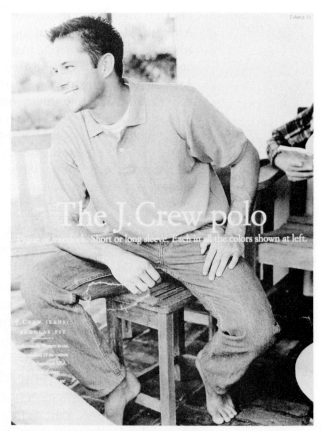

**Figure 13.3.** The varieties of catalog personae. What's a shirt? Lands' End thinks it's a well-made thing; J. Crew thinks it's less a thing than a lifestyle; and J. Peterman believes it's neither—it's a state of mind. Courtesy of: Lands' End, Inc., The J. Peterman Company, and J. Crew, 1992.

Zhao Lei & Li Na

Vigorous research, vivid specifics, a warm voice, and sheer will-to-sell combine and triumph. No item is ever allowed to be simply a thing.

## Each catalog creates its own persona

As a writer, you must shape your prose to fit a distinct marketing niche and voice. For example, the J. Crew clothing catalog targets a younger, hipper crowd than Lands' End. This catalog is more determinedly visual, and its photos and copy are more stylish, have more attitude, than the straight-forward, good sense that is Lands' End.

Here the copy is also particular, not about product specs, but about lifestyle:

> The barn jacket. Lightweight canvas. Ultimately layerable. Seen placing a bid at Christie's. Fly casting in Ketchum. Mucking out stalls near Santa Fe. Browsing flea markets in both Soho's. Strapped to a backpack at the foot of Mt. Fuji. Boarding a first class carriage on the Venice-Simplon railway. Observations that establish the stylish versatility of our famous barn jacket. Generously cut of prewashed cotton canvas on the outside, plaid cotton flannel on the inside....

Taking this approach—selling the romance of items instead of their utilitarian selves—one step further is the J. Peterman Company catalog, which does not even show photographs, relying instead on mere gestural sketches of the items. In the near-absence of product, the copy voice becomes everything. Eccentric and literate, singular and self-assured, the voice is almost Gatsby-esque in its evocation of the romance of life. This is warm, winning, very well-written copy that cleverly wraps the product up in a feeling. Notice that you really want to buy the voice and its attitude, so you buy their correlative, the product:

> Via Tornabuoni
>
> Spend 3 minutes walking along this ancient, elegant Florentine street and you could see anything.
> Spend 4 minutes and you can see everything. Or hear, smell, touch, taste, or buy it. Everything.
> There are the pickpockets, mother and daughter. In the honking black Alfa a descendent of the Medicis. Behind that closed doorway, a secret courtyard, and liquid water-music from a fountain, and thousands of white clematis climb....
>
> [We are working our way toward a cotton sweater.]

There are many more catalogs and voices. Find them. Learn from them.

**Study catalog headlines**

Whenever you're advertising anything and have gotten lost in the funhouse of witty headlines and wacky ideas, drifting farther and farther from any real selling promise, pull out a catalog and see how headlines by Lands' End or Sharper Image express—in a condensed but pungent way—the selling argument. They'll help pull you back from the jokes-for-jokes'-sake of your errant headlines. You'll appreciate again how well catalog writing stays inside the selling idea, dramatizing the benefit and positioning the product.

Here, for example, are some headlines in The Sharper Image catalog, a compendium of upscale, urbanite accessories. Notice how each pinpoints product and benefit:

> For an electronic, pocket-sized Spanish/English translator: "5 lbs. of Spanish on a microchip."
>
> For a teensy, clip-on reading light: "Marriage saving light for bookworms."
>
> For a compact home workout machine: "Tunturi squeezes 15 great exercises into 3 ft. x 4 ft."
>
> For a 2-in-1 travel product: "Hair dryer elopes with the travel iron."
>
> For a car cover that automatically gathers itself up: "Self-retracting instant garage."
>
> For talking scale: "Your weight, well spoken."
>
> For a car cushion: "Leave stressed. Arrive massaged."

These may seem too blunt for some advertising purposes, and they are. They may also be unsuitable examples of how to write national-brand headlines, their assertiveness too hard for the softer, more understated approaches of attitude or image advertising. Nevertheless, they serve as miniature lessons in persuasion, almost haikus in the poetics of ad copy, pure forms of the selling impulse. Learn from them and apply them when you can.

## Direct-response TV and radio advertising

The advent of cable television and the already-present narrowcasting of radio, both of which deliver specific audiences so well, have led to abundant direct-response advertising in these media. The special obligations of direct-response copy we've been discussing hold true here as well: Hook your audience with a strong lead and then write longer and straighter, sell harder, be more complete, and close with a call to action.

While 15- and 30-second spots can work for traditional TV and radio, here you must give yourself more room: no less than 60 seconds for radio, two minutes (or more, up to the long-form, 30-minute infomercials) for TV. Here is how you might break down a two-minute direct-response TV ad:[4]

*5–10 seconds:* attention-getting step

*65–75 seconds:* describe the product, with benefits, demonstrations, testimonials; the complete sales argument

*15 seconds:* the call to action (Do we get anything if we act now? Why should we act?)

*15–30 seconds:* ordering information; be complete and clear and repeat yourself.

## *RETAIL/NEWSPAPER ADVERTISING*

There's no better place for a young writer than in retail advertising. You learn the limits of aesthetics. You discover the world has no time for self-indulgence. You have to write ad after ad, and meet deadlines that force you to be fast. And every ad is judged on the basis of sales—period.
—Tom McElligott, founder, Fallon McElligott[5]

Retail advertising is local advertising for merchants—supermarkets, chainstores, department stores, bakeries, dry cleaners, and so on—all the commercial people selling products to final consumers for their personal use; that is, all the retailers. What should you know about it? For one thing, retail advertising makes up almost half of all the money spent on advertising; for another, most of it is placed in newspapers (55 percent of expenditures, as of 1989, with direct-mail second at 14.8 percent).[6]

---

[4]Huntley Baldwin, *How to Create Effective TV Commercials,* 2nd ed. (Lincolnwood, IL: NTC Business Books, 1989), pp. 276–277.

[5]"McElligott's Got It," interview with Tom McElligott, *Creative Leaders Advertising Program,* p. 32.

[6]J. Thomas Russell and Ronald Lane, *Kleppner's Advertising Procedure,* 11th ed. (Englewood Cliffs, NJ: Prentice Hall, 1990), p. 598.

While in many ways what works with print advertising in general works here too, there are distinctions. I once watched a friend rapidly turning the pages of our large Sunday newspaper. Page after page, section after section, she kept flipping, wetting her fingers with her tongue as she went. Mesmerized by her zippiness, I asked what she was doing. Her matter-of-fact response: "I'm shopping." And so she was—looking for commercial news—what was on sale, when, and where.

What does her behavior tell you?

## 1. Be fast, clear, and simple

Your readers are literally news-gathering. They use a less leisurely, more no-nonsense mindset than when reading magazines; they're scanning language and images more than dwelling in them. Hence, the need to catch attention, visually and verbally.

And since retail ads exist in a crowded medium, they must be simple: Give your ads a border and/or white space to establish a little elbow room on the page, and employ one dominant visual/verbal idea. If a number of things are being announced or included in the sale, then a good, clean layout assists mightily in keeping things from becoming a jumble.

## 2. Be aggressive

Retail ads are often the last thing consumers read before buying (or the last thing they see and hear; much retail advertising is on TV and radio). Make your appeal strong enough—driving the price, announcing the news, or in some way communicating an appropriate sense of urgency. Retail ads are meant to work immediately, not slowly like so much national advertising. Get to it.

## 3. Sell the retailer

Remember, too, that retail ads support retailers, not national brands. People have already formed their attitudes toward brands and products via general advertising; now the retailers of such products are fighting it out among themselves on the bases of price, service, quality, location, and other differentials. National advertising sells products and brands; retail ads sell the stores and the deals.

## 4. Don't succumb to clichés

Much retail advertising is repetitive: It must be hung on recurring news pegs like seasonal sales and other events with commercial tie-ins (Mother's Day, Valentine's Day, July 4th, and so on). It must also incorporate coupons, announce changes in prices, hours of service, and the like again and again. Sometimes you'll wonder just how many ways you can say "sale."

Quite a few, if you think about it. Examine these retail ads in Figures 13.4, 13.5, and 13.6 to see how they treat traditional retail obligations with panache.

**Figure 13.4** Retail ads that prove you can handle obligatory sale and price announcements with flair. Courtesy of *The Baltimore Sun*; Domain, Norwood, MA; and Scali, McCabe, Sloves, Inc.

**Figure 13.4** (continued)

**Figure 13.5** More retail ads that make the ordinary extraordinary—even that most boring of ad formats, the coupon offer. Courtesy of: American Greyhound Racing, Inc.; The Hardware Store (Art Director: Mike Gustafson, Copywriter: Bruce Hannum, Photographer: Chris Grajczyk, Agency: Bozell, Minneapolis, Client: The Hardware Store); and "Lil Red" Eden Prairie Grocery.

**Figure 13.5** (continued)

## 5. Study retail advertising

Because local advertising can be screamy and schlocky, some
people think it's a rat's nest of bad work. This impression can be
magnified if local newspapers are weak, the market is small, or
area retailers don't demand good advertising. But as my examples just showed and you'll verify by looking through *The Washington Post*, the *Los Angeles Times*, or any major metropolitan
newspaper, retail advertising can be stunningly good. Those
traditional demands of retail—its price orientation, the emphasis
on news and sale specifics, and the clearinghouse nature of many
ads (clusters of products grouped under arbitrary banners)—do
not conspire to deaden creativity. In fact, they demand it—and
in the great ads they get it. As an advertiser, you can serve such
strict masters and still do first-rate creative work. It can be every
bit as exciting to work on retail ads as other, more "prestigious"
kinds, and the pace alone will teach you plenty.

Vincent van Gogh, Self-Portrait with a Straw Hat. MMA, Bequest of Miss Adelaide Milton de Groot.

The Metropolitan Museum of Art
Now Open Fridays And Saturdays Until 9 pm.

Find Out Who'll
Win What's Behind
The Curtain.

You've heard the promises, now see the results.
For complete election night coverage, analysis and
what it all means to you, turn to Channel 5 and
CBS News. When the
ballots are cast, choose
the team with experience.

5 KCTV

KCTV 5 NEWS AT 6:00 PM

DAN RATHER AND
CBS NEWS AT 7:00

Experience. ◉ CBS News & KCTV News Campaign '92

**Figure 13.6** Can *any* announcement be made memorable? Certainly, as these great headlines demonstrate. Courtesy of CBS, Inc. and The Metropolitan Museum of Art.

## *OUT-OF-HOME ADVERTISING*

*Out-of-home* is the current term for what used to be called *outdoor advertising.* Its major formats are outdoor boards and transit ads, but there is much innovation: We discover little placards on our shopping carts, sponsored bulletin boards in schools and health clubs, and many other techniques, seemingly every day. It usually functions as a supplemental medium (only occasionally as a campaign's central medium) and seems to work best to help introduce new products, build rapid brand awareness, add reach to a campaign, or serve as reminder advertising for well-known brands and products.

## 1. Speed is of the essence

If advertising must be simple in order to be quickly comprehended, out-of-home advertising must be telegraphic. After all, people are cruising a highway at 65 mph or dashing down an airport concourse or taking steps two-at-a-time on their way to class. If a public ad is too wordy or too complicated, it's shrugged off as an incomprehensible blur (although cards inside buses and subways are an important exception; seated passengers can study them for a while, so these can be much more text heavy). Generally, however, think in terms of one image and a few words. Or perhaps just a few words and the logotype.

## 2. Think big

One of the main strengths of outdoor boards is that they invoke our respect for the monumental. Where else are you given the chance to shout at the world with letters and images up to 20 feet high and 48 feet long? This monumentalizing ability is something Marlboro has played like a tune over the years, with its great Montana skies and mountain ranges, massive horses and horsemen, buckles and boots, the huge Marlboro logo riding over it all. You're in a medium that can inspire awe; take advantage of it.

## 3. Regard it as a poster

Conceptually, outdoor advertising is like a poster, the selling idea reduced to one strong visual/verbal relationship. Advertising writers Hafer and White refer to such compression as "the nutshell principle or the poster principle" and believe, along with ad legend John O'Toole, that it is the essence of advertising, that if you can create a good outdoor board, you can create any other kind of advertising.[7] A good board can be completed into a magazine ad, newspaper ad, radio or TV spot. Like a nutshell, it can be opened out. (Verbal metaphors can prove especially effective because they allow you to say something funny and fast with enough meaning to stick. For more on verbal metaphors, see The Toolbox.)

## 4. Take advantage of placement

With out-of-home advertising you often know, in a way you never do in other media, just exactly *where* you are; placement of this advertising can be quite specific. That means that you often have a clear idea of who your audience is and what's on their minds. For example, a sign in front of a Dairy Queen in a residential district said simply, "Scream until Daddy stops the car." See Figure 13.7 for two more outdoor boards that know where they are.

## 5. Consider manipulations and sequences

Outdoor boards, bus cards, subway cards, airport posters, and the like also allow, even invite, successive manipulation over time and/or space. You can say something on a board and then add to it the next week, add to that a week later, and so forth. Or you can ask a question on one board and answer it further down the highway or airport walkway or subway line (like successive ads in a magazine). Or you can begin something on one board and complete it on another. Or demonstrate your product's benefit by making changes in the board.

All of us have seen such techniques in local out-of-home advertising and found them not only attention-getting but frequently amusing, memorable, and persuasive. Many such boards get tremendous "bounce," being covered by the local media and generating much word-of-mouth interest and curiosity. (See Figure 13.8.)

## *BUSINESS-TO-BUSINESS ADVERTISING*

Much advertising writing is not directed to the ultimate consumer at all. It's from one organization to another: An insurance company is talking to a college about handling its faculty's medical coverage; a plastics manufacturer is trying to interest a milk producer in shipping products via its packaging; a magazine seeks to convince advertisers to use it.

[7]W. Keith Hafer and Gordon E. White, *Advertising Writing,* 3rd ed. (St. Paul, MN: West, 1989), pp. 244–246.

**A WOMAN IS RAPED EVERY SIX MINUTES.**

**UNFORTUNATELY, YOUR BUS ISN'T DUE FOR ANOTHER FIFTEEN.**

Rape is not a crime against just one woman. Rape is a crime against all women. Help stop the violence. Call 920-4642 for more information.

**The Violence Against Women Coalition**

Remember, you're allowed two carry-on items.

**Figure 13.7** The *Tribune* ad was placed along the concourses at Midway and O'Hare International airports in Chicago. This bus shelter ad (in Minneapolis) was so "successful"—frightening those waiting for buses—that it had to be discontinued. A rare instance of an ad that worked *too* well. Courtesy of the *Chicago Tribune* and The Violence Against Women Coalition/Fallon McElligott.

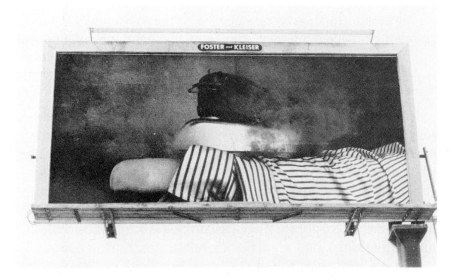

**Figure 13.8** This sequence of outdoor boards for Pacific Bell (first we see the dangerous iron, then we're asked the question) wittily dramatizes an obvious benefit of telephones. Courtesy of Pacific Bell, A Pacific Telesis Company, copyright 1986.

## Why it's hard to write

Technically one person is *not* talking to another, and often enough the product also seems vague—some corporate service somehow is supposed to help the gears of some other large corporation run better. Business-to-business advertising can seem too amorphous to write well—there's no simple thing or service, no ultimate consumer, like you or me, to put it on our hair, wear it, or drive it to the beach.

## What to do

The first [technique] is "role-playing." That is, playing the client's role, just as an actor would, expressing the client's personality and point of view. Role-playing ads will all be written in the first person; I can't remember the last ad I wrote that wasn't in the first person.
—Howard Gossage[8]

The good news is that your difficulties are mostly an illusion. Everything you've learned about how to write ads to the ultimate consumer will apply here, too. Treat the company as a person, both companies as two people, and you'll be fine. Bad business-to-business advertising wrongly assumes that there is a corporate mentality different from our human one, so it talks stiffly and engages in corporate meta-discourse (talking about talking about something). Bad idea. Boring headlines, boring copy.

We *are* ourselves when studying business proposals, just more seriously so. We define self-interest in a broader sense—what's good for our company?—so your advertising's *attitude* and *tone* become critical. If you're too flip, hip, and in-our-face (a voice that often works well in consumer advertising, especially for products where risk or ego-involvement is low), then you might alienate us. We're at work, after all, and in some sense our jobs are on the line. We want to make the right decision, not just an interesting one. Your voice must be serious enough to be trustworthy but singular enough to be human. Here, for example, is copy from an informational brochure for a company selling computer networking capabilities. Notice how it sounds human, understands our problems, and offers solutions:

> Telecommunications
> Deregulation not only opened the door to widespread competition, it created an information free-for-all. Nowadays virtually every customer has at least two providers, local and long-distance. An on-line database makes three. A cellular phone makes four.
>
> Maybe various divisions of your company are providing all those services and you'd like to combine billing or support resources. Online credit verification will be faster. And you'll know which customers are likely to benefit from new services you're planning.
>
> Sounds reasonable enough. Until you start trying to figure out how to tie the various networks together and how to access all your data regardless of where it is. And people start recommending you consider major hardware, software, or network modifications.
>
> At Covia Technologies, we understand that your network is your business. We can help you implement a single communica-

[8]Howard Gossage, *Is There Any Hope for Advertising?* (Urbana and Chicago: University of Illinois Press, 1986), p. 61.

tion standard that can work across any system, network, or application. So you just move data. Not mountains.

Finding this balance is one of the major difficulties of business-to-business writing. Too often copy errs on the safe side—it's sober and serious but never speaks with enough verve and authenticity to reach us. It's boring and dead—and the reason why many people stereotype business writing as interchangeable clap-trap. Be your own interesting self, inject your humanity into the corporate voice as you write it. Remember, we didn't leave ourselves at home when we came to work. We brought along our needs and anxieties, our hopes and plans—our whole humanity—so write to us as real people, and your copy will have the life it needs. After all, corporations never look at ads, people do.

> Most advertising, by playing it safe, by never sticking its neck out, is sort of an eyeless mask that effectively prevents the people behind it from talking to the people in front of it, or even from seeing them....Until advertising really believes that there is someone out there and talks to them—not in advertisingese, but in direct, well-formed English—we will never develop the personal responsibility toward our audience, and ourselves, that even a ninth rate tap dancer has. The audience is our first responsibility, even before the client, for if we cannot involve them what good will it do him?
> —Howard Gossage[9]

## Do your homework

One real difficulty with business-to-business advertising often isn't the speaker-subject-audience triangle. It's the writer not wanting to do the homework required. You've got to understand the businesses involved. What does Company A make or do, exactly, and what could Company B possibly get out of it? Who, exactly, will be reading this copy? And who else is a player in this game? What's their product like? If you're writing an annual report for a lumber company, what *are* the issues, both in the industry and in the environment? What would shareholders want to know, exactly? If you're writing a capabilities brochure for a semiconductor business or a third-party corporate reinsurer, then you've got some studying ahead, right?

Do enough research to wipe away the fog so that you can *see* the buyer, the seller, the product, and the competition clearly. You need to visualize the commercial situation well enough to write about it. But once you do, you'll realize that the whole large, vague scenario resolves itself into the usual transaction: A product helps someone solve a problem, and your task, as always, is to dramatize the benefit. (See Figure 13.9.)

[9]Gossage, *Is There Any Hope,* p. 17.

**Figure 13.9** Both of these are business-to-business ads. That they don't seem to be and are actually interesting to you and me is the point: Write to *people*, not companies, and you'll write well. (Airborne Express is targeting drug testing labs, and *Rolling Stone* magazine is addressing potential advertisers.) Courtesy of Airborne Express and Straight Arrow Publishers, Inc.

# CHAPTER 14

# HOW TO BE CREATIVE

## *ABOUT THE TOOLBOX*

What follow are techniques by which to help yourself have ideas. Think of them as tools. We accept the need for tools in other areas—no one thinks about working on wood without hammers and saws, or gardening without spade and shears, or playing baseball without bat, ball, and glove—but we'll try to think without anything at all. The techniques in chapters 14 through 21 are tools for thinking creatively about advertising. They lie like objects on a workbench. Pick up the ones that seem right for the task. Let them translate your energy into visible form; let them give shape to your ideas.

In this chapter, "How To Be Creative," I discuss some habits of mind and basic approaches that can help you find your own creativity. In the ensuing chapters, I present specific techniques that have been used to create great advertising, ones you can use, too. Many of them I have already mentioned in the text, directing you here to The Toolbox if you wanted a more complete discussion.

Creative skills, like any others, improve with practice, and creativity follows, however idiosyncratically, a method. You get better at being creative by exercising these inventive skills, and you improve your invention by going at it step by step. How to do so?

## *TECHNIQUES*

## Create a routine

> I need a fence before I'm motivated to climb out. So clarity and order are important. Establish a discipline up front, and then I feel free to explore.
> —Harry Jacobs, chairman, The Martin Agency[1]

Whenever solving any advertising problem, don't neglect practical matters. Establish working routines that follow your mental instincts. For example, I start early work on a clipboard, making lists of phrases, words, and strategy-like statements, all done as a gathering process. I am pulling words together that seem to belong to the problem. With the advent of computers, I've taken this list making into the screen, but for many early efforts, there's still nothing quite as comforting to me as a clipboard full of paper and a felt-tip pen. Art directors often think best with pencils, markers, and a big Ad-Art pad in front of them. The point is to find your own comfort zone and enter it; ritual and regularity here help.

## Let the assignment set some boundaries

> Great advertising requires pure creative spark within the context of a strategic assignment.
> —Tom Monahan, president, Leonard Monahan Lubars & Kelly[2]

The specifics of your advertising problem will help center your thinking. Are you writing copy for a corporate capabilities brochure? If so, you'll be thinking about what categories you should break the discussion into, how you'll organize the piece, and what will unify it, page to page (an issue you'll develop with the art director sharing the project). Maybe instead you're writing a series of newspaper ads for a local dry cleaner, so you realize that these will have to be quick and simple, probably price or service oriented. Perhaps you're writing a self-promotion piece for a photographer. The use of photos as samples is usually a given in such self-promotions, but what to say about them? It might be

---

[1]"Wild about Harry," interview with Harry Jacobs, *Creative Leaders Advertising Program,* collected reprints of its advertising series, published by *The Wall Street Journal,* 1991, p. 19.

[2]Tom Monahan, "Advertising: When Smart People Make Each Other Dumb," *Communication Arts* (September/October 1991), p. 112.

more original if your photographer mailed out only copy, no photos, in order to get attention. But what will he or she say? Or perhaps you're creating magazine spreads for a packaged good for your portfolio, in which case the only limits are those of your own devising.

In short, *how* you think through an advertising problem comes in large part from the nature of your assignment. It will head you in certain directions.

## Suspend judgment

Don't reject your early, often bad ideas. You must get material down in order to make material. Think of it as standing today on what you did yesterday; you usually can't simply leap to the great idea; rather you pile up the not-so-great ideas to provide a vantage point from which to reach that great idea, to just pluck it really.

If you're dumb today, thinking only obvious or inane thoughts, that's fine. The only way you'll be dumb tomorrow is by doing nothing today. So get those ideas, half-ideas, and nonsense ideas out of your system and onto the page. Returning to the example from Chapter 7, if you're selling peanut butter to adults as a breakfast alternative, then you'll need to say all the puns and obvious lines: "Go nuts," "Are you nuts about breakfast?" "A nutty way to start the day," and so forth. Until you noodle them out onto the page, you won't get on with solving the problem.

All those bad ideas either imply transformations or let other, related ideas slip out that would have stayed hidden otherwise. The next time you're brainstorming in a group or simply working inside your own mind, notice how pervasive is our self-critical editor, the "Oh-never-mind-it-was-a-stupid-idea" self who kills thoughts before they even hit the floor. Notice how often that voice interrupts conversation and how often it scolds silently inside your own skull. Suspend such judgments. Use them later, not now. As Edward de Bono says in *Lateral Thinking*, a very good book about creativity:

> The purpose of thinking is not to be right but to be effective. Being effective does eventually involve being right but there is a very important difference between the two. Being right means being right all the time. Being effective means being right only at the end....The need to be right all the time is the biggest bar there is to

new ideas. It is better to have enough ideas for some of them to be wrong than to be always right by having no ideas at all.[3]

## Use both lateral and vertical thinking

> You cannot dig a hole in a different place by
> digging the same hole deeper.
> —Edward de Bono[4]

Creating ads is an alternating process of expansion and contraction. That is, you must be abundant and uncritical—generating a variety of approaches, a number of different starts and little thumbnails and half-ideas (de Bono calls this "lateral thinking")—but then you must take the few that seem strong, the hot spots, and worry them into shape. You must exercise analytical skills—see what's wrong with a headline and fix it, prune extraneous images to their essentials, take that half-idea and really think it through, and so on. (de Bono calls this logical, analytical process "vertical thinking.")

Accustom yourself to shifting between these two kinds of thought. Each needs the other: You must find ideas outside the boundaries of the obvious, but then you must make them work. As you think up your ideas and then sweat them through, notice how you alternate modes—dreaming and judging, inventing and refining, thinking loose and thinking tight, being generous and being cold-blooded.

Throughout exploratory thinking, you will continually wander as well as leap away from your strategy. This is inevitable. The trick is to keep your strategy/objective in your mind like a porch light while you wander around in the dark. When you feel too out-there-in-nowhere, come back to that light: *What, exactly, are you trying to communicate and to whom?* Always use the strategy as your centering device. Come back to it after exploring in the dark for that big idea.

## Start with basic thinking techniques

If you've taken a creative writing or thinking course, you've probably encountered discussions of **free association, brain-**

---

[3]Edward de Bono, *Lateral Thinking* (New York: Harper Colophon—Harper & Row, 1973), pp. 107, 108.

[4]de Bono, *Lateral Thinking*, p. 13. Specified selections from pages 107-108, 13, and 132 of *Lateral Thinking* by Edward de Bono. Copyright © 1970 by Edward de Bono. Reprinted by permission of HarperCollins, Publishers, Inc.

storming, and **list making**. They're how we provide some structure to the notion of having ideas. They're the first techniques,
really, the first how-to's.

## Use free association and free writing

**Free association** is, of course, the process of letting one idea
suggest another, one word imply the next, one image beget two.
(**Brainstorming** is such a process performed by a group, in which
the members become one speaking, collective mind.) Free association of either sort must be fast and loose—a rapid-fire, auto-
matic-thinking kind of thing. No one can really prescribe anyone
else's free association because the connections in our brains are
so individualized. But I can offer suggestions.

First, give yourself a working topic, a focus for the free
association. If we're using the peanut butter problem, it would
be "peanut butter as a breakfast alternative," or some variant of
that idea, perhaps "why peanut butter makes a great adult
breakfast." (Let's assume, of course, that you've already done
research on the product and the target audience, so you have a
store of information.) The key is writing down rapidly whatever
comes to mind *as* it comes to mind. Don't stop. Peter Elbow, the
nationally influential teacher of writing, calls such a thing **"free
writing"** and suggests that you write for 10 minutes without
stopping.[5] The only way to do a free writing "wrong" is to go
slowly and edit your thoughts as you have them, deciding which
are worth saying and which not, what's grammatical and what's
not, and so on. Any such interference defeats the purpose of
scanning your brain and letting it, at speed, show you its connections. If you slow down, your associations become less free, more
arranged. You can't surprise yourself if you peek around every
corner first.

Later you can reread the free writing or free association to
see if any interesting ideas, phrases, or images have emerged and
then, as Elbow suggests, use each of these hot spots as the topic
of yet another 10-minute free writing. It's like peeling the layers
of the onion, this inward focusing on a core idea. Don't stop in
the middle of any of the timed writings. You can be analytical
and critical later, when you read them, but for now simply go.

One way to free write/free associate is to imagine that the
product itself is a friend, and you're explaining the relationship.
Imagine that you're the target market, and try to say what you
get out of using the product. Write it like a letter to someone

[5]Peter Elbow, *Writing Without Teachers* (New York: Oxford University Press,
1973).

about the relationship; confess: "The thing I really like about Wheaties is their athletic associations and their goofy orange box. I feel more like a 4-square guy when I eat them. They're American, they're traditional, they taste good, no frills, not a complicated food. Somehow they center me for the day. They also go great with fruit in the summer since they're flakes and they..." (This can work as a strategy creator, too, since you can investigate such confessionals for *strategic* ideas.)

## Make lists

A more organized approach than freewriting is **list making**. Go fast but use phrases more than whole sentences, and keep them all subsumed under a given category. For example, using peanut butter, here are some lists you could make:

### *Kinds of lists*

**1.** The fundamental list is *resayings* of your strategy. Continuing with our example, say this argument of peanut-butter-as-healthy-breakfast as many ways as possible so you can walk around it.

**2.** Collapse the data you've amassed from your market research into key lists. Our example would yield:

- the health benefits of peanut butter
- reasons why it's generally not considered as a breakfast alternative by the target audience
- reasons why it should be
- target audience's feelings about peanut butter itself, both positive and negative
- what is and isn't satisfying to them about current breakfast alternatives
- what cultural trends peanut butter rides with or against (for example, demand for convenience and portability in breakfast food, demand for nutrition, concern over fat)

Any of these lists might contain the word, image, or idea that will drive the ad and deliver your message. For example, a list of food already eaten at breakfast might spring something loose: toast, cereal, eggs, bacon, coffee, orange juice ("Ah, orange juice and peanut butter! ...What's so funny?"), ham and eggs, toast and jam, danishes and pop tarts ("You are what you eat. Looked at your breakfast lately?").

**3.** You can, of course, make as many lists as you wish. They're easily generated. You may want to create lists of morning rituals, morning attitudes and emotions, kitchen utensils, and so on because these obviously contain images which may provide a spark. Since dictionaries and thesauruses are repositories of words, let them help, too. At any point you can use them to give you items for a list or new categories by which to make a list (for example, looking up *peanut* or *butter* or *breakfast* or *crunchy* or *spread* or *energy*).

**4.** One list you ought to run past yourself is the *kinds of strategies* from Chapter 6. While you may already have a pretty firm sense of what kind to use, advertising is finally art rather than science. Great ads are constantly being made that combine categories, that use brand imagery where hard facts seem more logical, that find facts to sell emotional products, and so on. This list can serve you *tactically* as well as strategically. Right now you're looking for ideas. Here it is again:

### Product-oriented:

1. Generic claim: Sell the product category, not the brand.
2. Product feature: Sell a product feature; appeal to reason.
3. Unique selling proposition: Sell a benefit unique to the brand.
4. Positioning: Establish a distinct and desirable market niche.

### Consumer-oriented:

5. Brand image: Create and sell a personality for the brand.
6. Lifestyle: Associate the product with a way of life.
7. Attitude: Associate the product with a state of mind.

### How to use lists

The common error with early work is to rush past items, closing each up and going on, rather than letting them linger open. When you've made lists, suspend yourself in each word or phrase, let yourself nurture it for a while. What does it suggest? What images do you see? How might it lead to an idea?

The value of lists is that they give you things to think *with*; they help give expression to your selling ideas. As de Bono says,

"In a sense the whole point of language is to give separate units that can be moved around and put together in different ways."[6]

## Go past your first ideas

> All excellent things are as difficult as they are rare.
> —Spinoza[7]

> Genius is the art of taking pains.
> —Claude Hopkin[8]

Creativity doesn't arrive; it's earned. Don't get frustrated because a great idea simply will not come when called. Its elusiveness does not mean that you're "uncreative"; it simply means that good ideas require work and that problem solving resists short-cuts. Cultivate open-mindedness and relaxation when facing the "I-don't-have-an-idea-yet" state. Too many people feel anxious over this uncertainty and rush to end it with the relief of an idea, any idea. Learn to suspend yourself in a problem without being panicked by the sense of weightlessness that comes with no-idea-yet. It's not an easy skill to acquire, but as you solve advertising problems, going from nothing to something, you'll get accustomed to both the free-fall and the saving parachute of a good idea.

Here is Bill Westbrook, corporate creative director at Earle Palmer Brown, on the difficulties, even at a major creative shop, of finding a good idea:

> There's basically a time line when the writer and art director sit down to do an ad. The first things they think of are all the puns and clichés and the really stupid answers that their psyche knows from somewhere else. Then they go through a period where they think they're hacks, they don't have a clue and they think they're worthless: 'How did I get into this business?' And then they come out of that into getting very smart and focused on what they have to do. And they get a good idea. [If you rush yourself,] your answers can't be as smart or as sophisticated as they should be because you haven't had time to be stupid yet. You still have to go through that time line to get the really good work.[9]

[6]de Bono, *Lateral Thinking*, p. 132.

[7]Spinoza, quoted in John Bartlett, *Familiar Quotations*, 13th ed. (Boston: Little, Brown and Company, 1955), p. 283.

[8]Claude Hopkins, *My Life in Advertising & Scientific Advertising*, rpt. (Lincolnwood, IL: NTC Business Books, 1991), p. 272.

[9]Bill Westbrook, quoted in *Communication Arts* (March/April 1991), p. 46.

## Learn to multiply your points of view

> We subscribe to the 360-degree approach. We walk all the way around the problem, look at it from every direction, explore every possible approach. You can't tackle every problem from the same perspective; when you limit your thinking, you limit your solutions.
> —Sean Fitzpatrick, vice chairman-director of creative services, Lintas: Campbell-Ewald[10]

I think most of us in our educations get a pretty good dose of analytical ("vertical") thinking. We are taught to take things apart, label constituent parts, analyze (literally, "loosen throughout.") But one of the skills you'll need most in advertising is the opposite habit of mind: "lateral" thinking. Simply put: Given an advertising problem, how many *different* solutions can you find—and how quickly? Are you able to see a problem from multiple points of view? How dissimilar are your ideas from each other? Can you leap around, or is each idea just a logical half-step away from the last?

If you'd like to develop your "lateral thinking" skills, if you'd like to have more and more different ideas, you can. Like every other skill, lateral thinking develops with practice and insight. Here are some practical-minded texts for generating more ideas:

1. Edward de Bono, *Lateral Thinking* (New York: Harper Colophon—Harper & Row, 1973). This is his best known book about creativity, but he has written a number of them.

2. James L. Adams, *Conceptual Blockbusting: A Guide to Better Ideas*, 3rd ed. (New York: Addison-Wesley, 1986). A book that takes its title seriously: the breaking of the blocks that inhibit our creative capacities.

3. James L. Marra, *Advertising Creativity: Techniques for Generating Ideas* (Englewood Cliffs, NJ: Prentice Hall, 1990.) Many how-to-be-creative books don't narrow themselves to a subject, so we must transport their ideas to advertising. With this book we're already there.

4. Robert H. McKim, *Experiences in Visual Thinking*, 2nd ed. (Boston: PWS Engineering, 1980). A wide-ranging discussion, with many exercises, of how to see better. A good corrective for those of us who equate thinking with thinking verbally.

[10]"Sean Fits," interview with Sean Fitzpatrick, *Creative Leaders Advertising Program*, p. 13.

And when you're tempted to settle for having created a so-so ad, one that could be better if you'd dig deeper or elsewhere, think about this comment. Perhaps you'd even like to put it up where you work as challenge and inspiration:

> A lot is said in this business about excellence and order, but not enough about mediocrity and chaos. Too many ads don't intrigue, don't work. They are worse than forgotten—they are never even noticed. Forgettable is unforgivable.
> —Jay Chiat, co-founder, Chiat/Day/Mojo[11]

[11]Jay Chiat, quoted in Marilynn Milmoe, "Aspen," *Communication Arts* (September/October 1987), p. 91.

# CHAPTER 15

# THE POWER OF FACT

*I would want to tell my students of a point strongly
pressed, if memory serves, by Shaw. He once said that
as he grew older, he became less and less interested
in theory, more and more interested in information.
The temptation in writing is just reversed. Nothing is so
hard to come by as a new and interesting fact. Nothing so
easy on the feet as a generalization.*
—John Kenneth Galbraith[1]

*The more particular, the more specific you are, the more
universal you are.*
—Nancy Hale[2]

*God is in the details.*
—Mies van der Rohe[3]

## THE EVERYDAY POWER OF FACT

This book has argued that you cannot know too much about your
product, and that digging out facts is an especially important part
of your research. But not only can facts inform an advertisement,
they can control it. Find a strong enough one and let it be the
headline, let it run the concept. If people distrust generalities (and
they do) and if they distrust advertising (and they do), then
present facts with which they cannot argue.

[1]John Kenneth Galbraith, excerpt from *Annals of an Abiding Liberal* (Boston:
Houghton Mifflin Company, 1979), pp. 290-91. Copyright © 1979 by John
Kenneth Galbraith. Reprinted by permission of Houghton Mifflin Company.
All rights reserved.

[2]Nancy Hale, quoted in Donald Murray, *Write to Learn*, 2nd ed. (New York:
Holt, Rinehart and Winston, 1987), p. 53.

[3]An aphorism popular with the architect, but one whose original source is
uncertain. See John Bartlett, *Bartlett's Familiar Quotations*, 16th ed. (Boston:
Little, Brown and Company, 1992), p. 783.

Recently I saw an outdoor board in Columbus that relied on fact for its effect. It said simply, "Roaches carry six known diseases," under which was the Orkin logo. Amazing—and, we assume, true.

Here's another example of the power of fact in an advertising world riddled with the overly general and the over-enthusiastic. I was driving behind a large, slow, diesel-powered city bus, never a pleasant experience. Since traffic was congested, I had plenty of time to read the signs on its rear end, one of which was: "Fully loaded, this bus replaces 40 automobiles." Suddenly, I felt better about its presence. Another of its signs read, "This bus in service since 1982." Since it was now ten years later, I wondered, why tell me this? Then I realized it was to let me know, with a dramatic fact, just how careful the bus company had been with taxpayers' money. I felt better yet.

Both dramatic facts had cut right into my consciousness in ways generalities like "City buses are working for you" or "Buses—the economical way to travel" simply would not. Those phrases don't have enough rhetorical flair, of course, but even if we made them rhyme or pun, I doubt that we could be as memorable or convincing as those two specific facts.

Let's assume, then, that you've found potentially interesting facts about your product. But how will you express them? A large part of their power comes from how you think about and write them. Here are some techniques.

## TECHNIQUES FOR EXPRESSING FACTS

### Give your facts as sharp an edge as possible

For example, it may be a "fact" that women are often paid less than men for equal work. It may also be a "fact" that a small, exclusive hotel offers good service. But both statements are vague; neither is interesting. Look at Figure 15.1. Each "fact" has now been made precise, quantified, and its specificity gets our attention.

Likewise, it may be a "fact" that England's Canterbury Cathedral is historically important, so we should preserve it. But say that specifically enough to get our attention, as this restoration fund headline does (also note the well-used parallelism):

> St. Augustine founded it. Becket died for it. Chaucer wrote about it. Cromwell shot at it. Hitler bombed it. Time is destroying it. Will you save it?

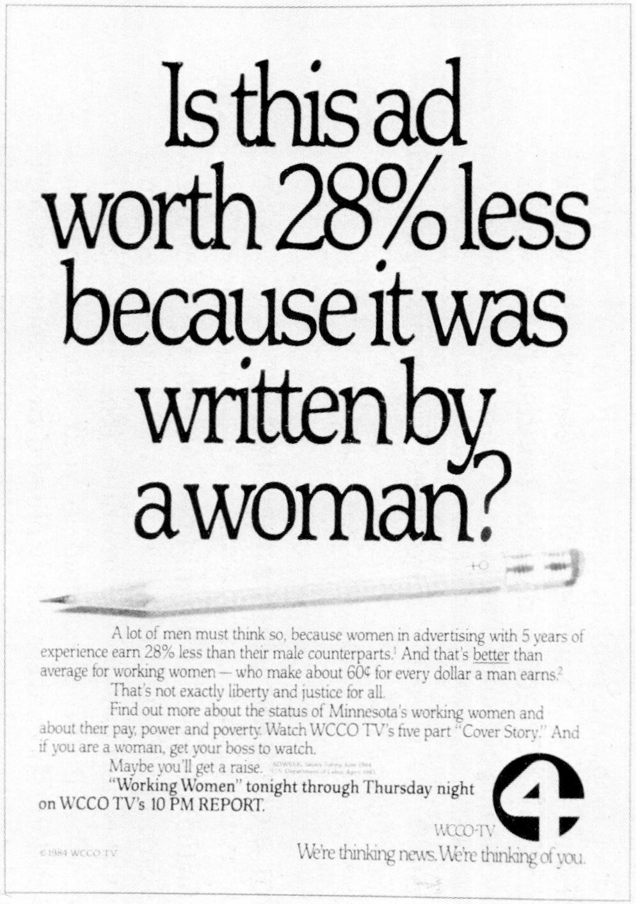

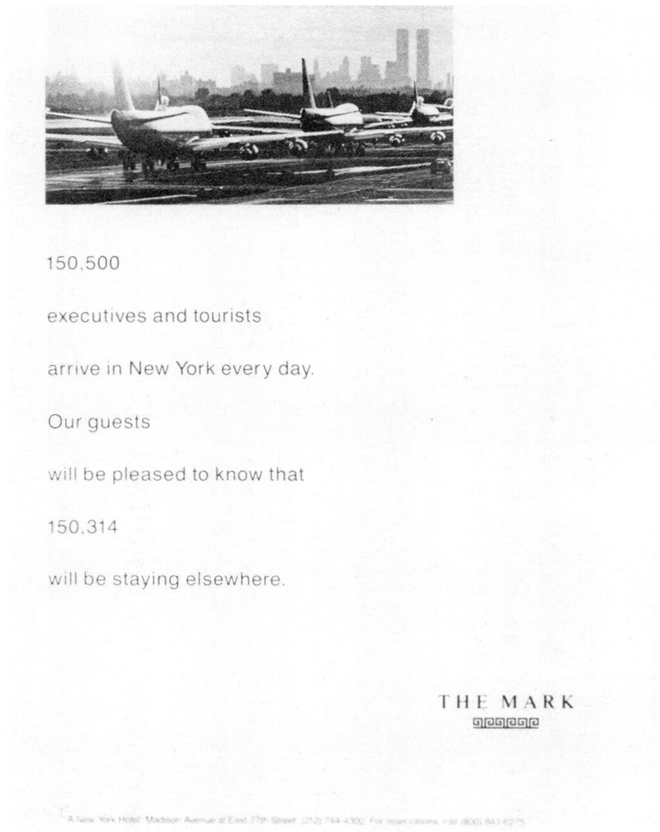

**Figure 15.1** Facts made precise. Courtesy of WCCO Television Advertising & Promotion Dept. Minneapolis, Minnesota, and The Mark Hotel, New York.

## Consider unusual quantifications

Can you quantify or measure your product in a way it usually isn't? Doyle Dane Bernbach's classic VW campaign did this repeatedly. One ad showed the Beetle with this headline: "$1.02 a pound." Another showed two VWs, with the headline, "There are a lot of good cars you can get for $3400. This is two of them." The cologne Bleu Marine for Men placed one drop from the bottle on the page, under the headline, "There are only 624 drops to a bottle. Plan each one carefully."

Any such unusual measurement of your product catches the mind with its unexpectedness. (See Figure 15.2.)

## Provide context for your fact

One problem with facts is that too often they're inert, just a big number, a small number, or some statistic that alone means nothing. Learn to lean your fact against things we do know about. Give it some context. Try to take its measure in human terms. If you just tell us, "Henry Weinhard beer has been brewed in Oregon since 1856," we're likely to say, "yeah, so?" The fact alone seems unimpressive, a number without enough meaning. But what if you say, "Oregon had a beer before it had a capitol."? Suddenly the fact becomes interesting, doesn't it? Likewise, you could say of Old Grand Dad whiskey, "First introduced in 1796," or you could say instead, "Introduced fifty years before ice cubes." (See Figure 15.3.)

## Look for a contrast you can exploit

A lot of factual ideas strike the mind because they present themselves as an opposition: This fact versus that one. The tension of facts-in-opposition powers the headline. (See Figure 15.4.) For example, what if you discovered in your research that New Balance athletic shoes were partly created by scientists at MIT? You could just say "The shoe that MIT created," or you could write a headline that gives that fact some contrast:

> Over the years, MIT professors have been responsible for 150 computers, 47 rockets, 6 satellites and one shoe.

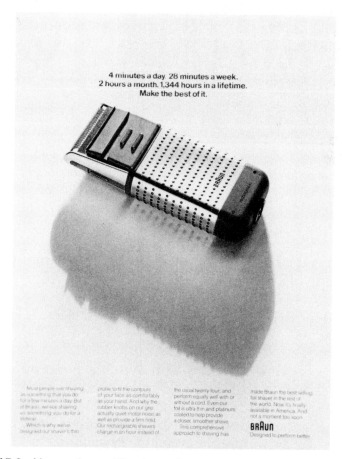

**Figure 15.2** Unusual quantifications. Courtesy of Austin Nichols & Co. and The Gillette Company.

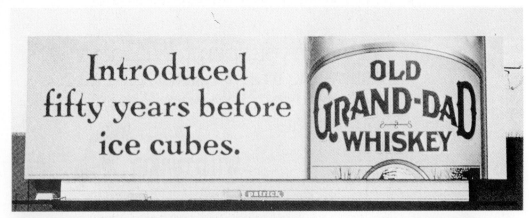

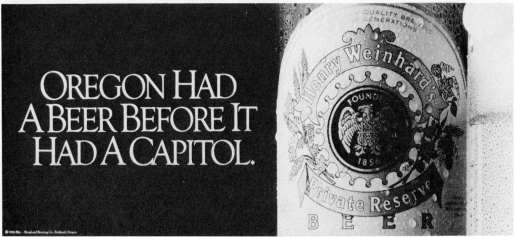

**Figure 15.3** Your facts may have more meaning if you give them human contexts, associate them with things we understand. Courtesy of Jim Beam Brands Co. and Blitz-Weinhard Brewing Co. (Agency: Ogilvy & Mather, San Francisco).

This is the headline for an ad promoting prunes (beside a photograph of a prune):

> There are five types of fiber your body uses. Here are four of them.

This copy line from a World Wildlife Fund ad similarly juxtaposes facts so that we better understand the issue:

> In the age before man, the earth lost one species every thousand years. Today, we lose one every twenty minutes.

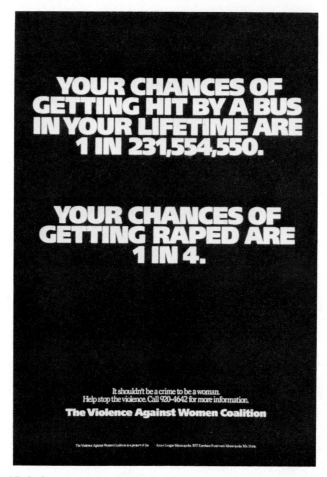

**Figure 15.4** An example of how contrast (and context) can give facts impact. This bus shelter poster made its statistic about rape even more disturbing by contrasting it with another one. Courtesy of The Violence Against Women Coalition/Fallon McElligott.

## Remember: facts about your product imply facts about theirs

For every fact you discover about your product, there is a corresponding fact about your competition. If your product has 1/2 the calories of its main competitor, then theirs has *twice* as many. If your product has 1/2 the market, then you sell as many as all the competition *combined*. In other words, consider your facts *in terms of* what they imply about the competition. You might be more impressive by using their facts in addition to or in place of yours.

## Facts can be visual, too

Sometimes we lock into thinking that facts must be statistics, quantifiable, verbal. We think the only way to express them is through words or headlines. But many facts are visual—or can be. (See Figure 15.5.)

The Complete Recipe for Gerber Peas:

*Fresh tender peas*
*Water*

All Gerber baby foods are perfectly prepared for your baby's nutritional needs, without added salt, artificial colors, flavors, or preservatives. These are the facts... Pure and Simple.

Gerber

Our tan line.

With over 6000 miles of beaches, it's always been easy for people to get a beautiful tan in Mexico.

And now, you'll find it equally easy to help people get here. Starting with vacation packages that are not only well-priced, but offer a wide variety of experiences. In addition, you'll find we've developed a program to make Mexico a good business

opportunity for you. And we're supporting it with an intensive advertising campaign promoting the unique beach and cultural opportunities that Mexico offers.

Also, we're starting a series of ongoing training seminars for travel agents about the benefits of Mexico and the best ways to sell it. To learn more, call our hotline: 1-800-44-MEXICO.

MEXICO
WE MEAN BUSINESS.

**Figure 15.5** Lots of facts can be *visualized*. The key fact about Mexico that the ad dramatizes is this, the first line of the copy: "The beaches of Mexico go on for over 6000 miles." Gerber is dramatizing the fact that its baby food contains only the vegetable and water, nothing else. Courtesy of Mexico Tourism and Gerber Products Company.

## Facts can drive an ad
## without being in the headline

Remember that an eye-opening fact does not *have* to be placed in the headline. For example, we may sense that being arrested for driving-under-the-influence is expensive, but until you tell us just *how* expensive, we probably won't think much about it. You need not, however, just type that number up and stick it in the headline. You can write a line that leads to it, that sets it up, as this ad does (Figure 15.6). Here the headline pulls us into the spec

**Figure 15.6** The crux of this ad *is* the number, but setting that fact up, as this headline does so well, provides a lot of the ad's impact. Courtesy of Mothers Against Drunk Driving.

sheet, and the number shocks us harder because it's ironically immersed in a wise-guy attitude. *Delivering* facts is as important as finding them.

## Consider a whimsical approach to "facts"

As valuable as straightforward facts are, even they can encounter consumer skepticism, and they're usually not funny either. So consider taking a whimsical or ironic approach instead. Make your facts up, just so long as the viewer/reader knows you're doing it. Joe Isuzu, the lying car salesman, with his outrageous facts and performance claims, exemplified such a joking approach to the idea of "facts." One of my students "counted" the bubbles in a beer and sold it that way: Over a close-up shot of a freshly poured glass was the headline, "2,124 reasons why Coors satisfies."

So ask yourself what outlandish "facts" might intrigue or amuse your target audience. Advertising that understands its own excesses, that jokes about its history of misusing "facts," can be effective.

## *DEMONSTRATIONS AND TORTURE TESTS*

> No argument in the world can ever compare with
> one dramatic demonstration.
> —Claude Hopkins[4]

Another kind of factual approach is the **demonstration** and/or **torture test**. It appeals to our interest in processes, in the suspense of something happening right in front of our eyes: Will the spot disappear? Will the sound break the glass? Will the ketchup ever come out of that bottle?

## How to think about them

First decide whether your product lends itself to demonstrations or torture tests. Are its benefits demonstrable? Do we buy it because of what it can do, and can you demonstrate that? Is it the

---

[4]Claude Hopkins, *My Life in Advertising & Scientific Advertising*, rpt. (Lincolnwood, IL: NTC Business Books, 1991), p. 64.

"toughest" or "strongest" or otherwise very high (or low) on some comparative scale of product virtues—whiteness, brightness, impact on the environment, susceptibility to rust, ease of use, and so on? Is it in a highly competitive market situation, and would something be gained by showing how it outperforms its competitors? Figure out what advantage your product really has over others and then show it.

## Be vivid, go beyond clichés

The key to a good demonstration is its dramatic freshness. Try to be witty and original while still demonstrating. You really can't just show Pile of Clothes A versus Whiter Pile of Clothes B or Dry, Unsmiling Face A versus Smooth, Smiling Face B, can you? You must supply some twist to the demo, reinvigorate it as a format. How to go beyond clichés? Start by listing all the obvious people who could demonstrate your product. List all the obvious demonstrations. Now:

### 1. Twist *who* demonstrates it

For example, to demonstrate an iron that shuts itself off if you forget, a TV spot opened with an elephant ironing, who then wandered off. We looked because *an elephant at the ironing board* was so visually arresting, and the ad had found the perfect "person" to demonstrate the iron—the animal supposed to have the best memory of all God's creatures. Our elephant is a twist of the demonstrator. What less than obvious person might be yours?

### 2. Twist *how* he or she demonstrates it

Change the location, for example. Audi demonstrated its ability to go in snow by driving *up* a snow-covered ski ramp. Cheer demonstrated cold-water cleaning power, not in the basement washroom, but by using a martini shaker and other small, hand-held "washing machines." What parts of your demonstration procedure or locale might be vividly altered?

### 3. Turn the demo into a torture test

Don't show how your product works in an ordinary circumstance. Show how it works under stress. Don't demonstrate it; abuse it. (See Figure 15.7.)

**Figure 15.7** A torture test that also shows you *can* demonstrate in print.
Courtesy of Volvo.

## 4. Consider a whimsical approach

As with any factual approach, some of us don't want to believe
demonstrations, sensing hidden mirrors, sleight of hand, or some
such trick of the eye, mind, and camera. This cynicism can make
selling by straightforward demonstration difficult. You may
want to create a whimsical demonstration instead of a literal one.
Timex watches, for example, reintroduced the "It takes a lickin'
and keeps on tickin'" theme used for so long, but this time with
tongue in cheek, merely pretending to torture the watch (remember the "psychic" TV spot in Chapter 11?). Other demos similarly
exaggerate the product claim as an attention-getter. (See Figures
15.8 and 15.9.)

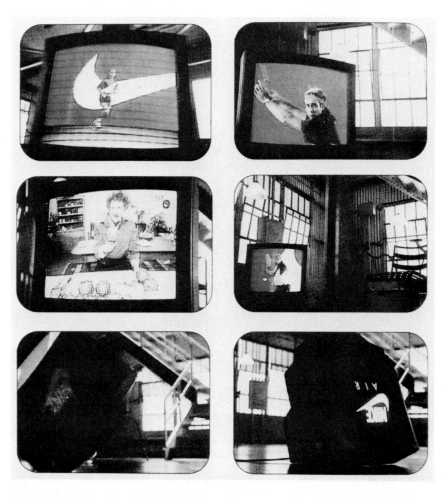

**Figure 15.8** A whimsical demo. Here the power of tennis is "strong" enough to screech, slide, and eventually flip over a TV set tuned to the match. Funny, unexpected, and effective in communicating Nike's energetic brand image. Courtesy of Nike, Inc.

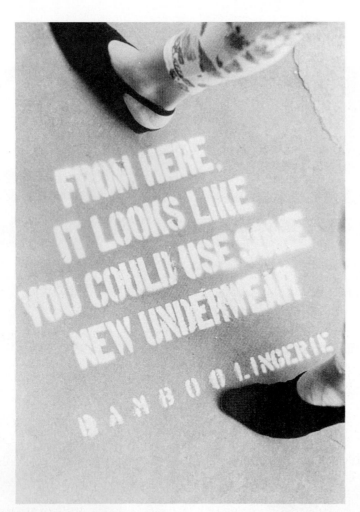

**Figure 15.9** Another whimsical demonstration. Sidewalks in front of Bamboo Lingerie retail shops were stenciled with a message both clever and unexpected. (Note: these are the photographer's feet—not part of the stenciled ad.) Courtesy of Kirshenbaum & Bond.

# CHAPTER 16

# TESTIMONIALS: The Power of Personality

*Personalities appeal, while soulless corporations do not. Make a man famous and you make his creation famous.*
—Claude Hopkins[1]

*In the future everyone will be world-famous for 15 minutes.*
—Andy Warhol[2]

One of the most durable of advertising techniques is the testimonial or endorsement. Someone speaks *for* the product. This may seem a creatively uninteresting approach, but let's examine just how many ways you can execute it.

**1. Unknown regular person** (just like you) testifying that he chose Blatz in the beer test and will drink it from now on, claiming that she won't trade her peanut butter for anything else, or being surprised that the restaurant coffee has been switched with Folgers crystals. Often used with a "hidden" camera in TV spots. (See Figure 16.1.)

**2. Unknown expert** testifying that he or she knows the field and chooses a certain brand. Car mechanics, bakers, chefs, and so on, all claim that they use Blotto and they know what they're talking about, so you should listen up. (A variation on this is Mr. Goodwrench, the personification of the mechanic we all wish we had. He is, of course, not a real person, but he seems to be. There are many such symbolic spokespeople in Adland.)

[1]Claude Hopkins, *My Life in Advertising & Scientific Advertising*, rpt. (Lincolnwood, IL: NTC Business Books, 1991), p. 148. Used by permission of NTC Publishing Group.

[2]Andy Warhol, quoted in James B. Simpson, *Simpson's Contemporary Quotations* (Boston: Houghton Mifflin Company, 1988), p. 243.

**Figure 16.1** Timex watches found unknown people (and occasionally animals) whose remarkable brush with catastrophe made them memorable spokespeople for the durability of the watches. This dog, buried after being hit by a car, dug his way back from "death." He endorses a watch with an in-built compass. Courtesy of Timex.

**3. President/CEO** who functions, in a way similar to Mr. Goodwrench, as a personification of some corporation that otherwise we would think too big, too corrupt, too remote, or too something. So we saw Lee Iacocca tell us Chrysler was back, we heard Victor Kiam say he liked the Remington shaver so much he bought the company, and we were asked, "Why does every Ferrari shipped to America come with American Eagle radials on it?" "Because Mr. Ferrari wants it that way," whereupon he stepped, snarling and smiling, from one of the cars.

**4. Famous people** testifying for the product constitute an endless category: Charles Barkley and many other athletes—plus Spike Lee—for Nike athletic gear; Bill Cosby for Kodak; Michael J. Fox and Hammer for Pepsi; Heather Locklear, Glenn Frey, and Cher for Scandinavian Health Spas; Jay Leno for Doritos; Michael Jordan for almost everything...

A clever twist of the celebrity endorser was a Chiat/Day campaign in 1986 for Drexel Burnham, the financial service, that used athletes famous for their size (Willie Shoemaker, Kareem Abdul Jabbar, William "The Refrigerator" Perry, and others), each of whom utters the line, "I thought I was too small for Drexel Burnham." The ads got our attention and in the same stroke communicated the campaign strategy: Drexel Burnham handled *all-sized* accounts.

The following ad, one of *Advertising Age*'s 10 Best Print Ads of 1989, combined the testimonial idea with news in what was both tribute and ad: Its visual was a silhouette of a figure at a grand piano, with the headline, "A Steinway will never sound quite the same again," and at the bottom of the ad, "Vladimir Horowitz 1903–1989."

**5. Not-quite-famous people/understatement.** We overdose so quickly on celebrity testimonials, deluged as we are, that you might play off the idea, tread softly on the form's clichés. For example, don't mention the name of the celebrity: Actress Lauren Hutton's print ads for Barney's New York and catalog appearances for J. Crew never mention her name, catching us with the surprise of "Say, isn't that...?" Other advertisers pick sort-of-famous people: Amaretto di Saronno liqueur and Gap clothing have both featured relative unknowns as models/spokespeople, identified only in small type or not all, a tactic which makes us double-take on our notions of fame.

You may want to subordinate the celebrity to some larger or higher value, as a recent American Express card print campaign did by regarding celebrities, not as themselves, but as photographic art, having them say nothing, often not even face the camera. (See Figure 16.2.)

Or you may want to bypass the celebrity altogether and just use something associated with him or her, as a Spiegel catalog campaign did, showing us the silk gown Bianca Jagger bought or the shoes Priscilla Presley bought from the catalog. There was an extra poignance to this use of a metonym (a part standing for the whole) in place of the celebrity, and more involvement by us as viewers. The same holds true for Reebok's use of handwriting as metonym. (See Figure 16.3.)

It's even possible to use the celebrity, not as endorser, but as attention-getting metaphor. These inventive student ads from Atlanta's Portfolio Center use famous faces to talk about qualities of paint. (See Figure 16.4.)

**6. The wrong person.** This is little used but shouldn't be, since it's far enough away from a cliché to get our attention. The

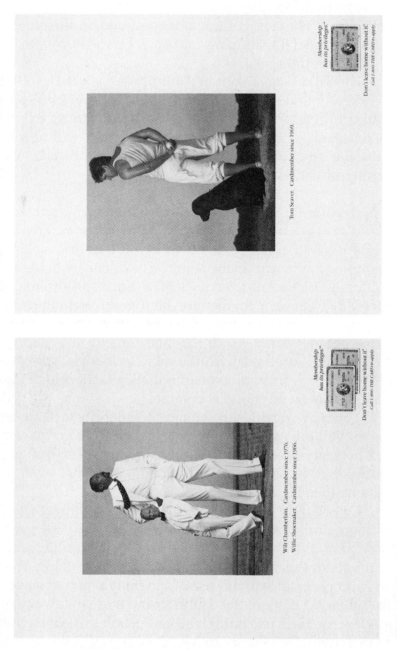

**Figure 16.2** Celebrities as art. Courtesy of American Express, Inc.

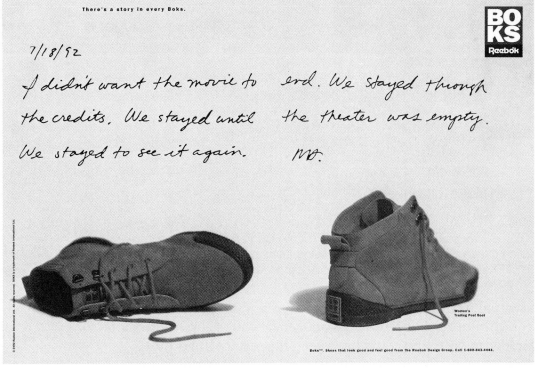

**Figure 16.3** Both the clothing and handwriting stand in place of the people, creating more poignance and viewer involvement. Courtesy of McConnaughy Barocci Brown and Reebok International Ltd.

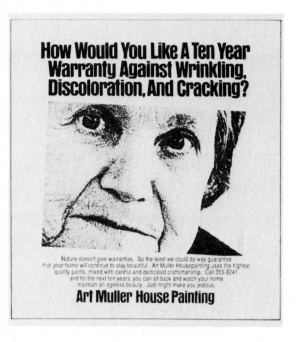

**Figure 16.4** Clever student work (from The Portfolio Center) that exploits the arresting quality of celebrity faces while using them as metaphors. Courtesy of The Portfolio Center (Bill Karow, AD and Mary Gould, CW.)

quintessential example may be Fallon McElligott's print campaign for a Minneapolis hair salon that used famous people with bad haircuts, people who could have used the service but didn't. The centerpiece of that campaign was an ad with a photo of Albert Einstein, hair all messed up as always, and the headline: "A bad haircut can make anyone look dumb." A great idea. (See Figure 16.5.) Similarly, Del Monte introduced shelf-stable, micro-

A bad haircut is a real tragedy.

7 South 8th for Hair
804 LaSalle Avenue / Call 333-3376 for appointment

A bad haircut can make anyone look dumb.

7 South 8th for Hair
804 LaSalle Avenue / Call 333-3376 for appointment

A bad haircut can take you out of circulation.

7 South 8th for Hair
804 LaSalle Avenue / Call 333-3376 for appointment

**Figure 16.5** By its witty use of the "wrong person," this campaign avoids hair salon ad clichés (manes of healthy hair, fashion-ad approach, and so on), thus creating a distinctive image for its client. Partly *because* these are so unlike hair salon ads, one supposes that this place knows its business. Courtesy of Avant Hair & Cosmetics, Inc.

wave vegetables by using horrified kids as spokespeople. Their unified fear: If vegetables are this easy to prepare, now we'll have them *all* the time. Ugh!

A memorable Jell-O ad showed us a Chinese child in his highchair with a bowl of Jell-O and his chopsticks—crying—and the headline, "There's nothing quite like Jell-O." Very funny, very sweet, and a dramatization of Jell-O's wiggly uniqueness. Is there something about your product, unique to it, that might be so dramatized by using a "wrong person"?

Often we're persuaded to buy things because of a negative endorsement. If a teenager's parents don't like a product, that could be all the reason necessary for wanting it. Spend some time thinking about who doesn't use or doesn't like your product. Can you twist that negative into a positive? Could your product be sold by someone unlikely? Who? How?

**7. Ironic testimonials.** You may want to go further and *devalue the seller*, make jokes on the idea of credible spokespeople. Given our cynical attitude toward advertising and endorsements, such ironic testimonials gain absurdist power. Remember Joe Isuzu, the lying car salesman, whose overstated promises the spots ridiculed? Or Bartles and Jaymes, two rubes who apparently sold the wine they made from their front porch? We were invited to laugh at their cardboard nostalgia—two guys too dumb to know they needed an ad agency. More and more ads play ironic jokes on their own clichés, sharing a wink with us at the genre, so think about subverting, subordinating, or in some way altering the usual position of the spokesperson as authority speaking for the product.

**8. Unreal people.** The person in the testimonial need not even be real. Characters from history, legend, the movies, and so forth can be used for their attention-getting quality as well as their unusual "relationship" (frequently humorous) to the product.

For example, Koss headphones used "famous people" for outdoor billboard advertising: a mummy wearing headphones with the headline, "Wrap music"; a Picasso painting, complete with headphones, and the headline, "PiKosso"; George Washington wearing headphones, "Father knows best"; Abraham Lincoln announcing, "Not all headphones are created equal"; Noah in front of his ark with the headline, "Noah's favorite pair"; James Dean not wearing headphones, "Rebel Without a Koss," and, later, wearing a pair, "With a Koss."

Do these ads sell Koss headphones? They certainly don't make specific product arguments—those await a salesperson's expertise, brochures, or more specific magazine ads—but the

Koss name and a positive feeling for the mind behind the product, the corporate sensibility, have been planted. Anyone who makes jokes this good must, we assume, also make a good product.

Thus, you do not need to limit yourself to living people, nor do you need to be reasonable. We've seen Laurel and Hardy used to sell windshield wipers, Abbott and Costello to sell bran cereal, James Dean for tennis shoes. Even Hitler can been used to sell things. (See Figures 16.6 and 16.7.) So feel free to rampage through history or famous people or fictional characters. Just try to make them work.

BOB LAMBERT · RETOUCHING · 835-2166

**Figure 16.6** Our "what's-wrong-with-this-picture?" feeling drives the concept, while its subject proves that almost anyone can provide a testimonial. Courtesy of Robert Lambert & Assoc.

**Everyone's taking Presidents' Day off, except us.**

While other banks are taking it easy on Presidents' Day, TCF will be working. And that's good news for you. If you open a certificate of deposit that day, we'll add an extra ¼% to our regular rate. That's a ¼% increase in the annual rate normally payable on a CD of the same amount and term. Stop into or call any TCF office on February 20th. Because while everyone else is sleeping in, you can start raking it in. For current rates, call TCF-RATE.

**TCF**

**IF SOCIETY CAN PROVIDE HOUSING FOR A MAN LIKE THIS, CAN'T WE DO MORE FOR THE HOMELESS?**

In the United States, we take better care of convicted killers than we do innocent homeless people. Help us correct this injustice. Call the Mayor's Voluntary Action Center at 212-566-5950.

No shrink.
Pre-washed cotton clothing from ACA Joe.

Rosedale • Calhoun Square • World Trade Center

**ACA JOE**

**Figure 16.7** Famous and infamous figures can gain attention while delivering the selling idea. Courtesy of Agency: Chuck Ruhr Advertising/Client: TCF Bank; Peter Cohen/Coalition for the Homeless; and Fallon McElligott.

## Exercise:

Who might testify for your product, and how so? If your product is, say, Noxzema, an obvious spokesperson will be a lifeguard, who uses it in the summer for protection from sunburn. But how will you have him or her endorse it? What twist will you use? There are a million lifeguards in the world. Why should we look at yours? Or maybe you want to use an instantly recognized face. Same problem: What to say? (See Figure 16.8.)

In the real world of advertising, of course, testimonial approaches become complicated. (Are the celebrities available? What will they cost? What are the legal implications, if any, of using a pop culture or historical figure? And so on.) But you can make testimonial ads for your portfolio without worrying about these complications. What you *don't* want to do, though, is simply present the celebrity—"Hi. I'm famous. I use Blotto. Buy it."—and let him or her do all the work. As my examples have shown, *spin* your testimonials, make them fresh enough that we're looking not just at the famous person but at your *idea* about that person.

Remember that the transit from novelty to cliché in our media-saturated existence is swift: There's often a short shelf-life to "celebrities." Spin-offs on Bart Simpson were terrific fun for about two weeks, but it's too late to use him now. Who do we want to look at this week? (Remember, too, that in locating the celebrity-of-the-moment, you must make a connection to your product. Bart Simpson's "Don't have a cow, man" would only have worked with vegetarian restaurants or pet stores or in some context that would re-invigorate it and make it funny all over again. That line worked for him in his context, but what about yours? Make the testimonials work for *you*.)

DROP OUT OF SCHOOL AND YOU CAN STILL GET THE KEY TO THE EXECUTIVE WASHROOM.

BREAK THE RULES
NOURISH YOUR MIND. BURGER KING

(continues)

**Figure 16.8** With all the oh-so-clever, celebrity testimonials, can "normal people" with an obvious relationship to the product still be effective? Certainly, as this campaign shows. Even though the spokespeople are the most obvious ones possible—school drop-outs—the smart headlines prove attention-getting, amusing, and psychologically powerful. As always, even with testimonials, good ads aren't the result of lucky choices. They're the result of thought and labor: You make them good, or you make them bad. Courtesy of Burger King Corporation.

# CHAPTER 17

# "TWO-FERS": Comparisons/ Before and After/ and Other Dualities

A fundamental way to organize information, get attention, and be persuasive is through paired imagery, what we might call **"two-fers": comparison and contrast, before and after,** or any of a number of similarly paired images. We remember many such ads with side-by-side visuals: On the left she is fat; on the right she is skinny. Once he was bald; now he has hair. This shirt had chocolate stains; now it's white again. The dry hamburger droops on the left; the fat, juicy one awaits us on the right. And so on.

## *THEIR VARIETY*

Although these examples seem to suggest clichés, "two-fers" are really a neutral category waiting to be used imaginatively. Lots of *great* ads exploit this A/B structure, and you can use it to your advantage as well. Usually you consider this format only when comparing your brand with brand X or in a before/after scenario—and "two-fers" work well to express such intentions. (See Figures 17.1 and 17.2.)

But you need not restrict yourself to those categories, nor must you be so literal minded in using this format.

**Other uses:**
"Two-fer" ads may be any number of things:

1. A comparison between versions of the same product.

**Figure 17.1** Comparisons with the competition need not be boringly straightforward. The dogs work as metaphors, simplifying a complicated product, enlivening a potentially dull distinction, and warming up our sense of the company itself. Classic Lite writes a great headline to make its straightforward comparison memorable. Courtesy of Informix Software, Inc. and Con Agra.

**Figure 17.2** Two more straight-ahead comparisons. Notice the aggressive tone in the Episcopal church ad, the tie-ins to culturally fashionable psychological talk in the almond ad. The headline and copy voices energize these comparisons. Courtesy of Hallberg Schireson & Company.

2.  A way to show two different benefits, purposes, kinds of consumer, and so on of a single product. (See Figure 17.3.)

3.  A comparison between *unexpected things*, perhaps between the product and something fundamentally dissimilar that nevertheless looks the same or works the same. (See Figures 17.4, 17.5, and 17.6.)

## STAY ON STRATEGY

Look at what you're trying to communicate and see if you can express that strategy as a "two-fer." Is it that your product has an old image but now a new reality? An old use but now a new one, too? Is your product good not only for one kind of person

**Figure 17.3** "Two-fer" formats work well to communicate different benefits or versions of the *same* product. Courtesy of The Keds Corporation/The Kinney Shoe Corporation, Borden, Inc., and Saab Cars USA, Inc. (continues)

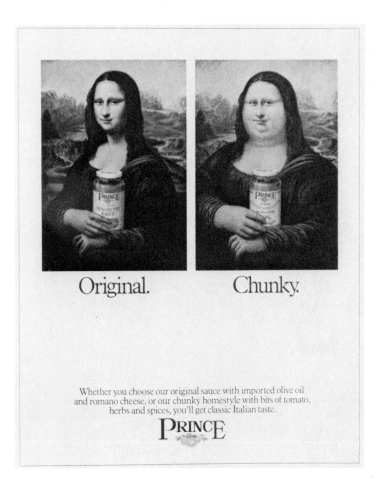

**Figure 17.3** (continued)

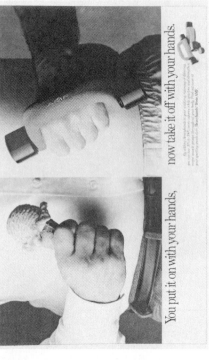

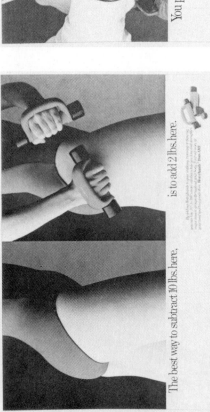

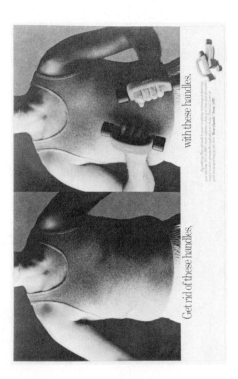

**Figure 17.4** This great campaign seems to make more sense than it really does, thanks in part to tight visual and verbal parallelism. For example, eating with our hands doesn't lead to any necessary wisdom in exercising with them, but it seems to, doesn't it? The "two-fer" format lends its rhetorical weight to the argument. Courtesy of American Athletic, Inc.

but for another one as well? Are there two versions of it we should know about? Two benefits? Can you show the product one way and then add to it in the other image? Can you take two benefits and fuse them into one doubled image (for example, half-man—half-whatever; one arm this, one arm that; one half of the product shape this, one half that, and so on)?

Also once you see two pictures or one split picture, how will you work the headline? Cast the words into two short bursts? Use one long question or statement that runs across the gutter and applies to both images? What? Remember, a large part of the success of these is in how you introduce or explain or title your imagery.

**Figures 17.5 and 17.6** Effective comparisons can be made with almost anything. These examples are strong and unexpected, and all were generated by considering what aspects of product and situation could be cast into binary relief. They show that "two-fers" are as creative as you are and work when you make them work. Courtesy of the Madison (WI) Advertising Federation, the AIDS Awareness campaign, October 1990; Nike, Inc.; The Lee Apparel Co.; American Honda Motor Co., Inc.; and Richmond Police Department. (continues)

**Figure 17.5** (continued)

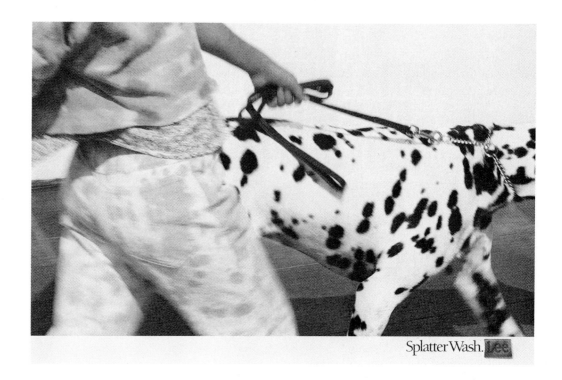

**Figure 17.6**   (continues)

**Figure 17.6**   (continued)

## *MANY VISUALS ARE POSSIBLE*

For example, if you're selling a waterbed by arguing that it's superior to regular mattresses, you could compare one with a regular bed, and just headline the regular bed "Sleep" and headline the waterbed, "Sleep improved." That would be okay, as would others showing just a regular bed and a waterbed. However, think of the other things that could be compared: number of turnovers per night in one versus the other, a well-rested look versus a not-so-well-rested look, water itself versus stuffing and springs, one bed-shape versus another (or these days a "Guess which is the waterbed" ad, with two identical visuals), or one backbone versus another, or a waterbed sleeper and an embryo (both float!). Or the waterbed and a shot of the Pacific Ocean, with the headline, "We took a great idea and made it a little smaller."

## SEQUENTIAL ADS

One widely used, interesting approach to "two-fers" is the **sequential ad:** a series of two ads or more that occupy, usually, the same space on succeeding pages in a magazine. Thus, we see an incomplete message and then turn the page for the rest. Or we get an apparently complete message that either varies or builds on itself with each ad in the series. These gain cumulative power: If we page past the first ad, the repetition (with variation) of succeeding installments eventually registers, and we notice the whole series. It's one way to beat clutter: repeat yourself until we notice. These are also called **fractional** ads. (See Figure 17.7.)

## OTHER MEDIA

**Other media** besides magazines and newspapers use this technique as well. Outdoor boards often evolve, frequently adding information to an incomplete message in the weeks after it's put up, gaining initial attention because of its incompleteness and then sustaining attention with the incremental additions to the message. For example, a series of outdoor boards in Columbus, Ohio, said "MOO" for quite a while. "MOO" was all over town. Only after several weeks of increasing interest was this completed into "MOOLAH in the Morning," a radio station cash-giveaway promotion. Chiat/Day created boards for Nike in which broad jumper Carl Lewis took off from one board and landed on another across the freeway, and another combination in which then Oakland Raiders quarterback Jim Plunkett threw a football in one board and tight end Todd Christensen caught it in another.

    **TV** spots can use "two-fers," either within a given ad or by splitting up ads. A man announces a headache and takes the aspirin in one spot, and after a few intervening ads, returns to tell us his headache is gone. Crispix cereal proved its crispness by having a man pour milk on it in one spot and after similar intervening ads return to demonstrate that the cereal was still crunchy.

    But you need not limit yourself to such straightforward demonstrations with TV "two-fers." A Soho soda campaign contrasted "natural" and "artificial" images to the tune of a Zydeco accordion, to great effect. We were shown a man, at first bald and then wearing a bad toupee; a German short-haired pointer followed by a bow-ribboned poodle; a sky with moving clouds contrasted with belching factory smokestacks; and so forth, all metaphorically persuading us that natural was indeed better than artificial—that, like the images, Soho Natural Soda was better than pop. (See Figure 17.8.)

**Figure 17.7** We encountered each of these small-space ads sequentially, one to a page, finding our interest piqued as the argument unfolded. Courtesy of Volvo.

**Figure 17.8** A TV spot employing a comparison/contrast format to good, whimsical effect. Created by Chiat/Day/Mojo, courtesy of Soho Beverages, Inc.

## Exercise

No matter what medium you're using, think first about strategy and 1–2 combinations. Make a list of the possibilities. What are your two images, your two benefits, your two whatevers? Make these add up to your intended selling idea.

Bad ads are simply two images that occurred to the person; they contain no selling idea, no commercial point—or they're off strategy. So do better. What two things make advertising sense? Think it out. Write them down. Create your ads from that list. Let it guide you.

# CHAPTER 18

# REVERSAL

*One thing we look for when we look at junior books is a sense of fun and abandon. For the rest of your lives, you are going to have some creative director or client pulling you back. Now's the time to go nuts.*
—Martin Canellakis, copywriter, David Deutsch Associates[1]

All great ads employ reversal: Something significant has been put in, left out, inverted, photographed oddly, colored wrong, talked about differently, or in some way had violence done to its ordinariness. Otherwise, if our preconceptions have been fulfilled instead of violated, we'll be looking at clichés. If a tire ad looks exactly like a tire ad, if the housewife is smiling about her floor wax, if the whiskey is just sitting there in its glass—in short, if *no* stereotype is changed, then great advertising is not before us. We won't even blink because nothing has moved out of its same-as-usual spot.

If you want us to look, you've got to make us look, and that's where reversal comes in.[2] Study, for example, this quintessential VW ad (Figure 18.1). It took the American maxim, "Think big," and reversed it to "Think small." It also ignored an advertising maxim—use the whole page to display the product—and instead wasted the page with emptiness, sticking an itty bitty VW Beetle, the product, up in the corner. The ad reversed our expectations twice: once as users of clichés and once as viewers of ads.

Similarly, advertisers for Chivas Regal and Seagram's Crown Royal have done things other than simply show us smiling, successful couples gathered around their drinks. They break the bottle: "Ever seen a grown man cry?" Or empty it: "If you think people buy Chivas Regal just for the bottle, try selling this one." Or they simply print the label on a white page ("If you buy

[1]Martin Canellakis, quoted in Jack Haberstroh and Paul D. Wright, eds., *Copywriting Assignments from America's Best Advertising Copywriters* (Englewood Cliffs, NJ: Prentice Hall, 1989), p. 9.

[2]I owe the title of this chapter and some of my thinking to Edward de Bono's *Lateral Thinking: Creativity Step by Step* (New York: Harper & Row, 1990).

**Think small.**

Our little car isn't so much of a novelty any more.

A couple of dozen college kids don't try to squeeze inside it.

The guy at the gas station doesn't ask where the gas goes.

Nobody even stares at our shape.

In fact, some people who drive our little flivver don't even think 32 miles to the gallon is going any great guns.

Or using five pints of oil instead of five quarts.

Or never needing anti-freeze.

Or racking up 40,000 miles on a set of tires.

That's because once you get used to some of our economies, you don't even think about them any more.

Except when you squeeze into a small parking spot. Or renew your small insurance. Or pay a small repair bill. Or trade in your old VW for a new one.

Think it over.

**Figure 18.1** This ad may have created a longer ripple effect than any other single ad in this century. Its approach remains influential, both graphically and conceptually, over 30 years later. Courtesy of Volkswagen United States, Inc.

Chivas Regal just for the label, we can save you $11.00."). Seagram's has buried the bottle, replaced it with a chalk outline as though in a murder mystery ("The butler did it."), had it stolen from its pedestal by the photographer, and so forth. In short, both companies reverse expectations by putting the bottle in jeopardy, showing us what happens if things go wrong, or what happens if we don't buy the product. And the reversal—provided it communicates a selling idea—is what pulls us into the ad and makes it work.

## *HOW TO THINK IN REVERSE*

### Reverse visual clichés

List the stereotyped **visual clichés** that come to mind with a product. Then try to reverse them.

For example, if your product is liquor, we expect to see it over ice cubes in a nice glass. We expect to see well-dressed couples holding the glasses. We expect the bottle to be prominently displayed in an expensive interior setting, the room to be darkly lit, the colors to be dark themselves. These constitute the visual stereotypes, the visual clichés, of liquor advertising.

If you start thinking in reverse, you might contemplate *no* ice. Or perhaps the unopened bottle *beside* some ice cubes with a headline like "Some assembly required," or maybe you could say, "Get some old friends together tonight." Or you can reverse other aspects of the stereotyped visual. No glasses. No colors. Bright colors. An outdoor setting. And so on.

If your product is a car, we expect to see it on a mountain road after a rain—so show it still on the boat from Korea; possible headline: "Every Hyundai comes with 6,000 miles on it". Or we expect to see it sitting on a page surrounded by lots of type—so just show a part of the car, as VW did once, displaying only the engine underneath the headline, "Introducing the 1981 Rabbit" (their point was that nothing else had changed). (See Figure 18.2.)

### Explore negative space

Artists talk about the negative space of an object: not the tree but the broken-up sky that interpenetrates it, not the model's fingers but the space that wraps itself around them. Artists learn to draw, not just the contour of the object, but also the contour of the space around it. They learn a different way of seeing.

Similarly, you can think about the negative space of a product, the "un-things" around it: the nonuses and wrong places and wrong times and wrong people for the product. Ask yourself:

- Who doesn't use the product?
- Where don't you find it?

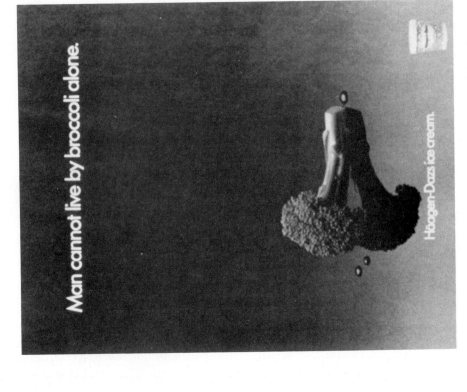

Man cannot live by broccoli alone.

Häagen-Dazs ice cream.

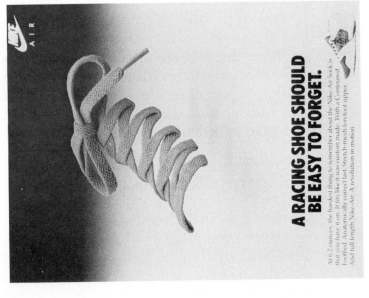

A RACING SHOE SHOULD
BE EASY TO FORGET.

At 6.2 ounces, the hardest thing to remember about the Nike Air Sock is that you have it on. If it fits like it was custom made. With a Contoured Footbed. Anatomically correct last. Stretch-mesh notched upper. And full length Nike-Air. A revolution in motion.

**Figure 18.2** Reversing visual expectations. Ads for expensive running shoes must give us a beauty shot of the shoe itself. Ads for ice cream must show us the creamy, luscious product to stimulate our taste buds. Or must they? Courtesy of Nike, Inc. and Haagen-Dazs.

- When isn't it used?
- What's an unusual use for it?
- When is the one time it *won't* come in handy?
- If it has lots of features, what *doesn't* it have?
- If it will solve lots of problems, what problem *won't* it solve?
- How can it be placed out of context?
- What's an odd point of view from which to see it?

In other words, explore the empty, absurd areas around a product. (See Figures 18.3, 18.4, and 18.5.)

## Say it "wrong"

Instead of taking a reasonable idea and reversing it into unreason, this time do something less extreme. Take that reasonable idea and simply reverse the way you say it. Invert the normal expression of a benefit. If your airline serves lots of cities, then there are some that it doesn't. One of Pan Am's benefits was that it flew more places than other airlines. But saying "more places than, greater than, the most number of" and the like is a cliché. So in a moment of genius, they took a photo of a cluster of penguins strolling past an ice floe in the Antarctic and said, "It's easier to remember where we don't go." Similarly, Volvo wrote the headline, "It does 60 to 0 in 4 seconds flat," a nicely inverted way to express braking capability.

Examine your list of straightforward benefits, asking how each could be said backwards. (See Figure 18.6.)

## Turn deficits into assets

Every artist knows that sunlight can only be pictured with shadows. And every good biographer shows us, as Boswell did, that only the faults of a great man make him real to us. But in advertising we are afraid of this principle, hence less convincing than we might be.
—James Webb Young[3]

---

[3]James Webb Young, *Diary of an Ad Man* (Chicago: Advertising Publications, Inc., 1944), p. 68.

**Figure 18.3** Exploring negative space. Here the bathing suit becomes more intriguing out of context and water more strongly evoked by its absence. Likewise, the cigarette warning is reinvigorated by being placed in a new context. Courtesy of New York Lung Association and Speedo (Europe) Ltd.

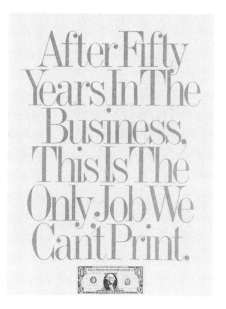

**Figure 18.4** Examples of negative space: what the product can't do, what it doesn't have, what problems it won't solve. Here the printers tell us what one job they can't do. The athletic shoe shows us one problem it can't solve. Other ads in the shoe campaign featured a snow-covered tennis court and a water-splashing truck. Courtesy of Spencer Printing and Brooks Sports, Inc.

**Figure 18.5**   Makes you want to go, doesn't it? Courtesy of Duffy Design.

I can't remember when I first noticed that a very good approach to problem solving was: If you're stuck with a lemon, make lemonade out of it.
—Howard Gossage[4]

Every product has perceived liabilities, but most advertising simply ignores a product's deficits and concentrates instead on making good seem better. Great campaigns, however, have been built on turning deficits into assets.

Here's an example of a campaign predicated on a liability of Bazooka chewing gum. If you've had Bazooka, you may remember that it's hard to chew at first, more like hard candy than chewing gum. Most advertisers wouldn't even consider that problem. Not Chiat/Day, whose campaign theme was, "Bazooka

---

[4]Howard Gossage, quoted in Dick Coyne, "Only Yesterday...," *Communication Arts* (May/June 1989), p. 97.

**Figure 18.6** Examples of "saying it wrong." The Volvo headline gets our attention and provokes us into reading the ad to resolve the apparent contradiction. Instead of saying that it's sleek and modern, the RCA TV ad communicates hip design with this brash headline, "No imitation walnut finish." Courtesy of Volvo and Thomson Consumer Electronics, Inc.

chewing gum. If you're tough enough to chew the hard stuff." One TV spot had a close-up of a man starting to chew a piece to the soundtrack of a car trying to start and then stalling out. The voice-over: "It's harder to get started, but once it gets going, it never stops." Clever and memorable. And it successfully differentiates the brand, no small feat in a category chocked full of look-alike, taste-alike competitors about which it's hard to find much to say.

## Reposition the competition

We discussed this briefly in Chapter 6. Find a deficit in what is otherwise the strong position of the market leader. Point out Mr. Big's liabilities. For "offensive warfare" that repositions the leader, marketing experts Trout and Ries give this advice: "Find a weakness [inherent] in the leader's strength and attack at that point."[5] For example, Coca-Cola for many years had virtually no significant competition, and its distinctive 6 1/2-ounce bottle shape was its symbol. So in the late 1930s when Pepsi went after Coke, it attacked the bottle. Its key selling concept was a 12-ounce bottle for the same nickel, and the strategy worked.[6]

### How to do deficit/asset thinking

Make a list of all the reasons your target audience would *not* want to buy the product. Then examine these perceived liabilities to see if you can flip one around—turn a deficit into an asset. You'll probably do one of two things:

a.  Take your deficits and show how they're really assets, or

b.  Take the competition's assets and show how they're really deficits.

That is, you push yourself up or the competition down, by arguing that an apparent weakness is really a strength or an apparent strength is really a weakness.

The following example does both. Royal's golf ball isn't exactly #1 among the Tom Kites, Greg Normans, and other

---

[5]Al Ries and Jack Trout, *Marketing Warfare* (New York: McGraw-Hill, NAL Plume, 1986), p. 70.

[6]Ries and Trout, *Marketing Warfare,* pp. 117–136.

touring pros; they play Titleist and other brands. So Royal simply took a close-up picture of a Royal golf ball resting on the grass and put on it the headline, "Play the ball the pros ignore." Although they also wrote a lot of copy to explain why, the nervy headline alone challenges and intrigues us, don't you think? (Their slogan at ad's bottom was, "The perfect golf ball for the imperfect golfer.") This approach re-positioned the Big Boys; playing the ball the pros play now looked like a bad idea. And the ball-from-nowhere, the also-ran Royal, suddenly seemed more special, its humility appropriate to ours.

## *FINAL ADVICE*

Working with reversals helps you take chances, but it's a difficult way to think. It runs so counter to our usual desire to make sense, plus it deliberately puts your product in jeopardy, creating a *non sequitur* from which you must then make sense follow. It's a tough technique—on both your product and your brain. But remember the great ads and campaigns you've admired. Not one was a straightforward presentation of the traditional way of seeing a product, with the usual arguments for buying it. Each one jolted you by reversing some expectation. As a creative person, you are dedicating yourself to transcending clichés. Try these techniques. We both know that in the great work, upside down is indeed right side up.

# CHAPTER 19

# METAPHOR MAKING

*But the greatest thing by far is to be a master of metaphor.
It is the one thing that cannot be learnt from others;
and it is also a sign of genius, since a good metaphor implies
an intuitive perception of the similarity in dissimilars.*
—Aristotle[1]

One of the most powerful advertising techniques can be metaphor, but you need to know when to use it. As consumers we like to think we choose among products on the basis of what we can see, hear, feel, taste, and touch about them. In other words, we make our judgments via *tangible* distinctions. Is this a good hamburger? Let's taste it. Is this a good car? Let's drive it. Does this shampoo get our hair soft? Let's wash with it and feel our hair.

But what happens when we can't literally apprehend the product, a phenomenon much more frequent than you might suppose? Services are not things the way goods are, so often the product is itself *intangible*—we cannot see insurance or feel banking or test the plumpness of a college education with our finger—but we certainly demand a strong sense of a service's effectiveness before we buy it. Just as often an otherwise tangible good—that car, for example—offers *intangible* benefits that need expression, such as feelings of power or freedom or security. These don't literally adhere to the hardware, yet they're part of why we buy cars and ought to be part of how you sell them. Some goods, like computers, are too complicated to apprehend with our senses, while others—most packaged goods, for example—are shielded away from our immediate senses by tin, plastic, or

[1]Aristotle, *Poetics,* in *The Complete Works of Aristotle,* rev. Oxford trans., ed. Jonathan Barnes (Princeton, NJ: Princeton University Press, 1984), two, 2334–2335.

cardboard. All these instances invite the advertising use of met-aphor—talking about one thing in terms of something else—be-cause the product's "one thing" is intangible, allowing the metaphor's "something else" to vivify it.

In short, when we can't apprehend the product's benefits with our senses—either before trial or ever—then we rely on substitutes, images that stand for those things. As Theodore Levitt notes, "Metaphors and similes become surrogates for the tangibility that cannot be provided or experienced in advance."[2] And while you'll primarily think of using metaphors in specific ads, consider the general point here—it explains why IBM insists on a rigorous dress code for its people; why Apple went to such lengths with the package, product, and graphic design for its computers; why you'll often put a plastic binder on your English essay or laser print it. Here is Levitt again: "The less tangible the generic product, the more powerfully and persistently the judg-ment about it is shaped by the 'packaging'—how it's presented, who presents it, what's implied by metaphor, simile, symbol, and other surrogates for reality."[3]

## *HOW METAPHORS WORK*

Think of all the insurance companies that use a metaphor or symbol to stand for the security they offer: Nationwide's blanket, Prudential's Rock of Gibraltar, the Travelers' umbrella, Hartford's elk, the "good hands" of Allstate, and so on. Since insurance is less a thing than a feeling or a state of mind, these metaphors help define the feeling, give us something to grasp in the absence of any tangible *thing*. Metaphors need not always be visual images, either. They may be stated in the copy line or slogan, or in the case of State Farm insurance, sung: "and like a good neighbor, State Farm is there." What's an insurance com-pany like? It's like a good neighbor, that's what.

A **metaphor,** of course, is a figure of speech in which one thing is talked about in terms of something else; a comparison is made between *dissimilar* things. If you compare Ohio State and Penn State or compare the Cleveland Browns and the Chicago Bears, then you are making literal comparisons between similar things. But if you say that a college is the lengthened shadow of one man or that a football team is like a harnessed set of horses,

[2]Theodore Levitt, "Marketing Intangible Products and Product Intangibles," in *The Marketing Imagination,* new, expanded ed. (New York: Free Press, 1986), p. 97.

[3]Levitt, *The Marketing Imagination,* p. 98.

you are making metaphors. (Remember that a **simile**, which uses "like" or "as," is a kind of metaphor.) Here are other examples of metaphors:

All the world's a stage,
And all the men and women merely players;
They have their exits and entrances,
And one man in his time plays many parts,
His acts being seven ages.
—William Shakespeare[4]

When you write, you lay out a line of words. The line of words is a miner's pick, a woodcarver's gouge, a surgeon's probe. You weild it, and it digs a path you follow.
—Annie Dillard[5]

His grin was taut, nailed on.
—Raymond Chandler[6]

I lift my face to the pale flowers
of the rain. They're soft as linen,
clean as holy water.
—Mary Oliver[7]

## WHY METAPHORS WORK

As an advertiser, your job is to communicate the essence of a product to consumers. Sometimes the best way is through metaphor: The qualities of the chosen image transfer to the original thing or idea and help explain it, make it more vivid or understandable. For example, a snowball rolling down a hill is a good metaphor by which to explain rumors—snowballs gain momentum and gather up material, becoming bigger, more dangerous, and more out of control, just like rumors. The power of metaphor derives from our ability to make such connections, to comprehend the similarity between apparently dissimilar things. (See Figure 19.1.)

[4]William Shakespeare, *As You Like It,* act II, scene 7, lines 139–143, in *The Riverside Shakespeare* (Boston: Houghton Mifflin Company, 1974), p. 381.

[5]Annie Dillard, *The Writing Life* (New York: Harper & Row, Publishers, 1989), p. 3.

[6]Raymond Chandler, *Farewell, My Lovely* (New York: Vintage Books—Random House, 1976), p. 10..

[7]Mary Oliver, "Spring," lines 1–3, *American Primitive* (Boston: Little, Brown and Company, 1983), p. 45.

# You wouldn't do it to your baby.
# We wouldn't do it to our babyfood.

The make-up on this little girl's face contains no less than 100 chemicals.

It seems outrageous to do such a thing to her delicate baby skin. (And of course we didn't. We re-touched the photograph.)

But what about her delicate baby stomach?

It's quite within the law to add some 4,000 artificial additives to baby foods.

When you think about it, that's even more outrageous.

Young babies are particularly vulnerable to the adverse effects of artificial additives.

Because the mechanisms which provide protection against these substances are not fully developed.

For that reason, we'd like to tell you what we don't put in any Cow & Gate babyfood. Or juice. Or rusk. Or yogurt.

**No artificial colouring.**

Since when did a baby complain that our Vegetable Casserole and Pasta looked a bit on the pale and pasty side?

Or our Strawberry Fool looked a trifle dull?

The value of artificial colouring is purely cosmetic. And you all know what we think about that.

**No artificial flavouring.**

When we first mixed up our Lamb Dinner, we decided it wasn't as tasty as it could be.

But the last thing we thought of adding was artificial flavouring.

We simply added a few carrots.

That way we improved both the taste, and nutritional value. And that's the way we make all our babyfoods.

**No artificial preservatives.**

Many manufacturers go along with adding artificial preservatives. Granted, that's one way of doing it.

We prefer to employ some 400 people checking, sterilising or pasteurising, double-checking, then vacuum sealing.

We even put a 'safety button' on baby-meal jars. So you can check that the food is in perfect condition.

**No added salt.**

Young babies don't have fully matured kidneys. If they are over-loaded with too much salt, it can build up in their blood.

Besides that, the foods we use naturally contain any salt a baby needs.

So salt is one thing you'll never find on our tables.

**No need to guess.**

We want you to know exactly what goes into our babyfoods.

On every Cow & Gate label, there's a complete list of ingredients. Plus nutritional information.

In addition, the 'tick' system means each item can be checked for additives, at a glance.

If you'd like a leaflet that goes into even more detail, write to Consumer Affairs (G.N.), Cow & Gate, Trowbridge, Wiltshire BA14 8YX.

- ✓ NO ADDED SUGAR
- ✓ GLUTEN FREE
- ✓ NO ARTIFICIAL COLOURING
- ✓ NO ADDED PRESERVATIVES
- ✓ NO ARTIFICIAL FLAVOURING
- ✓ NO ADDED SALT
- ✓ ADDED VITAMIN C

Clearly, we shy away from the use of anything artificial. Only adding Vitamin C to our drinks. Or a tiny sprinkling of sugar to some of our fruit puddings. But only enough to overcome the natural tartness of the fruit.

So when you pop Cow & Gate food into a baby's mouth, you can be sure it's as natural as we can possibly make it.

Babies being babies, they may end up with their faces covered in food. But at least you know it's not covered in artificial chemicals.

**Cow & Gate**
The Babyfeeding Specialists.

**Babymeals. Baby Juices. Liga Rusks.**

**Figure 19.1** Just as make-up is garish and inappropriate on a baby's face, so too are additives in baby food, this company argues. Here we see the power of metaphor: This claim may or may not be "true," but our transfer of belief from the metaphor to the claim lends it credence. A good instance of argument by analogy. Courtesy of Cow & Gate Nutricia Ltd/Abbott Mead Vickers BBDO, London (Copywriter-Lynda Richardson, Art director-Andy Arghyrou, Photographer-Steve Cavalier).

We can "read" all sorts of images *as* metaphors or symbols and are happy to do so. If we see an unfinished skyscraper, its steel I-beams still visible, paired with the headline, "It's not what's on the outside, but what's on the inside," in an ad for Big Brother or the YMCA or a college, we understand that the skyscraper's gridwork is a metaphor for internal values, values these services imply they can provide. We thus read the image, not as literal building, but as metaphor for human potential.

An argument for the product is made and vivified; we "get it"; and what's more we like ourselves for getting it. Metaphors require our participation; when we get them, we pat ourselves on the back for being smart. (When we don't get them, all we do is turn the page or gaze away from the TV screen, and as an advertiser you have been clever but obscure. The point? Metaphors can be tricky and are high risk, but when they work, they are wonderful.)

## HOW TO USE THEM

First, decide on the essence of the product, what you need to communicate. Using a teen-age suicide prevention service as an example, you might ask yourself what a lonely teen-ager thinking about killing himself or herself is like. A broken twig? Like something with lots of pressure on it, maybe an egg squeezed into a very small box? Or like a forlorn object, something little and away from others, maybe a grounded bird in an open field?

Instead of expressing the essence of the problem, you could find metaphors for its solution. What is a metaphor for receiving help when one is suicidal? What images communicate deliverance? Sun shining in through a window? Rainbows breaking through clouds? (Maybe too clichéd.) A rope being mended? (Maybe too homely.) An icy river beginning to melt?

## PURE METAPHORS
## VERSUS FUSED METAPHORS

The preceding examples we might call **pure metaphor;** that is, there is no teen-ager anywhere, just an object or situation meant to represent him or her and the problem. However, you may want to **fuse** the teen-ager with a metaphor (that is, make a metaphorical modification of the teen-ager). You could, for example, show his or her face but make it out of cracking plaster or stamp *fragile* (or a product expiration date) across the forehead. Or, as earlier, you could try to show the solution rather than the problem: Maybe paint the kid in rainbows or use his or her shape but fill it with birds in flight or maybe make the face a jigsaw puzzle coming together. In short, use *literal* parts of the situation (in this case the teen-ager) but modify them metaphorically, metamorphose them. (The next chapter, "Fused Metaphors," gives you a long list of possible metamorphoses to perform on a subject or product.)

Each of these approaches—pure metaphor and fused metaphor—has its strengths. (See Figures 19.2 and 19.3.)

Fusion helps keep ads focused *on the product.* If all I see is river ice melting (a **pure metaphor** since it stands for something else), then it will take words to make me contextualize that image. I will think automatically of the Sierra Club or some environmental issue until your language steers me toward the real subject of suicide prevention. If, however, I see a child's shape with birds in it (a **fused metaphor** since it uses something already part of the subject and then modifies it), then I will think "children" from the outset.

**Figure 19.2** Two pure metaphors. Otherwise abstract situations are made more concrete by metaphors, which show us what they are *like*. Courtesy of Fallon McElligott, photography by Rick Dublin; and Barnett Banks, Inc. Jacksonville, Florida.

HERMAN WOUK'S
# WAR AND REMEMBRANCE

Beginning Sunday November 13

**Figure 19.3** Examples of fusion: A rose's stem as barbed wire for a drama about WW II and Nazi concentration camps; *Time's* cover becoming a chalk board to suggest its use in a classroom; and an image cleverly fusing skiing and eating for a Vail restaurant. Courtesy of Agency: Grey Entertainment & Media (New York, NY)—Client: Capital Cities/ABC, Inc.; Time, Inc.; and Manor Vail Lodge.

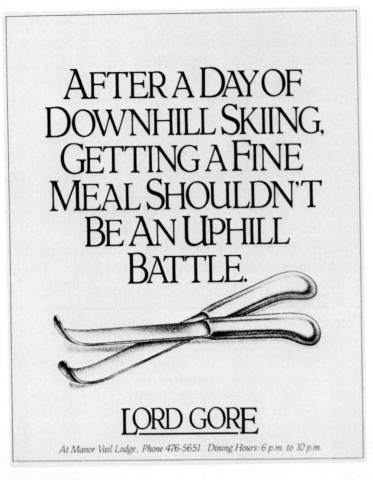

**Figure 19.3**  (continued)

Even though a fused image helps center us, pure metaphor can be powerful. I once saw this poster in the public library: A hiker with backpack was pausing in a glorious solo trek through the Grand Canyon; I could see the awesome spectacle looming over his shoulder. The only headline was "Knowledge is free." I understood it. I knew that ideas and books and all the things in the library were as big as the Grand Canyon, that going to the library was like an odyssey through immense, spectacular country. It was an inspiring, arresting poster, and I doubt that any metaphorical modification of a book, a library card, the facade of the library building, or any other part of libraries would have been better. The pure metaphor worked all by itself.

## ADVICE ON GRAPHIC PROBLEM SOLVING

Pushing two things together into one image often creates a powerful graphic solution. Get in the habit of looking for latent pairs in whatever advertising problem you're working on. For example, if you're selling a home security system, you could use a house and then metaphorically do something to it. Or you could begin with a lock or barbed wire or an armed guard and then metamorphose that. A lot of arresting images are really a *fusion* of the product and a metaphor or a fusion of two aspects of the problem.

Look at these two corporate symbols. (Figure 19.4.) Even though you don't know exactly what the companies do, you can figure it out. The eye with a lightning bolt through it says, "powerful insight," and the firm's name is, in fact, Insight Electronics. The light bulb, with gears for rays, visually says its name, "Idea Works"; it's the symbol for a specialist in business communications. Both images manipulate clichés or symbols associated with their subjects, and the fusion creates memorable, visually arresting work—images that deliver meaning and punch.

Photographer and art director Henry Wolf, famous for his conceptual work for *Esquire, Harper's Bazaar, Show,* and other magazines, worked frequently with metaphors and explained how he thought them through:

> The working method that accomplishes these results [shock and surprise] is not easy to quantify. There are two major categories: *addition*—in which one or more elements are added to an image; and *substitution*—in which part of an image is replaced by another that does not normally belong with it.[8]

Wolf is talking about fusion, and the two examples we just discussed illustrate his point. The eye **adds** a thunderbolt, and the light bulb **substitutes** gears for rays. Think in terms of addition and substitution when you're working visually. (See Figures 19.5 and 19.6.)

Also when dealing with images, don't be too literal minded. Try to find metaphors that capture the psychological essence of a problem more than simply its external reality. Let's say that you're doing a poster announcing a seminar in business fundamentals for graphic designers, one called "The Business Primordial." You may start thinking of cave men and clubs—clubs as felt-tip markers, business cards made out of stone, cave men dressed in business suits, and so on. In other words, you try to fuse some image of business or graphic arts with some "primordial" image. But you don't have to. A visual of two dogs in a tug of war (a pure metaphor) can also express the psychological

[8]Henry Wolf, *Visual Thinking: Methods for Making Images Memorable* (New York: American Showcase, 1988), p. 14.

**Figure 19.4** Examples of graphic fusion: The power of these images comes from combining two clichés, symbols, or aspects of a situation into one new image. These corporate symbols "say" their names: Insight Electronics (the eye) and Idea Works, a business communications firm (the light bulb). Courtesy of Agency (Design Firm): Retail Planning Associates, Columbus, Ohio/ArtDirector-Designer-Illustrator: Tim Smith; and Loretta Smith/Ideaworks.

**Figure 19.5** A clever substitution of Donna Karan's logo in place of "Don't." The copy: "Introducing DKNY shoes. Because everyone walks in New York." Courtesy of The Donna Karan Company (© 1992 The Donna Karan Company).

**Figure 19.6** Examples of addition. Courtesy of Penn Racquet Sports and
J. Coby Neill, Brian Brooker, and James M. Goss.

essence of basic business difficulties but do so less obviously. It's a metaphor off to the side; the dogs symbolize not the thing, but the emotional center of the thing. They're unexpected but appropriate.

## *LET WORDS HELP*

Look up a key word of your advertising problem in the thesaurus and scan the synonyms and antonyms for metaphors. All language is metaphorical, and the ones hidden inside words can spark visual ideas. Using the library problem as an example, if you look up *knowledge,* you find:

"acquaintance," suggesting perhaps the library card as a hand to shake.

"conceive," an obvious birth metaphor.

"have at one's fingertips" and "know by heart" both offer visual suggestions.

"impression" might suggest thumbprints pressed into books or the literal impressions books and ideas leave (casting some such phrase in relief?).

"lettered"—placing letters all over someone?

"ken" implies sightlines, horizon lines, and landscapes.

"insight" and "glimmer" both use light as a metaphor for knowledge. You might do something with light slanting through windows, coming through open doors.

If you change the key word and look up *progression*—because one promise of the library is getting ahead in life—you find "make rapid strides," "on the high road," "flood-tide," and "go with the current," each suggesting a possible image.

In all these cases, you still must do the work, but thesauruses can quickly put a lot of different metaphors in front of you. They give you access to more ideas than you'd locate unaided.

## HEADLINE ADVICE

Remember, if your visual is loud, then you can speak quietly, as was done with the Grand Canyon/library poster. It didn't scream, "Whole Worlds of Awesome Ideas!" It said simply, "knowledge is free." So if you shout visually, think about whispering or making a little joke verbally, and vice versa.

And, of course, never resay in words what you show in pictures. *Marry* the headline and the visual. In the Warner Amex home security problem, if you show a house all wrapped up in barbed wire or a great big padlock on the roof, don't shout, "Lock up Your World With Great Protection!" We can see and hear your image. Perhaps show that visual and then below it say, "Or call Warner Amex." See?

## METONYMY AND SYNECDOCHE

Metonymy and synecdoche, two figures of speech closely related to each other and to metaphor, can be helpful. Metonymy is the use of a thing or idea associated with the item in its place; thus

**Our neighborhood is the finest in the world.**

**But it's getting a little crowded.**

Years ago, when Gallo first came to California's famed Sonoma and Napa growing regions, the neighborhood wasn't quite so crowded.

There were the Beaulieus, the Mondavis, and the Martinis.

And just over the hill, lived the Kenwoods.

But when the rest of the world discovered the extraordinary quality of our wine grapes from Sonoma County and the Napa Valley, we had folks moving in from just about everywhere.

Now there are the Heitzes, and the Jordans, and the Montelenas, and some folks with rather odd names, like the Duckhorns, and the Stag's Leaps.

Yet today, even though there are more folks around, Gallo still makes more wine with premium Sonoma and Napa grapes than any other vintner.

And we still continue to experiment with new strains of varietal grapes, better methods of growing our grapes, and improved harvesting and winemaking techniques, as we have since we first came here.

Because we're never satisfied with being just the same as folks next door. **Today's Gallo.**

We want to keep improving the neighborhood.

**Figure 19.7** Using the metonym of mailboxes for wineries helps us think of Gallo, not as a large winery facing multitudes of smaller competitors, but as the oldest, best neighbor in a valley crowded with newcomers. It humanizes the corporation for us. Copyright, E. & J. Gallo Winery, 1986, used with permission.

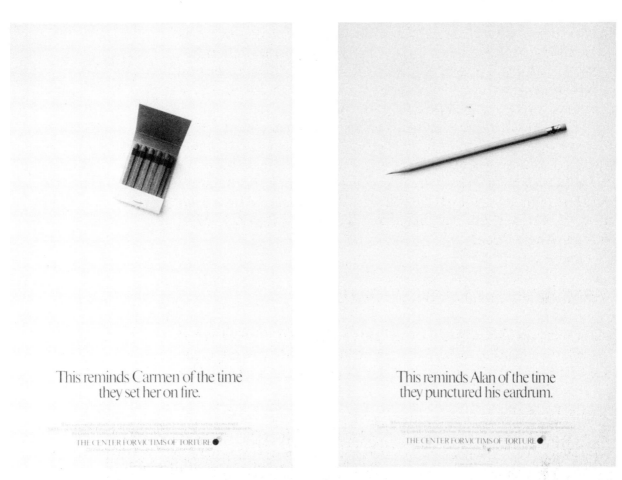

**Figure 19.8** Another metonym. Here the items associated with violence have a stronger emotional power than we'd think such "empty" pages could have. They make us imagine the abuses, and, as with radio, our imaginations prove strong, don't they? Courtesy of The Center for Victims of Torture.

"the pen is mightier than the sword" employs those two items to stand for writing and warfare, just as "the White House" stands for a presidential administration. Synecdoche is the use of a part to represent the whole, so "the long arm of the law" stands for a police force and its effectiveness, and "a trained eye" really means perceptual skill. (The distinction between the two figures of speech can be slippery; think less about what to call them and more about how they work for you.)

Both devices provide the graphic impact of visual shorthand. They work like cropping does in design, which eliminates part of the image—crops it—pushing part of it off the page, thus providing power, immediacy, and an invitation to us to complete the image. Don't neglect synecdoche and metonymy. And notice just how often both are used in advertising, where speed and power are everything. (See Figures 19.7 and 19.8.)

# CHAPTER 20

# FUSED METAPHORS: The Metamorphoses

*Ideas do not need to be esoteric to be original and exciting....What Cezanne did with apples, Picasso with guitars, Leger with machines, Schwitters with rubbish, and Duchamp with urinals makes it clear that revelation does not depend upon grandiose concepts. The problem of the artist is to defamiliarize the ordinary.*
—Paul Rand[1]

One way to defamiliarize the ordinary is to perform various metamorphoses upon it. Objects which are "wrong," which have been "mutilated" or assaulted in some way, are attractive to us, more so than unmodified ones. Unmodified images are really just clichés. For example, one of David Ogilvy's famous ideas is The Man in the Hathaway Shirt, who wears an eye patch and is thereby more interesting than a man who doesn't. He isn't just the cliché of hunk #119; he's a wounded, brave, singular fellow with a story to tell. Similarly, Chivas Regal and Seagram 7 liquor ads do things to their bottles: they are empty, used up, broken, and therefore "wrong" enough to gain our attention. Absolut Vodka has been metamorphosing their bottle in various amusing ways for quite some time now: turning it into a swimming pool for "Absolut L.A.," fogging it in for "Absolut San Francisco," blowing off its letters for "Absolut Chicago," and so on. Many other ads gain some of their visual strength from a "what's wrong here?" approach.

As we discussed in the last chapter, "Metaphor Making," this technique is **fused metaphor**—taking some literal part of your advertising situation and then metamorphosing it, fusing it, with something else. While pure metaphor often works best

[1] Paul Rand, *A Designer's Art* (New Haven: Yale University Press, 1985), p. 45. Used by permission of Paul Rand.

with intangible services (insurance, banks, and the like), fused metaphors can work very well with tangible products.

Take the product you're selling (or something associated with it, as a toothbrush is associated with Crest, for example, or hair and combs are associated with hair care products) and metamorphose it, fuse it with something else. Try for images that are suggestive, provocative.

## *THE METAMORPHOSES*

Set it on fire.

Stamp a label on it (RUSH, FRAGILE, and so forth). For example, fabric-care symbols for "delicate washable" were placed on the nape of a woman's neck to sell a gentle soap. Our world is replete with peel-off stickers and buttons of all sorts. Can one go whimsically, ironically, or dramatically on your product?

Put a zipper on it (Howard Cosell's mouth has been zipped as an illustration for a magazine article on him, "The Mouth That Roared." Bananas have been zippered to indicate freshness.)

Make a paint tube or paint bucket out of it.

Plastic-wrap it or put it into a baggie.

Make it into a tin can or tin can label, or otherwise give it the packaging of another product.

Take its label and wrap it around something else.

Put a wind-up key on it (for example, Rodin's "Thinker" with a key in his back was used as the cover illustration for the book *Mechanism of Mind*).

Humanize it in some fashion; that is, give it eyes, ears, a mouth, fingers, and so on.

Make it part of a roadsign, a freeway exit sign, and the like.

Make it cast a shadow of something other than itself; for example, Audi Foxes in TV spots cast shadows of real foxes, not of the car.

Put postage stamps or other postal markings on it.

Put bandages, adhesive strip(s), or splints on it.

Cross section it, perhaps to reveal unexpected insides.

Break it. Disassemble it. (See Figure 20.1.)

Replace some part of it with an ironic substitute (for example, replace the bristles of a toothbrush with tiny drill bits).

Regard the logo or symbol or product as a vessel and drain it or change what's in it. Or replace its typeface with another distinctive one. Or "mutilate" the logotype; for example, Vuarnet

**Figure 20.1** Metamorphoses from the list: changing an object's shape (the tennis ball); breaking it, or changing its scale (the candy bar). Courtesy of Penn Racquet Sports and Hershey Canada, Inc. (Oh Henry is a registered trademark.)

has presented their logo in day-glo colors instead of the usual red and blue, splashed paint across it, and cut some of it away, each of which makes the logo more graphically attention-getting. (Enough such work, however, and they literally dismantle their own logo, and by extension, our impression of the corporation itself.)

Tattoo it or use it *as* a tattoo.

Put hair on it, human or animal. If it has hair, change it; for example, a cat striped like a skunk, for a brand of cat litter: *Headline*: "A cat without Kitty Litter Brand seems like a whole different animal."

Fold it up or crumple it up as if it were paper.

Peel off its surface to reveal another texture or substance or thing beneath it.

Make it electric; that is, stick a socket on it or hang a cord off it.

Or use the computer versions of sockets and plugs. (These have become as familiar as electric sockets and plugs by now and can communicate more twenty-first century suggestions.)

Put a dial on it or make it a dial, for example, weight scale dial, radio dial, microwave dial, and so on. Or use an LED meter instead, since they're the new dials.

Give it antennae, either a TV's or a moth's.

Turn it into a hand grenade or a handgun or a rifle or a missile.

Paint it. Make it rainbow colored. Paint it gold or camouflaged. Splatter it. Jackson Pollock it. (The distinctive Apple symbol, that graphic apple-in-profile, has been metamorphosed twice: It's been rainbowed as well as bitten into, and we understand the symbolism of each.)

Large category: give any animal characteristics to it.

Turn it into a pill; for example, place your product's name or logo on aspirin tablets.

Give a light bulb filament an unusual configuration or the light bulb itself an unusual shape or texture.

Inhabit a famous logo; for example, put *your* product logo in the place and shape of Superman's, GE's, Nike, and so on.

Make it into a food: Put it on a plate, make it ice cream or ice cream topping, add it to a sandwich or soup or cereal.

Turn it organic: Hang it off a tree as fruit or make it part of a vine.

Turn it technological: Give it circuitry, control panels, or some other features of a high-tech product.

Put holes in it. Perforate it.

Change its shape: Make it a cube, a sphere, flat, pyramidal, and so on. (See Figure 20.1.)

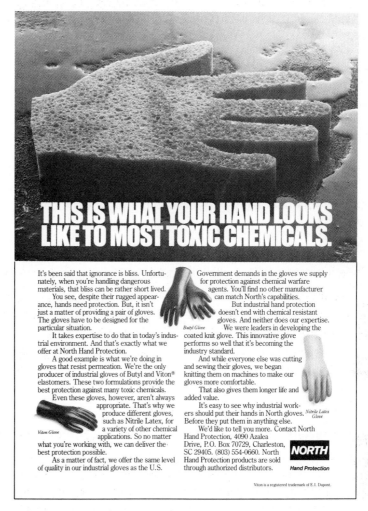

**Figure 20.2** Changing an object's texture (or depending on the object with which you begin, giving it human characteristics). Courtesy of Siebe North, Inc.

Turn it into a liquid, a gas, a solid, a jelly, a milkshake, a sno-cone.

Stick a straw into it.

Make it hot or cold: Make it into ice cubes or make it give off steam.

Weave it, make it a quilt, or turn it into a needlepoint picture.

Turn it into a leaf or a tree, give it leaves, make it a flower.

Make it leak, spill, or bleed.

Change its texture—LOTS of possibilities here. Make it out of sand, glass, wood, stone, brick, and so on. Find a texture that's surprising but communicates the product's essence or benefit; for example, a burnished, golden VW logo with the headline, "Invest in precious metal." (See Figure 20.2.)

Make it a candle or a flashlight.

Make it one item in an unfolded Swiss Army knife. Give it characteristics of any carpenter's tool.

Fuse it into another object, make it half itself and half something else. (See Figure 20.3.)

Change its color; if it's ordinarily white (like popcorn), show it multicolored; if it's certain colors, change it to white or skin-colored or some unexpected color (for example, black popcorn for a Stephen King movie).

Turn it into a feather or put feathers on it. Turn it into a metal or put a metal jacket on it.

Turn it into a microchip or put it within the gridwork of a microchip.

Give it a computer screen or metamorphose it into the computer box.

Wrap it up like it's a candy bar.

Change its scale; that is, make it much larger or much smaller relative to its surroundings.

Change its proportions; that is, make some part of it larger or smaller relative to the rest of it.

Superimpose it, as film, on some other surface or thing; or superimpose other images onto it; for example, Talking Heads have projected typography and lyrics on their own faces in their music videos; a Cyndi Lauper video projected a moving car onto her body.

Make it talk or think, as in comic strips, with words in a bubble over its head.

## *HOW TO THINK WITH THEM*

Hold your product (or that thing associated with it) in your mind and then move it through the items on the list, one by one. Pause at each metamorphosis long enough to create a mental picture and then imagine how that image might work. Go slowly, give each one a chance, and never try to do them all at once—unless you want your brain to metamorphose into a pretzel.

Obviously not all of these will work or be interesting, but some will be provocative, seem neat, suggest an arresting way of communicating a product advantage. Write down the good ones. Always work toward trying to sell something. How can this image sell your product? Is it an example of what goes wrong with hair if you *don't* use the product? Is it an example of how the product will make you feel? How fresh it smells? What? Push

**Senior Advertising Graduates' Portfolio Review**
monday, may 2  9:30-11:30  v-hall  room 214
WE INVITE YOU TO PREVIEW OUR ADVERTISING
SENIOR PORTFOLIOS.
LEND YOUR EXPERTISE AND ENCOURAGEMENT
TO THESE FUTURE PROS.

**Figure 20.3** Metamorphoses in action: A graduate's mortarboard is transformed into an artist's portfolio; a weakling becomes a strongman. Used by
permission of Tim Smith and American Athletic, Inc.

always in the direction of *advertising the product*—expressing
some benefit of using the product or liability of not using it, or in
some way providing an image that helps sell the product. That's
the whole value of this list: not simply stunners but commercially
effective stunners. So get words on these images. Try to find
headlines, language that goes with the image. If you showed
thus-and-such, what would you say?

These metamorphoses can begin interesting ideas, and they certainly deliver visual stunners, but you've got to finish them off. You've got to make them work.

Incidentally, many illustrators use this conceptual approach in their work. If you look through *Print*'s annuals or *Communication Arts* Illustration Annuals, you'll see how illustrators communicate a visual idea by metamorphosing aspects of it.

# CHAPTER 21

# VERBAL METAPHOR — Or Give It Another Name

Ads we skim past or ignore on TV are ones in which nothing seems amiss: expected imagery is accompanied by expected language; nothing is out of place.

Here is another method for moving things out of their clichéd resting places. Rather than metamorphosing the product or replacing it with a metaphor, put it in another language system. Instead of making your product "wrong" visually, try calling it by the "wrong" name.

## HOW THE WRONG NAME CAN BE THE RIGHT ONE

Not only do you gain attention when you call something by the wrong name, but verbal metaphor also helps sell products by renaming them. Often we don't want things themselves unless we can be made to see that they aren't just regular, boring, ordinary things, but are instead Something Else Real Important or Nifty. As an advertiser, you often want to reposition products in our minds, make us reimagine them as something more than they might otherwise seem.

For example, Club Med calls itself, cleverly, "the antidote to civilization." This is verbal metaphor (a comparison between dissimilar things). Literally, they are a vacation service; only metaphorically are they some prescription for an illness. But it's a good line that makes a vacation seem like much more than that. Similarly, Royal Viking cruise lines has headlined ads, "The 7 day refresher course for those who have forgotten how to live."

This is metaphor too, since, of course, a cruise vacation is not literally a life-skills course at all. But both these services have given themselves metaphorically appropriate names. They have talked about themselves using language associated with something else or language literally meaning something else. Thus they catch our attention, and with the logic of metaphor, elevate the services in the process.

## VERBAL METAPHOR ABOUNDS

This idea of inviting us to reimagine a product is so fundamental an advertising strategy that once you begin to look for verbal metaphor, you will see it everywhere. Here are a few examples:

Below a close-up shot of a bowl of soup Campbell's has written the headline, "Health Insurance." And it is, isn't it?

A famous ad for Volkswagen's convertible shows it with the headline, "Topless entertainment." Cute, funny, and true.

A dramatic photo of a destroyer at sea is accompanied by this headline in a poster for the U.S. Navy: "Begin your career at any of our branch offices." The dramatic punch of this is the purpose of verbal metaphor. You hear good advertising in this example: a smart selling idea targeted to a specific market segment and delivered with wit and energy.

American Airlines shows a photo of one of its jets landing under the headline: "The On-time Machine," and the tagline for American is "Something Special in the Air."

*The Wall Street Journal* likes to rename itself to avoid the deadly notion that it's just a compendium of business statistics. Its primary verbal metaphor has been "The Daily Diary of the American Dream." That makes us look at a financial newspaper in very positive ways—presenting the highest possible benefit of the *Journal*, plus personalizing the paper by calling it a diary. Another phrase, used on their boxes on the street, has been: "The Most Powerful Business Machine Ever Invented." That's good, too, in part because it gains extra meaning by being on the metal newspaper box.

"The MCI card—It *is* America's business card." This is the theme for TV ads featuring various businesspeople and salespeople making calls from anywhere—pay phones and such—that is, taking their offices with them. So a phone card *is* a business card.

"Share a little piece of America." This theme is sung in TV ads for Wrigley's four gums. It's a nice slice-of-life spot and a good way to elevate chewing gum. We're not just adding sugar to our system, relieving stress, or idling away time: We're passing on America itself!

Signs on Central Ohio Transit Authority city buses: "COTA. AN ENVIRONMENTAL SOLUTION YOU CAN TAKE SITTING DOWN." Wit with a purpose, a very good way of seeing the service at its highest possibility.

When Apple was introducing the Macintosh computer and its revolutionary mouse, ads featured a hand in a racing glove, finger poised on the mouse, with the headline, "Take a Macintosh out for a test drive," and the campaign encouraged precisely that. We were invited to sample the computer by taking it home overnight, discovering if it truly was easy and fun. This approach transcends its witty headline to become a great marketing idea, since sampling helps reduce consumer fears about new products, especially technological ones that we believed demanded a long learning curve.

TV spots often create verbal metaphor by running a soundtrack that is technically "wrong" over the imagery. Operatic arias sung as mayonnaise is being spread or while monkeys listen to Sony Walkmans are verbal metaphor, because the incongruity makes a kind of sense and humorously elevates the product. Notice how often TV soundtracks bear an ironic relationship to the visual and function as verbal metaphor—asking us to see the product a new way.

## HOW TO THINK ABOUT VERBAL METAPHOR

Shop around in your mind. If you had to call the product something else, what would it be? If you had to compare it to something else, what would it be? How does it function? What does it do? What's the best possible way of regarding it? What's its highest possible benefit? What other things does it allow you to have more of—leisure, time, recreational possibilities, love, money, what? Start by making this list of benefits.

Always ask yourself, what *is* this product? For example, what *is* a car? Is it an investment? Durability on wheels? A reward for hard work? A mobile home? A comment on you? An exercise in rationality and sensible spending? Simply a way to get from point A to point B? Similarly, what is a Sony Walkman? A portable concert? A hearing aid? A privacy rite? Ask yourself, what is this product doing here? What is its real purpose? What do people go to it for?

## *EXPLOIT LANGUAGE SYSTEMS AND CLICHÉS*

Also, are there any clichés that are associated with the product, category, or target market that you might be able to exploit? What language does your audience use? (For example, Honda has placed "multiple choice" and "Roads Scholar" headlines above their cars in ads aimed at students because a college audience speaks that language, understands those phrases. Can you apply your target audience's language to your product?) Get some words out on the page. Fiddle around with them. You don't just have to use nouns either.

Sometimes the Other Name is language brought in from a similar place but not necessarily a noun, a thing. Maybe it's a command. For example, we've all heard the phrase "Dress for Success." It was the title of a best-selling book about how to dress for the business world. You could show a picture of someone kayaking down a river or scaling a mountain, his or her rugged-but-stylish Patagonia gear clearly visible, and use the headline "Dress for Success." See what I mean? This headline has some "pop" because it's been moved out of its normal place, yet it "fits"—unexpectedly—here as well. Hence the jolt of surprise. Shop around, break and enter other language systems.

Just remember, if you're selling jeans, you can't call them jeans; you must think of them as something else. Maybe you see a good-looking hunk of a guy in jeans jackhammering at a construction site. You could take a photo of him (focusing on those jeans) and title it "Construction Sight." That is probably a visual pun more than a metaphor, and it's probably too quiet a pun, but it is in the area. You could have a subhead or tagline, "Levi Jeans—on the job for 134 years."

What else are jeans? Where else are they? Work to find new ways of looking at and talking about that old product.

## Exercise:

Think about your product and try to call it other names. When you do this, imagine your product in various settings and from various angles—from behind, in use, empty, just sitting there, in the driveway, in the showroom, and so on. With different visual expressions of it might come different verbal headlines. Many verbal metaphor ads do simply show the product sitting there in air, with the witty headline, but many others derive their relationship between headline and visual from some specific visual placement or view of the product. So think it out visually as well as verbally. You may wish to focus on only part of it, as this punning ad does (Figure 21.1).

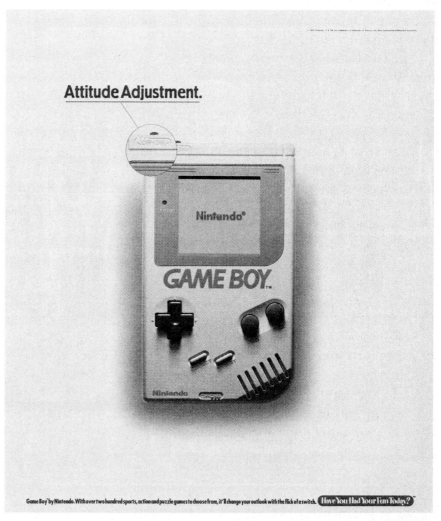

**Figure 21.1** Since we commonly think of "attitude adjustment" as a change in psychology, the phrase gains stopping power when relocated, here to summarize the product's benefit. This ad gains extra power by punning on "adjustment" as well. ©1993 Nintendo, used courtesy of Nintendo.

*Important Note:* You may go beyond just naming it, and write whole sentences, tell us what functions it serves in our lives, and so forth. You are creating headlines, so they can be sentences, commands, and such. I call this technique Verbal Metaphor to get you in the habit of pulling in language from elsewhere. But many great headlines do more than rename. For example, Hyundai car makers, on outdoor boards, say this: "Use your mind more than your money." That's not exactly a renaming of the car itself, but it is a reimagining of the act of buying one, as well as smart positioning of this particular car. Be great. Then worry if it's exactly verbal metaphor. (For examples of verbal metaphor, see Figures 21.2–21.4.)

**Figure 21.2** Verbal metaphor is widely used because of its obvious virtues: It's startling, often funny, and quickly and memorably communicates a product benefit. Courtesy of Reebok International Ltd., Woodland Park Zoo, and YMCA of Metropolitan Minneapolis. (continues)

## Exercising regularly at the YMCA causes visible side effects.

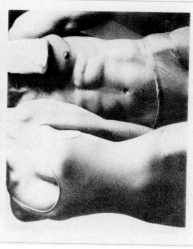

Like excellent muscle tone all over your body. It also relieves stress and creates self confidence. So start enjoying some side effects you can live with. Join the YMCA. Call your local Y for information.

**YMCA**
Don't put it off.

## Simple instructions for changing your spare tire.

Join the YMCA.

## Learn how to defy gravity at the YMCA.

The older you get, the more gravity seems to work at pulling parts of you down. So don't let your physical condition fall into decline. Join the YMCA. Call your local Y for information.

**YMCA**
Don't put it off.

**Figure 21.2** (continued)

**Figure 21.3** Verbal metaphor works well in outdoor advertising because you can say a lot without using many words. Courtesy of Levi Strauss & Co. (Canada) Inc.; Volkswagen United States, Inc.; Blitz-Weinhard Brewing Co. (Agency: Hal Riney & Partners); and Goodby, Berlin & Silverstein.

OPEN ON LOCKED SHOT OF A PORSCHE PIT AND CREW. A
962 PULLS INTO THE PIT AND THE CREW SWARMS OVER IT
CHANGING TIRES, CLEANING WINDSHIELD, AND REFUEL-
ING THE CAR.
**SFX:** Natural throughout.
**ANNCR VO:** At Porsche, key personnel meet on
a regular basis to discuss alterations and
refinements.
THE DRIVER AND SEVERAL TECHNICIANS (SPEAKING
GERMAN) ENGAGE IN A HEATED DEBATE ABOUT SOME
DETAIL OF THE CAR'S PERFORMANCE.
**ANNCR VO:** At these times, many important con-
tributions are made in the perfecting of our cars.
THEIR WORK COMPLETE, THE CREW STANDS BACK AND
THE CAR ACCELERATES OUT OF CAMERA.
**ANNCR VO:** We try to keep the meetings short.

**Figure 21.4** Verbal metaphor also
works well in TV spots. By showing
us one thing while talking about it in
unexpected language, you're using
irony. You hook us with the incongruity while making us re-see the product. Copy of advertisement used by
permission of Porsche Cars North
America, Inc. Porsche, and the
Porsche crest are registered trademarks of Dr. Ing. h.c. F Porsche AG.

# INDEX